How Women Must Write

SRLT

NORTHWESTERN UNIVERSITY PRESS

Studies in Russian Literature and Theory

SERIES EDITORS

Caryl Emerson

Gary Saul Morson

William Mills Todd III

Andrew Wachtel

Justin Weir

How Women Must Write

Inventing the Russian Woman Poet

Olga Peters Hasty

NORTHWESTERN UNIVERSITY PRESS / EVANSTON, ILLINOIS

Northwestern University Press
www.nupress.northwestern.edu

Printed in the United States of America

10 9 8 7 6 5 4 3 2 1

Library of Congress Cataloging-in-Publication Data

Names: Hasty, Olga Peters, author.
Title: How women must write : inventing the Russian woman poet / Olga Peters Hasty.
Other titles: Studies in Russian literature and theory.
Description: Evanston, Illinois : Northwestern University Press, 2019. | Series: Northwestern University Press studies in Russian literature and theory | Includes bibliographical references.
Identifiers: LCCN 2019019812 | ISBN 9780810140936 (paper text : alk. paper) | ISBN 9780810140943 (cloth text : alk. paper) | ISBN 9780810140950 (e-book)
Subjects: LCSH: Russian poetry—19th century—History and criticism. | Russian poetry—20th century—History and criticism. | Russian poetry—Women authors—History and criticism. | Women and literature—Russia—History—19th century. | Women and literature—Russia—History—20th century.
Classification: LCC PG3051 .H37 2019 | DDC 891.713099287—dc23
LC record available at https://lccn.loc.gov/2019019812

For Kate

Contents

Preface

> To make a poem, you first have to invent the
> poet to make it.
> —C. K. Williams, "The Poet"

The title of this book comes from Evdokiia Rostopchina's poem "Kak dolzhny pisat' zhenshchiny," translated as "How Women Must Write," to underscore the compunction and conjecture entailed in attitudes toward women.[1] "Must" in its two meanings—the prescriptive and the speculative—encapsulates the dictates imposed on women poets and the assumptions projected onto them. Both are crucial to my exploration of how women who make poems are variously invented in nineteenth- and early twentieth-century Russia. The inventors include (1) the woman poet herself, (2) readers who read the gender biases she subverts back into her poems, and (3) men who fabricate women poets and their poems. The vantage points they provide on how the woman poet is variously constituted direct attention to the woman's complex interactions with her readers and the shifting sociopolitical and cultural contexts that shape these interactions. This allows me to focus on women poets not as passive victims of gender-driven constraints but as purposeful actors negotiating a system rife with disincentives that they turn to advantage. To this end, I look closely at strategies of enablement that the foremost Russian women poets of the late nineteenth and early twentieth centuries develop in response to inhibiting constructs of gender in the rapidly changing but consistently inhospitable cultures of their time.

How Women Must Write is neither a history of Russian women's writing nor a comprehensive record of the steadily growing number of women poets who emerged in the periods under consideration.[2] Each of its six chapters centers on an episode from Russian literary history that concretely registers how "the literary problem of being female"[3] manifests itself in the culture of the time and how individual women poets address it. My purpose is not to theorize about the woman poet but to study the lived experience of her efforts to come into her own in a world intent on determining her. The study moves from an emphatically masculine Romantic age to a modernist period preoccupied with women's creativity, but also its containment. Within this framework, I explore illuminating examples of the woman poet's three-fold project to fulfill herself creatively, to heighten readers' receptivity to her poems, and to secure a rightful place in the tradition. This means considering her in the very thick of the changing sociopolitical and cultural climate in which she works and which governs the fluid constructs of the woman to which she responds. It also means attending to the specific terms in which the poet chooses to assert herself and what she uses these terms to convey.

This book, which studies women poets in confrontation with patriarchal norms that inhibit their creative self-realization and deny them full valuation, is informed by and contributes to Russian women's studies of the past four decades[4] and, more broadly, feminist scholarship. In keeping with feminist theorists' recognition that gender does not figure in isolation from broader historical, sociopolitical, and cultural forces, each chapter draws attention to multifarious conditions that influence the woman poet's interactions with the culture of her time, her reception in it, and how she is regarded. This leads me to engage other perspectives as well. The foremost of these come from (1) seminal writings on political censorship and its effects on the relationship between writers and readers;[5] (2) Wolfgang Iser's reader response theory,[6] which, though not overtly discussed, underpins my conceptualization of "reader-imposed censorship"; and (3) mystification theory, which draws attention to how power structures are alternately undermined or supported by fictitious information[7] and masquerade.[8]

This multifaceted approach is driven by the case study methodology I use for my inquiry. Recognized as an efficacious means to challenge and inform theoretical assumptions, case study methodology preserves individuating characteristics that theoretical abstraction subsumes.[9] Privileging particularity and process, this book complements the generalizing thrust of theory with close attention to the unique circumstances in which individual women poets project their creative identities and in which they are received. The cases I explore are rooted in close readings of works that maximally foreground women poets' strategic self-affirmations and map their advancement toward recognition. The reception of these works documents the resistance of the male establishment to that advancement. Reserving center stage for the poets themselves, I regard them from an experiential angle, supplementing theoretical approaches with the kind of close, contextualized individuation routinely accorded to men poets.

Observing that Nikolai Golitsyn's 1889 *Bibliographical Dictionary of Russian Women Writers* (*Bibliograficheskii slovar' russkikh pisatel'nits*) comprises more than twelve hundred entries, Suzan van Dijk and Ursula Stohler note that "there are still many Russian women authors who have not yet received proper scholarly attention."[10] The present study redresses a different egregious imbalance—that between what women invest in their poems and how they are read and evaluated. The sociopolitical structures and the changes in Russia during the period under consideration affected women and men differently. Accordingly, I foreground the woman's perspective on the conditions in which she wrote and examine individual poems for what prompted their composition and shaped the messages they carried. In keeping with what Van Dijk and Stohler describe as "an increasing interest among feminist scholars in investigating the writings of female authors before 1900 and in situating them within the cultural context of the time of their production,"[11] this brings to light deeper levels of meaning in women's poems. That these levels of signification remained without attention is the function of two problematic tendencies. The first is that gender biases left readers disinclined to look beyond the surface of a woman's poems, adversely affecting their critical evaluation. The second is the remarkable staying power of authoritative male critics' assessments that remain unchallenged and continue to influence how women poets are regarded. Thus, for example, I show how frequently anthologized poems that are touted as articulating their authors' poetic credos are consistently subjected to readings that are retrograde to the messages encoded in them. Deep reading of these poems rectifies this situation and is essential to fuller appreciation both of their authors and of the women for whom they subsequently serve as role models.

Individualizing the women poets I consider in this book, I study the impact of gender on their lives and works, but also their resolve to prevent it from being the determinant of how their creative identities and their writings are received. As I recuperate what is vested in women's poetic self-inventions, I uncover the strategies of enablement that they develop and show how readers' gender biases defuse them. Illustrative of their times, the individual case studies in this book reveal also an underlying continuity both in women poets' accomplishments and in the resistance they meet. The implications of my findings go beyond the individual poets and poems I consider in this volume, as do the terms in which I discuss them. Here I focus on women poets working in a specifically Russian context. But my approach with its emphasis on detailed, context-sensitive analyses of individual works that subvert power structures and on how these writings are received can be applied productively to marginalized groups and individuals of other times and places as well.

Unless otherwise indicated, the translations in this book are my own. In the interest of space, I include only English versions of cited Russian prose except in instances when the original conveys something essential that is lost in translation.

Acknowledgments

Addison tells us that "there is no more pleasing exercise of the mind than gratitude," and I fully agree. Thanking those from whom I learned and received support—tangible and intangible—as I worked on this book is indeed a pleasure. The thinking of many scholars, whom I duly note, has enriched my project. Many have helped me directly, inspiring by example and giving generously of their time. Among these is Kirsti Ekonen, whom I commemorate here for her exemplary scholarship and thank for our discussions of women's writing in the Silver Age. I owe gratitude to Milica Banjanin for what she taught me. I am grateful to Sibelan Forrester for her invigorating scholarly and creative work, her contagious enthusiasm, and helpful feedback on chapter 3. I thank Diana Greene for opening new ways to approach women's writing, for the Rostopchina materials she shared with me, and her encouragement. Lazar Fleishman, a master of close reading, generously supplied me with valuable material relating to Cherubina de Gabriak, for which I thank him. I am deeply grateful to Irina Shevelenko for her pathbreaking work on the modernist period and for the books and ideas she has shared with me. Many thanks go to Alexandra Smith for the bountiful sources she provided and her long-distance friendship. Two readers of my manuscript gave unstintingly of their time to offer valuable insights and suggestions that have meaningfully improved this book. To these anonymous individuals I express my profound gratitude.

Many thanks go to Trevor Perri, Acquisition Editor; Anne Gendler, Managing Editor and Director of Editorial, Design, and Production; and to my eagle-eyed copyeditor, Mike Ashby, who guided the manuscript into book form.

Princeton University abundantly provided the means that allowed me to pursue work on this project and a stimulating environment in which to do so. I am grateful to all my colleagues and students who enlivened me intellectually. I thank Ellen Chances for her positive energy and her philosophy of clear space. I am indebted to Maxwell Parlin for his generosity of spirit and the scrupulous, intelligent attention he gave to the manuscript. I thank writer and philosopher Leeore Schnairsohn for poetic insights and fruitful discussion of the early chapters. To the talented New York actor (and former student) Jake Austin Robertson go enormous thanks for his help with editing and proofreading and for his awe-inspiring work on the stage.

I was extremely fortunate to have the support of friends and family to see me through this project and everything that happened as I pursued it. I thank my dear friend of many decades Susanne Fusso and her husband Joe Siry for their unfailing love and kindness. I thank Peter Greenleaf for the incomparable generosity and thoughtfulness with which he brought beauty and light into dark days and added valuable books to my library. Barbara Lee and Jim Begin were always there for me as friends and models of bighearted-ness. Peggy Skemer has been a staunch friend and walking companion who kept me going when things got rough. I greatly appreciate the inspiration and wisdom that Christine Dougherty (a.k.a. die Muse) abundantly supplied as I worked on all my projects, including this one. I also thank Natalie Medvedev and Tatiana Ermolaev for their warmth and kindness and our many lively roundtable discussions.

Above all, I am grateful to Kate Hasty, who gives my life meaning and improves everything around her, including what I think and write. Special thanks go also to Loren Pfeiffer for his loving support, to my mother, who has always been a model for hanging in, and my deeply caring family, all of whom give unstintingly of love and joy. Lastly, I thank my four-legged pal Zeus, who expressed no qualms about my manuscript.

How Women Must Write

Introduction

WHEN THE WOMAN POET made her way into the literary arena in nineteenth-century Russia, she confronted not a static set of demands and expectations but complex, shifting configurations of cultural and sociopolitical constructs of the woman that demanded skillful negotiation. Men directed the competing, often heavily politicized images of the woman and the platforms these images were used to support, and even the heroines of men's fictions had a normative function. Whether or not they accorded with the woman poet's creative self-realization, the various concepts of the woman affected how she was regarded and how her poems were read. This demanded that she respond to them in the course of her self-invention. Inasmuch as the woman poet sought to make her way into the tradition and not to overthrow it, this response involved finding ways to position herself within available options that she could potentially reshape to her own ends. However she construed her gender and her calling, the woman poet had to remain alert to the various ways in which "woman" signified in the culture of her time as she developed a viable creative identity and the means to project it.

This culture was itself undergoing steady change. By the 1840s, the male Romantic movement was losing momentum and the status of poetry was waning as the aristocracy ceded its control over literature to civic-minded liberals who called for realist prose. Literary debates revolved increasingly around the advancement of a new social order. Progressive thinkers saw in the newly imagined woman a disruptive force that could be turned against the patriarchal tsarist regime, while conservatives warned against freeing the woman from domesticity. One underlying principle remained invariant for liberals and conservatives alike: determining how "woman" signified was a male prerogative.

It was in the dynamic contexts of her chosen genre, its status in the culture of the time, and the sociopolitical emblem "woman" that the women poets this book opens with worked to invent themselves and to enter the poetic tradition. Though challenging, this multifaceted indeterminacy offered a space of possibility, expanding the range of images the woman poet could draw on for her self-fashioning, enlarging opportunity for encoding additional layers of meaning in her poems, and allowing her to play off different notions about women against one another. By strategically manipulating assumptions that were projected onto her, the woman poet could deflect attention from her transgression of limiting norms, smoothing her entry onto the poetic arena and into print. Such derivation of enablement from restrictive conditions gained the woman poet agency and removed her from passive victimhood. Significantly, the capacity to work within strict limitations accorded with (1) the genre of poetry, which establishes exacting norms within which the poet must learn to write freely, and (2) a poetic tradition that flourished under the constraints imposed on it by government censorship.

This eloquent argument in favor of the woman poet's inclusion in the tradition was not immediately apparent to its male gatekeepers, who were inclined to see her as a charming guest and not a full-fledged member. Nor did readers apprehend the subtlety and the import of what a woman poet invested in her poems. She remained in a tenuous position inasmuch as the preconceptions that her authorship undermined continued to dictate how her poems were received. The biases that the woman poet subverted as she wrote were thus reinstated as she was read. Indeed, the quality of the reading accorded to women's poems was demonstrably inferior to that commanded by poems authored by men. Having secured access to publication, the woman poet had yet to secure readers who were prepared to give her poems the serious attention that would uncover their deeper layers of meaning and thus also their author's message and command of the idiom.

PART I—CONTENTIONS

Part 1 of *How Women Must Write* centers on frequently anthologized but, as I show, underappreciated poems by Karolina Pavlova (1807–93) and Evdokiia Rostopchina (1811–58), the two leading women poets of the nineteenth century. These lyrics, which capture the complexity of how Pavlova and Rostopchina positioned themselves in the culture of the time, show their authors projecting creative selves that are adequate to their own expressive needs and yet acceptable to the male establishment whose authority they destabilize. This brings me to the question of how a readership thoroughly schooled by the government censor in the fine art of reading between the lines could suddenly go blind to subversive content that a woman concealed in her poems. While this very blindness allowed women to register their resistance to prevailing norms, it also left the deeper layers of their poems without notice. Extending scholarly thinking about government censorship[1] to gender-driven sociocultural prohibitions, I develop the concept of "reader-imposed censorship" to designate the reading of gender biases back into poems that subvert them, thus effectively blotting out the woman poet's challenges to established norms. A more intense variant of reader-imposed censorship appears in instances of "the invisibility of the unthinkable," which describes readings that demonstrate a cognitive failure to perceive deviations from the norm, thus documenting the intransigence of prevailing assumptions.

Chapter 1 examines the lyrical contretemps between Pavlova and Rostopchina that stemmed from their divergent solutions to the problem of reconciling their gender with their calling. In her work, Pavlova consistently denies gender a definitive role in the constitution of the poet, whose art, as she sees it, subsumes such distinctions. Rostopchina, on the other hand, accentuates her womanhood and, as I show, uses feminine masquerade to advance her ends. Notably, Pavlova and Rostopchina developed as poets in a time when the patriarchal autocracy and the domestic ideology that supported it were confronted with Fourier's socialism and George Sand's shattering of gender norms that took Russian liberals by storm. Accordingly, how they position themselves as women and the terms in which they do so have sociopolitical implications as well as poetical meaning.

Central to this chapter is "We are contemporaries, Countess," Pavlova's apostrophe to Rostopchina of 1847, in which she couches their differences in the contrasting images of an authored self who works within the precepts of domestic ideology and an authored Rostopchina whom she styles a "*zhorzhsandistka*"—a George Sandian—who breaks with these precepts. Although repeatedly singled out as articulating Pavlova's poetic credo, the poem suffers from superficial readings that take this schematic contrast at face value. This leaves its author undermining Rostopchina's poetic worth and supporting a backward-looking order that is deleterious to the woman poet's advancement. Beneath this surface, however, is a strategic effort on Pavlova's part to counter the image of the woman poet as a disruptive element. Ever the advocate of responsible action and self-governance, Pavlova presents the woman poet who, like her male counterparts in the Russian tradition, can attain creative self-fulfillment undeterred by restrictive external conditions. Establishing close ties between the marginalized woman and the increasingly marginalized poet, she uses the ability to write in inimical circumstances to validate herself as a poet and to inscribe herself into the Pushkinian tradition. This image of the self-contained woman poet was in urgent need of defense in the aftermath of a political scandal caused by the publication of Rostopchina's allegorical ballad "A Forced Marriage," which government censors, deceived by her feminine masquerade, allowed into print in an instantiation of the invisibility of the unthinkable. Pavlova's masterful encoding veiled her allusion to the "Forced Marriage" scandal from government censors only to fall victim to readings that reduced her poem to an endorsement of patriarchal norms.

Chapter 2 elaborates on reader-imposed censorship and the invisibility of the unthinkable, focusing on self-affirmations that Rostopchina veils in protestations of modesty and homage to leading male poets. Unlike Pavlova, who claims parity for the woman poet, Rostopchina moves to assert her ascendancy. What are best described as her "retaliatory self-inventions"[2] enact compliant femininity in a way intended not simply to undermine a restrictive status quo but to turn the tables on the dominant group that upholds it. Men, as Rostopchina argues, have the most to lose from limiting women's self-expressivity. Unlike Pavlova, who works toward a seamless absorption of the woman into the extant tradition, Rostopchina undermines the male establishment and challenges men's political and cultural authority. Thus, as this chapter newly shows, in her poems to Pushkin and Lermontov, she does more than claim a place in the Pushkinian tradition: she maintains that it now depends on her for its perpetuation.

In "How Women Must Write," a poem often cited as articulating her poetic credo, Rostopchina enjoins writing women to remain within socially dictated bounds of propriety in their writings. It remains largely unrecognized that, like Pavlova's recourse to domestic ideology, Rostopchina's call for modesty in "How Women Must Write" has a subversive dimension. The argument Rostopchina advances in her seemingly acquiescent poem is that by limiting women's self-expressivity, men effectively bar their own access to the woman's emotional experiences and creative domain, thus limiting themselves.

Rostopchina's sabotage of established norms in the poems I discuss in chapter 2 was undone by the success of its concealment. Her rehearsals of conventional femininity deflected attention from her "unwomanly" poetic activity and spared her from being branded "mannish" as Pavlova was. At the same time, however, Rostopchina's feminine masquerade activated gender biases that left readers riveted to the surface of her poems and insensate to any deeper meaning. Rostopchina falls victim to the efficacy of her purposefully encoded insubordination. This demonstrates the effects of reader-imposed censorship and the invisibility of the unthinkable with which the woman poet contended beyond the government censorship that all Russian poets negotiated. A male poet could rely on perceptive readers to apprehend what he smuggled past the government censor. Women poets who undermined limiting constructs of gender were in a more difficult situation. Their reliance on the auspices of the poetic establishment left them veiling their sabotage of gender norms from male gatekeepers of the tradition who evaluated their work. This left their messages and successful encoding practices unacknowledged and their poems misconstrued. As long as reader-imposed censorship kept them in check, women could engage in literary activity, but not redraw the cultural landscape. Pavlova and Rostopchina were discredited as poets in their own time on, respectively, domestic and sociopolitical grounds. The concealed messages and enabling strategies their poems carried remained open for discovery by women writing after them.

Beginning in the 1840s, poetry steadily surrendered its position of generic dominance to the realist prose advocated by civic-minded critics. The viability of the woman poet was of little interest, and the contretemps between Rostopchina and Pavlova was dismissed as petty female jealousy. With the rise of George Sand's popularity in Russia, female sexuality was drawn into the male armamentarium for effecting social change. Though it suggested a new possibility for women, *zhorzhsandizm* failed to dislodge the long-standing conviction that women lacked self-governance and required strict male control. Indeed, the increased sexualization of women to which Sand in her various Russian refractions contributed complicated the woman poet's situation. Defending poetry in an age of civic prose meant, by extension, upholding a patriarchal order that was inimical to women's creative self-realization. Yet to embrace the new social order meant to renounce her poetic calling and to subscribe to an increasingly politicized image of the woman that intensified objectification and eroded the poet's agency.

PART II—FEMALE IMPERSONATIONS

When poetry regained its pride of place at the start of the twentieth century, interest in women's creative psychology ran high, and women gained unprecedented opportunities to make their way into print. Yet though the period was propitious for women poets' advancement, serious challenges persisted. The increasing ease with which women could publish marked a major improvement, but the degree to which they continued to be determined by male constructs and dependent on male support remained problematic. Widely circulating philosophical, psychological, and scientific studies of women were authored by men and continued to be normative rather than revelatory. The modernist urban aesthetic commodified women. The growing interest in the unique, expressly feminine creative domain that Rostopchina championed reflected a gain in cultural status but also sustained women's otherness. While it stimulated curiosity, the terra incognita of the woman's inner world fueled apprehension in the male establishment, heightened by fearful images of women in works of French Decadents popular at the time. Seeing women as potential sources of poetic renewal, men were also anxious to retain authority over them. This anxiety fueled controlling mentorship, sexualizing objectification, and an impulse to colonize the woman's creative domain. The situation finds vivid realization in two women poets invented by men. In the poems ascribed to these fictive women, the speculative and the prescriptive meanings of "must" come together as men's conjectures about women's creativity overlap with an urge to control it.

Chapter 3 is devoted to the first of these mystifications—Cherubina de Gabriak, the progeny of Maximilian Voloshin, a recognized writer, and the aspiring woman poet Elizaveta Dmitrieva, whom he directed in the project. Their asymmetrical collaboration instantiates the mentorship of women characteristic of the time and shows in concentrated form the woman's untenable situation between her own creative identity and the one projected onto her. The beautiful woman aesthetic of the time gave precedence to male fantasies over actual women and perpetuated their objectification in the name of art. The mysterious de Gabriak captivated readers by her absence and the exotic content of her poems, which readers used to invent and celebrate Cherubinas of their own. Dmitrieva bore no outward resemblance to the invented poet on whose behalf she wrote under Voloshin's tutelage. As de Gabriak took on a life of her own, this figment of the male imagination overrode Dmitrieva's creative selfhood. When the mystification was unveiled, readers—shocked by the disparity between the actual woman and the one they dreamed up—questioned not their own biases, but the authorship of de Gabriak's poems. Dmitrieva suffered a prolonged creative crisis. When, after five years of silence, she resumed writing, she used de Gabriak's name rather than her own. Voloshin publicly maintained that he designed the mystification to unleash the creativity he discerned beneath Dmitrieva's unprepossessing appearance but privately admitted that he needed her for inspiration. Appropriating the story of the mystification, he perpetuated the assumption that inventing the woman poet was a male prerogative. An instance of Symbolist life-creation (*zhiznetvorchestvo*), this episode and its aftermath capture the male establishment's ambivalence toward the rise of women poets and document the insuperable tensions between a woman poet's selfhood and the gender-driven expectations projected not just onto her work but onto her as well.

Chapter 4 is devoted to a woman poet contrived by Valerii Briusov— don of Russian poetry, influential critic, and self-styled Pushkin of the time. Briusov's dictatorial mentoring and sexualization of "poetesses" attest to an insecurity caused by the rise of women poets and a determination to maintain command over their development. When—some three years after Cherubina de Gabriak's huge success—Briusov brought out a volume of verse authored ostensibly by the woman whose name appears in its title, *Nelli's Poems*, some readers believed it to be the work of yet another woman debuting under his aegis. More discerning readers saw through Briusov's disguise. Nelli failed to win anything like the acclaim Cherubina de Gabriak had enjoyed and amounted to little more than a riddle of middling success. Written from the perspective of a courtesan who invites sexualization as she traverses the city, Nelli's poems create an implicit parallel between the woman who sells herself on city streets and the woman poet who publishes verse. The collection tells a story that rehearses—in new dress—the all-too-familiar warning of earlier centuries that a woman who seeks public recognition is doomed to failure in both her public and her private life. The impressive command of the poetic idiom that Briusov grants Nelli is offset by her commodification and her signal failure to attain either creative or emotional fulfillment.

With his debut as a woman poet, Briusov claims to access a creative domain posited as uniquely feminine and to master a purportedly feminine poetic idiom. In other words, he claims to penetrate that very space from which—according to the argument Rostopchina advances in "How Women Must Write"—men were barred by limitations they imposed on women's self-expression. Nelli's poems do nothing to lift these limitations. Rather, they ventriloquize the woman poet to reaffirm them, as Briusov has Nelli voice her own unsuitability for urban modernism. With this female impersonation, Briusov works to assert his command over women's writing by directing it from within. The psychosexual misogyny of works he wrote during this period and his sexualization of his mentees suggest that his proclaimed interest in "the psychology of the feminine soul" (*psikhologiia zhenskoi dushi*) was not benign.

PART III—RESISTANCE

For all the progress women poets made in the early twentieth century, they still had to contend with male authority and gender-driven expectations that the de Gabriak and Nelli mystifications emblematized. The growing number of women publishing at the time and the role models that they could find in women writing before them—Pavlova and Rostopchina foremost among them—offered potential support and suggested viable strategies of enablement. In asserting themselves, a number of women poets of the time—including Elizaveta Dmitrieva, Sophia Parnok, and Marina Tsvetaeva—challenged male authority by pointedly distancing themselves from Briusov and citing their freedom from his mentorship as constitutive of their creative identities. Such claims to agency reflected a developing awareness of the drawbacks entailed in women's reliance on male approval and the subordination to male authority and constructs of gender this reliance led them to accept. This acceptance, together with the objectification it fostered and the competition for men's attention it stimulated, leached women poets of agency and inhibited their unmediated self-realization. It also impeded the formation of supportive relationships among women poets and undermined a sense of continuity of women's poetry in the tradition. Notably, a number of articles written by men about Pavlova and Rostopchina in this period belittle them and dismiss their work as inconsequential. This compromised their potential value as role models, discouraging women poets from overtly connecting with their predecessors. This in turn denied a developing line of women's poetry and sustained the image of the woman poet as an aberration.

Another problem was that aspiring women poets of the day were not always cognizant of the deleterious norms that they themselves perpetuated in their effort to secure approval from the male establishment. Advancing the woman poet's cause thus involved raising her conscious awareness of her situation and urging her to react responsibly to it. In chapter 5, I show Marina Tsvetaeva working toward this goal. Strengthened by her private ties with Pavlova and Rostopchina and energized by her public opposition to Briusov, Tsvetaeva eschews male mentorship and draws on what she learns from her female predecessors. Accompanying Tsvetaeva's steadfast arguments against granting gender a determining role in defining the poet are her resolute destabilizations of the gender binary and her insistence on the ascendancy of women over men. Far from inconsistent, this multifaceted response integrates the divergent approaches that fueled Pavlova's and Rostopchina's disaffection and allows Tsvetaeva to address manifold disincentives and contradictory demands besetting the woman poet. Overarching this project is Tsvetaeva's definition of poet and poetry as all-embracing phenomena in which contraries productively coexist and into which the gender binary is absorbed.

The chapter centers on a "A Hero of Labor" ("Geroi truda") and "The Living about the Living" ("Zhivoe o zhivom"), Tsvetaeva's commemorations of her foe Briusov and her friend Voloshin, in which the two poets appear as negative and positive examples of how to relate to gender in general and to women poets in particular. In these otherwise dissimilar essays, Tsvetaeva draws attention to the woman poet's situation and presents an authored self as a model of responsible resistance to it. Like all the prose works Tsvetaeva dedicates to other poets, these essays are oblique self-presentations in which she leads her reader to participate actively in developing the arguments she advances. Notably, Cherubina de Gabriak and Nelli come under Tsvetaeva's purview in these essays. Her response to the former in "The Living about the Living" is an enabling rereading of the mystification that asserts the proximity of all women—whether or not they write—to the incorporeal realm of poetry. Nelli appears in "A Hero of Labor," only to be dismissed as an indicator of Briusov's creative insufficiency. Defining her own poetic debut in terms of her public challenges to his authority, Tsvetaeva adduces Briusov's obsessive concern with binaries—the gender binary among them—and his sexualizing objectification of women as proof of his antipoetical nature. Essential to her self-presentation, the rebellion against him she describes in "A Hero of Labor" is also an instructive rallying cry to writing women, whom she urges to stop courting male approval and to establish supportive relationships among themselves.

If Briusov is a poet against whom Tsvetaeva defines herself, Voloshin is a poet with whom she presents herself in mutual embrace. "The Living about the Living" is permeated with details that destabilize the gender binary and document the benefits of this destabilization. Voloshin appears in Tsvetaeva's essay not as an authoritative mentor but as a friend and an equal in whom male- and female-gendered traits coexist. In contrast to Briusov's binarism is Voloshin's span of contraries that validate him as a true poet. In the course of portraying Voloshin, Tsvetaeva again shows herself to be an astute reader of poets, poetry, and the myriad signs of their surrounding world. Here, as in all her major essays, Tsvetaeva's emphasis on the derivation of meaning and her demonstrations of how she herself reads teach her readers to follow suit. This leads them into the habitually neglected, deeper reaches of the woman's text. Heightening readers' mindfulness by drawing them into active engagement with her work, Tsvetaeva fosters a collaborative relationship between the author and the reader whose benefits extend to all writing and reading.

Chapter 6 studies additional examples of how Tsvetaeva promotes cocreative reading but focuses primarily on another problem besetting women poets that she addresses—their persistent opposition to one another by critics and readers. This tendency is detrimental to the woman poet in obvious ways, which include generating insecurities around differing modes of self-presentation, reducing the poets' complex creative identities to a series of reductive binaries, and creating tensions that inhibit the formation of supportive communites among writing women. Here I explore the relationship between Tsvetaeva and Akhmatova—the two leading women poets of the twentieth century, who are repeatedly contrasted—as it reveals itself specifically in what they wrote to and about each other. Studying the two poets' own perspectives on and responses to each other counters their reductive pairings by critics and, more importantly, foregrounds Tsvetaeva's pointed resistance to such juxtapositions. As in the relations between Pavlova and Rostopchina considered in chapter 1, there is more than gender at stake for Tsvetaeva and Akhmatova.

I first look closely at how Tsvetaeva positions herself vis-à-vis Akhmatova in a conscious effort to dispel any sense of antagonism between them. Motivating this effort on Tsvetaeva's part are differences in how she and

Akhmatova absorb gender into their creative identities, but also a deep appreciation of her poetry that overarches their differences. With the early poems she addresses to Akhmatova, Tsvetaeva validates her own creative identity and taps into the celebrity that Akhmatova enjoyed at the time, much as Pavlova did with the first lyric she addressed to Rostopchina. The differences between the two modernist poets are roughly analogous to those between their nineteenth-century predecessors. Akhmatova fit easily into the beautiful woman aesthetic of the early years of her poetic career. At this stage in her career, Tsvetaeva presents herself pointedly resisting it. Avoiding discord like that between Pavlova and Rostopchina, she promotes a vision that readily accommodates—indeed insists on—a plurality of women's voices and self-images.

Characteristically, Tsvetaeva enacts what she describes. The poems she addresses to Akhmatova demonstrate her absorption of that poet's idiom into her own, while her letters develop bonds and commonalities between them. Key to understanding how Tsvetaeva frames her relations with Akhmatova and her motives for doing so is the essay "An Otherworldly Evening" ("Nezdeshnii vecher"), written on the death of the poet Mikhail Kuzmin. The titular evening marks Tsvetaeva's poetic debut in St. Petersburg (then Petrograd), which Akhmatova could not attend. Into a context that undermines the gender binary, Tsvetaeva weaves an argument against expecting congruity between how a poet looks and writes. Important for Tsvetaeva's self-affirmation, this was essential also to her wider efforts to get readers past all surface appearances—and those of the woman and her poems in particular. Tsvetaeva celebrates the absent Akhmatova but stops short of either granting or claiming ascendancy to present two different but equal poets. The image Tsvetaeva creates of her relationship with Akhmatova offers an enabling model for other women. Paying homage to Akhmatova, she resists the "divide and conquer school of criticism"[3] and pushes against literary historians who judge women in order to "accord real victory only to one 'queen.'"[4]

Akhmatova's responses to Tsvetaeva offer insight into what motivates and nurtures her own self-fashioning. Akhmatova was less invested in the relationship, and her responses, though cordial, lacked the intensity and volume of the letters and poems she received from Tsvetaeva. Tsvetaeva's emigration broke off closer ties that might have developed between them. Akhmatova, who presented herself as refusing to abandon her country in a time of need, was contemptuous of those who chose otherwise. Her access to what Tsvetaeva wrote in emigration was limited. Tsvetaeva's repatriation in 1939, and the horrors both poets endured in Stalinist Russia, brought them together briefly. Deeply affected by Tsvetaeva's suicide in 1941, Akhmatova referred to her with increasing frequency in conversations and notebook entries. Her responses to what she was able to read of Tsvetaeva's works span praise and censure, while her own comments on Cherubina de Gabriak and Nelli offer another perspective on the mystifications. Akhmatova's poems "A Belated Reply" ("Pozdnii otvet") and "There Were Four of Us" ("Nas bylo chetvero") express profound ties with Tsvetaeva, while the subtextual presence of Tsvetaeva's lyrics in Akhmatova's later poems documents an absorption of that poet into her own creative space in an embrace of differences that accords with Tsvetaeva's project.

How Women Must Write ends with a brief conclusion that recapitulates subversive strategies that women poets developed to move beyond victimhood and to claim agency. It notes the persistence of reader-imposed censorship that continues to affect evaluations of the woman poet and her writings. Drawing attention to the staying power of pronouncements made by authoritative critics, it iterates the need to counter their reductive assumptions about women poets by giving close attention to their individual texts. My enabling rereadings of the poets and poems studied in this book are directed toward this end.

PART I

Contentions

Chapter One

Karolina Pavlova versus Evdokiia Rostopchina

> A woman must love the arts, but love them
> for pleasure, and not in order to be an artist
> herself. No, a woman author can never love nor
> be a wife and a mother.
> —Vissarion Belinsky, review of the Russian trans-
> lation of Mme. B. Monborne's *Une victime, es-*
> *quisse littéraire*

THIS CHAPTER STUDIES two poets who emerged in
the waning years of the Golden Age: Karolina Pavlova (1807–93) and Evdokiia Rostopchina (1811–58).[1] The focus is on their response to the twofold problem of how a woman might best project a poetic self within an
emphatically male tradition and how that self might best respond to the
changing sociopolitical and cultural constructs of the woman in nineteenth-
century Russia. As they negotiate between the acquiescence to prevailing
gender norms that wins them approval and the subversion of these norms
that is vital for their creative self-realization, Pavlova and Rostopchina find
different ways to deal with constructs of gender in their time. These differences could have been seen as introducing a welcome plurality into possibilities open to women poets. Instead, they fostered strife. Pavlova's and Rostopchina's contretemps—a sign of the self-consciousness and discomfiture
of women poets seeking approval from the male establishment—alerts us
to the strengths and vulnerabilities of the divergent strategies they developed in the effort to gain recognition. It also demonstrates that despite their
differences and the changing views on women in their time, one problem
remained constant: women poets depended on men for the evaluation of
their poetical and social gestures. Here the risk of being misconstrued that
stalks all poets was compounded for the woman by gender biases that readers projected onto her poems.

Pavlova's and Rostopchina's disaffection highlights challenges that all
writing women confront as they respond to the demand that individual expressive needs be tailored to the expectations of the dominant culture. Here
those challenges are studied in the context of issues specific to Russia in the

17

1840s and 1850s that affected individual women poets and the development of a line of women's poetry within the tradition. I begin by sketching the culture of the time in which Pavlova and Rostopchina worked to establish themselves as poets. Next, I use two poems in which Pavlova publicly disassociates herself from Rostopchina—"To Countess R" ("Grafine R," 1841, pub. 1863) and "We are contemporaries, Countess" ("My sovremennitsy, grafinia," 1847, pub. 1899)—as points of departure for exploring the two poets' distinct modes of self-presentation.[2] Tracing the personal, social, cultural, and political references that carried meaning in the time these poems were written and received, I uncover multiple levels of signification that are essential to understanding how Pavlova and Rostopchina respond to changing constructs of the woman in their time. This allows me to foreground the largely unrecognized strategies they develop to subvert gender biases in ways that proved consequential for subsequent women poets. In particular, I draw attention to how the two poets use cultural vocabulary of their time to encode subversive messages in their poems and to what I designate as reader-imposed censorship, which maintains the status quo that Pavlova and Rostopchina disrupt. The chapter closes with an epilogue that looks at the parodic "A Song on the Occasion of the Correspondence of a Learned Man and a No Less Learned Woman" ("Pesnia po povodu perepiski uchenogo muzha s ne menee uchenoi zhenoi," 1854), in which Rostopchina sides with the dominant group to belittle Pavlova. The discussion of the parody and what prompted it revisits concerns discussed in this chapter from another perspective and highlights the tenacity of prohibitions that aspiring women poets confront.

Pavlova and Rostopchina sought recognition in a transitional period. The Sentimentalists, who at the end of the eighteenth century promoted the feminization[3] of literature (though not writing women themselves), were supplanted some decades earlier by poets of the Romantic school,[4] who "remasculinized" it.[5] Relegating women to a lower status in a separate domain, the Romantics claimed a privileged subjectivity, made an art of public displays of self-reflexivity, and framed poetic expression as an affirmation of male sexuality.[6] Defined as an assertive, expressly masculine form of creative endeavor, the poetic enterprise moved beyond the range of activity allowed women, leaving them in a double bind. That women's expressivity was subject to strict social control bespoke a lack of confidence in their capacity for self-governance and insisted on their need for male guidance. Yet at the same time, prevailing norms denied women precisely those emotional and erotic drives that required the exercise of self-control. This left women little room for asserting a forceful poetic personality or for regulating the powerful feelings that, for the Romantics, give rise to verse.

Accompanying Romantic tenets was an intensification of domestic ideology, which made its way into Russia from Europe in the 1820s. The drive to remove women from the public domain and to relegate them to the domestic sphere reflected a cognizance of the role women played in the French Revolution and a tacit recognition of their capacity to disrupt the existing order.[7] This politically motivated wariness of enlarging women's orbit extended into the cultural domain as well. Encouraged in the early decades of the nineteenth century, aspiring women poets now contended with increasingly restrictive patriarchal norms that pushed them back into the private sphere. Ol'ga Demidova plausibly suggests that the reason for this withdrawal of support "may have been the competition which women's literature now began to afford men's."[8] The tsarist state and the (male) poets it curbed concurred in their reluctance to loosen men's governance of women.

By the 1840s, the masculinized Romantic movement that supplanted the feminized Sentimental school was itself giving way to new developments. In the latter part of the 1830s, the prestige of poets and poetry in Russia took a downward turn that paralleled the nobility's steady loss of dominion over the arts. The posthumous publications of Pushkin's and Lermontov's lyrics in the early 1840s was widely seen as representing the pinnacle from which poetry had fallen and not as a sign of the genre's vitality.[9] By the end of the 1840s, the poets of Pushkin's pleiade were dead, and critics, following Vissarion Belinsky's lead, were championing naturalist prose and civic verse. As E. M. Shneiderman summarizes, "There was, it seems, no other period in the history of Russian literature when poetry was in such disregard as in the 40s of the 19th century."[10]

Paradoxically, the awkwardness of making a poetic debut when the status of poetry was in decline combined advantageously with the even greater awkwardness perceived in a woman's attempt to establish herself as a practitioner of that art.[11] By rising to defend poetry in an ever less receptive cultural climate, women could join ranks with male poets of the day on more equal footing than they might otherwise have done. For its part, the Romantic school benefited from new allies, who, as Susanne Fusso shows, effectively prolonged the expiring movement: "The literary fact of Pavlova's gender enabled her to keep the Romantic hero alive a bit past his generally accepted date of death: in many of her poems, the feminine gender of the lyric speaker lends new meaning and depth, based on the position of women and especially women writers in Russian society, to the poet's alienation and separation from the crowd."[12]

That women poets could gain possibility from a declining, expressly male school of poetry and that the school itself should derive sustenance from them can be attributed in part to the fact that the limitations imposed on women's writing were partially offset by the broader demands of lyric poetry for constant redefinition of both the genre and its practitioners. Because the domain of poetry and the poet operating in it are continuously redrawn, the act of fashioning a viable creative self is within the purview of the genre itself. At the same time, however, domestic ideology exacerbated the self-consciousness with which the woman poet appeared in the poetic arena, making it more difficult to make her entrance appear natural. The ever-present danger of being misconstrued—whether intentionally or inadvertently—was compounded for the woman poet by the double threat of objectification and of not being taken seriously enough to merit close reading. The professionalization of writers beginning in the 1830s added to this discomfiture, for even as it opened a potential source of income, it threw an unsavory cast over the woman writer who received monetary compensation for appearing in public. Moreover, as Greene describes, with the concurrent rise of the publishing culture, "men literary gatekeepers . . . took virtually complete control of the means of literary production and distribution," leaving women in an even greater state of dependency on their approval.[13] The woman poet's efforts to enter this culture on equal footing with men demanded assurances that she was neither an aberration nor a disruptive element and prompted the need to explain the absence of women's voices from the tradition.

The self-invention in which poets engaged in their verse and social behavior was additionally complicated for women poets by the fact that the sociopolitical and cultural emblems of the woman were determined by men and remained in flux. The complexity and instability of how gender was framed and what it signified demanded that the woman poet respond to multiple, often conflicting currents. This affected how gender figured in her self-presentations and definitions of poet and poetry. It extended also to how she positioned herself vis-à-vis other prominent women—whether flesh-and-blood individuals or literary heroines authored by men. A cultural setting that problematizes gender intensifies women poets' need to win approval from the male establishment. This fosters strife between them,[14] deepening the woman poet's sense of isolation and intensifying the insecurities attendant on reconciling her gender with her literary aspirations.

Once the woman poet was published, there still remained the exigence of securing not just a readership but serious, engaged readings of her verse. Whatever strategies she developed, the woman poet depended on her reader to discern deeper layers of meaning that she embedded in her poems. In Russia, Aesopian writing that developed in response to government censorship complicated the subtle encoding that characterizes the poetic genre. Readers were thus doubly trained—poetically and politically—to apprehend multiple levels of signification in a poem. Yet when the poem was authored by a woman this well-exercised aptitude to read between the lines fell by the wayside. Readers tended to overlook deeper strata of meaning and to read assumptions about gender back into the very poems contravening them. Whether consciously or unconsciously applied, such reader-imposed censorship reaffirmed the status quo by reading the woman back into her place.

As she sought to position herself to best advantage, the woman poet remained aware of how she herself, her works, and other women (both fictional and real) were being read, and mindful, too, of a need to take an active role in shaping these readings. The creative self she projected—both in her social behavior and in her writings—figured in this project as a sort of paratext designed to influence the reader's approach to her poems. As with her poems, however, what her projected self-image conveyed depended on how it was read. This further intensified the anxiety attendant on women poets' self-presentations and made divergent self-images developed by other women seem threatening. One image was invariably productive: the woman poet could derive advantage from presenting herself as a reader—a role famously validated by Pushkin's heroine, Tatiana.[15] Women's readings of canonical authors, works, and heroines gained them a role in the male tradition and allowed them to enact the kind of reading that their own works merited. Such "enabling rereading," as I designate it, suggested a means to counter reader-imposed censorship.

Pavlova and Rostopchina did not explicitly promote the woman's right to self-realization that was implicit in their act of writing. They also resisted injunctions of progressive critics to sever ties with the Pushkinian tradition and to write civic-minded verse. This did not indicate a lack of awareness of the sociopolitical and cultural climate. On the contrary, their poems responded to the shifting contexts in which they arose and were received, as both women purposefully engaged vocabulary of their time to absorb gender into their creative identities. Pavlova's disagreement with Rostopchina was easy to dismiss as stereotypical female jealousy. Reading it with the attention it merits shows the two poets working deliberately—each in her own manner—to maximize possibility and to find ways to turn inimical circumstances to advantage.

At the height of their careers, Pavlova and Rostopchina presided over influential literary salons and engaged in lively exchanges with leading cultural figures of the time. Both were encouraged by prominent (men) poets, published in leading journals, and recognized as cultural figures. On the question of how to deal with gender in their self-presentations, however, they parted company. Pavlova used demonstrative dedication to the poetic calling to sidestep her womanhood, while Rostopchina developed a poetic identity that embraced it. Rooting her "pose of a poet of thought" in German idealism, Pavlova consciously modeled herself on Evgenii Baratynsky (1800–1844),[16] who privileged the imagination and insisted that emotions be reined in by the intellect. Emphasizing the activity of the mind, Pavlova downplayed the body in an effort to forestall objectification. For her, poetic language was a replacement for the body rather than a manifestation of its desires. Thus, for example, in the narrative poem "The Crone" ("Starukha," 1840), Pavlova has an old, emphatically desexualized woman enthrall a young, attractive male listener not with physical allure but with the story she relates to him. Exchanging her body for the power to wield language, Pavlova sought just such desexualization for the invented selves who appear in her poems and for the poet who authored them. As Olga Briker notes, even her poetry of the heart "features a poet-lover who speaks of love either as a quasi-religious experience or asexually, using fraternal and sororal images."[17] Pavlova's unconsummated love for the Polish Romantic poet Adam Mickiewicz, who briefly tutored her in his native tongue, remained a constant in her lyric autobiography.

Pavlova sought to have her erudition recognized as integral to her creative identity. She was known, in particular, for her grasp of Russian, German, French, English, Polish, and Italian. Her translations of Russian poetry into French and German and her translations of French and German works into Russian promoted the recognition of Russian letters in Europe and enhanced Russian familiarity with European writers. The praise she received at home and abroad for bringing Russian culture to the attention of a European reading public advanced her cultural status, albeit initially at the expense of her own verse. By presenting herself as a poet of thought and foregrounding the learnedness that she made a distinctive feature of her creative identity, Pavlova sought to deflect attention from her gender. This well-reasoned strategy, however, fueled allegations that she was not a real woman but an aberration and was used to devalue her as a poet. Ironically, her efforts to create a viable poetic self that bypassed gender precipitated the demand that she prove herself as a woman. In the latter part of her career, this circular argument compromised Pavlova's standing as a poet.

In a discussion of Pavlova, Catriona Kelly writes, "Her sense of poetry as an intellectual utterance, rather than simply an outburst of feeling, distinguishes her voice from that of her female contemporaries."[18] Nowhere does this difference seem more marked than in her juxtaposition with the prevailing image of Rostopchina. As Green describes, "While Rostopchina appeared to revel in the feminine role, Pavlova directly protested against the strictures that made it almost impossible for a woman to be strong and creative."[19] Like Pavlova, Rostopchina could boast the command of several languages, and the epigraphs to her poems show that she was remarkably well read. Unlike Pavlova, however, she did not shy away from combining this conventionally male-gendered aspect of her creative identity with enactments of conventional femininity. Indeed, in some poems, Rostopchina appears to court the objectification Pavlova went to great lengths to avoid, and there is no trace of desexualizing domesticity in her poems, from which her husband and children are conspicuously absent.[20] Broadly summarized, Pavlova's enactments of the poet were intended to camouflage the woman. Rostopchina's enactments of the woman were aimed to camouflage the poet. Underlying these divergent positions is the shared struggle to close the perceived rift between woman and poet and to gain admission into the Russian poetic tradition on equal terms with poets who were men. In the following chapter, I look more closely at Rostopchina's feminine masquerade, what she seeks to accomplish with it, and its consequences. Here I focus on how Pavlova positions herself vis-à-vis her sister poet for what it tells us about her own objectives and the inadequate choices available to her in the culture of the time.

In "To Countess R," the first of the two poems that she addressed to Rostopchina, Pavlova launches a spirited defense of Moscow, the old Russian capital that Rostopchina allegedly slights in her lyrics. As Pavlova upbraids her sister poet for abandoning traditional Russian values in favor of a cosmopolitan St. Petersburg lifestyle, the reader is led to understand that it is patriotic zeal that moves her to defend Moscow, which she styles as the locus of creativity—a Castalian spring that nurtures verse. Rostopchina's departure from Moscow, the city of her birth where she began writing, thus amounts to a betrayal of the poet's true, creative self. Notably, the reproaches Pavlova leveled at Rostopchina remained untested against that poet's Moscow poems and were uncritically accepted and repeated by commentators.[21] Yet even a cursory look at Rostopchina's "To Moscow" ("V Moskvu") and "A View on Moscow" ("Vid Moskvy") reveals them to be innocent of the breaches of fealty and gratitude to Moscow for which Pavlova castigates her. The aspersions that Pavlova casts on Rostopchina's poetic sensibilities are also no more justified by these poems than is the charge of disloyalty to the city. Indeed, when Rostopchina's "To Moscow" first appeared in *The Contemporary* (*Sovremennik*) in 1840, Belinsky singled it out for praise and spoke of it as "remarkable in its warmth of feeling and charm of expression."[22] Moreover, the ethos of Rostopchina's two Moscow pieces—with their foregrounding of memory and imagination, their privileging of the acoustic over the visual, and their expressions of longing for disappearing Muscovite customs—is in accord with Pavlova's own Romantically informed views on poetry and allegiance to the old Russian capital.[23] Given the poetic acumen documented in Pavlova's translations and her own verse, there is little doubt that if she misreads Rostopchina's Moscow poems, she does so purposefully. This calls out for attention.

Significantly, Pavlova composed her apostrophe to Rostopchina not when that poet's Moscow lyrics first came out in 1840 but only in the spring of 1841, when they appeared in her debut collection, *Poems of Countess E. Rostopchina* (*Stikhotvoreniia grafini E. Rostopchinoi*). Although Pavlova was no stranger in literary circles at this time, she earned praise primarily for her translations.[24] Her renown as a Russian writer had yet to peak as it did only in 1848 with the publication of *A Double Life* (*Dvoinaia zhizn'*). When Pavlova composed "To Countess R," Rostopchina was the better known poet. Stephanie Sandler and Judith Vowles describe this period as one in which "poetic identity was typically achieved in poems that established relationships with other poets, relationships themselves marked by assumptions about gender differences."[25] This applies directly to "To Countess R," which is an oblique self-presentation that taps into Rostopchina's celebrity and satisfies two conflicting demands: it puts Pavlova in the public eye yet allows her to remain within the bounds of modesty expected of women. Moreover, by addressing Rostopchina, Pavlova attracts male readers with the rhetorical allure of listening in on what one woman has to say to another, creating the impression that they are privy to a personal communication rather than a public act of self-affirmation.

Using terms familiar from the growing debates between the Slavophiles and the Westernizers—at this time still amicable and regularly conducted in her salon—Pavlova identifies with the grammatically feminine, Russian city of her birth in contrast to the new, masculine European capital. The ostensibly spontaneous outburst of patriotic fervor that she registers in "To Countess R" legitimizes what could otherwise be seen as immodest self-promotion that runs counter to the values that Pavlova champions in her poem. Pavlova would have her reader think that she addresses Rostopchina not to attract attention but out of an overpowering need to defend Moscow that makes her forget herself. Social norms governing women's behavior make allowances for just such outbursts of patriotic zeal, and "nationalistic or patriotic convictions allowed some women writers to strengthen their claim to authorship."[26]

Pavlova's show of patriotism was important also in that it allowed her to shore up the "culturally ambiguous status" that made her "sensible of, and sensitive to, the negative resonance of her status as foreigner."[27] On her mother's side, Pavlova's family was French and English, while, as her name and patronymic Karolina Karlovna proclaimed, her father's family was German. Noted even by her admirers, this background left her claim to the status of Russian poet insecure. "A veritable miracle!" one reader exclaimed, adding, "Her work gladdens us, only it is vexing that however you look at it, she still ends up being a German."[28] In the effort to establish a Russian cultural identity, Pavlova asseverates loyalty to a pre-Petrine order, maximally distancing herself from her European forebears. Indeed, she makes herself out to be more Russian than her St. Petersburg rival—a Muscovite whose husband (to whom Pavlova alludes in the poem) was the son of the governor-general of Moscow who, as was widely held, foiled Napoleon's plans to capture the city by setting fire to it. Pavlova's emphasis on the historical and cultural significance of Moscow reflects also the insecurity of the old Russian city vis-à-vis the modern European capital of Peter the Great. Although in the 1840s "Moscow entered a remarkable period of increased intellectual animation, a period of unprecedented literary activity,"[29] it paled before St. Petersburg in cultural significance. Pavlova—a woman, a non-Russian, and a denizen of Moscow—thus found herself triply marginalized. The oblique self-presentation that emerges from her poetical chastisement of Rostopchina speaks to all three areas.

Beyond promoting Pavlova's selfhood, "To Countess R" reflects her broader preoccupation with how women poets were perceived. As with any marginalized group, the missteps of one reflected badly on all. Pavlova's multivalent defense of Moscow signified in yet another way. With her rejection of Rostopchina's "cosmopolitanism," Pavlova rejected the image of frivolous society lady and promoted her own paradigm of the responsible, self-controlled woman poet. Inasmuch as nothing in Rostopchina's Moscow poems called for the city's defense, Pavlova's "To Countess R" was triggered apparently not by these lyrics but by Belinsky's review of the volume in which they were reprinted—*Poems of Evdokiia Rostopchina*, which came out that year (1841).[30] In his review, which marked the downturn of Rostopchina's literary acclaim, Belinsky initially praises Rostopchina but then goes on to brand her as a socialite, who is "chained to the ball."[31] Pavlova was keen to disassociate herself in particular and the woman poet in general from the feminine frivolousness that Belinsky invoked to devalue Rostopchina's cultural status. Indeed, with "To Countess R" Pavlova addresses not Rostopchina but the male establishment.

In January of 1847,[32] Pavlova addressed another poem to Rostopchina. The untitled lyric, which opens with the line "We are contemporaries, Countess," is a masterful negotiation of conformity and subversion, enacted now in a more volatile context where there is considerably more at stake. As in her earlier poem to Rostopchina, Pavlova seeks not to enter into dialogue with her addressee but to convey something about herself. Commentators repeatedly single out this poem as articulating Pavlova's artistic credo[33] but consistently overlook its deeper strata of signification. Because on its surface "We are contemporaries" appears to deliver its author's acquiescence to restrictive patriarchal norms and resistance to progressive ideas, shallow reading compromises the enabled self-image encoded in it, leaving the poem victim to reader-imposed censorship. A closer reading, which addresses the situation of the woman poet in the culture of the time, reveals Pavlova's masterful use of Aesopian language to put the woman poet on par with her male counterparts.

Pavlova opens "We are contemporaries" with what she and Rostopchina have in common. They are "daughters of Moscow," are of the same age, and influenced by the same poets—Byron and Pushkin. These similarities foreground the differences that now prevail between them. On the one hand, there is Rostopchina, featured as a beautiful, freewheeling George Sandiste (*zhorzhsandistka*) of St. Petersburg society, who, unrestrained, travels widely and expresses herself spontaneously. Opposite her is the invented self of Pavlova's poem—a wife content to remain within the confines of her Moscow home, who has no need for the "emancipations" she designates with a dismissive plural. The lines between "George Sandism" and domestic ideology are sharply drawn. The authored Rostopchina is aligned with the former, while the authored self, who accepts her husband's authority over her writing, falls squarely in the latter: "And I simply give my poems to my husband for stern judgment" (*I otdaiu ia prosto muzhu / Svoi stikhi na strogii sud*).[34] To apprehend what lies beyond this schematic opposition it is essential to read "We are contemporaries" in the sociopolitical context in which it arose and in light of the specific event to which the poem responds. Accordingly, I first sketch the impact of domestic ideology and George Sandism on constructs of the woman in the culture of the time and then describe what prompted the apostrophe to Rostopchina and the unlikely position that Pavlova assumes in it. This leads into a discussion of the broader implications of the poem's enabling import.

Patrick Vincent situates the discord between Pavlova and Rostopchina in "the culture wars of the 1840s," noting that "the women positioned themselves according to sectarian lines: Slavophile or Westernizer, Muscovite or Saint Petersburger, domestic or cosmopolitan." His account of the poets' disaffection as "stoked by an increasingly embittered exchange of poems between Slavophiles and Westernizers"[35] alerts us to the historical context and the terms in which Pavlova couched her objections to Rostopchina but not to what Pavlova engages this cultural vocabulary to convey. More than a rehearsal of debates conducted by men, Pavlova's poem documents the perspective of a woman poet as she considers how to best position herself within the limited options that these debates make available to her. Here it is important to remember that both the domestic ideology and the George Sandism invoked in "We are contemporaries" are fluid, polyvalent constructs whose effects on aspiring women poets extend well beyond the opposition around which Pavlova structures her poem. Read not simply as an enactment of male ideas and ideals but as the locus of the creative subjectivity that

Pavlova purposefully crafts for herself, "We are contemporaries" discloses a nuanced project.

It is helpful to begin commentary on the terms Pavlova uses in her poem by recalling that domesticity in nineteenth-century Russia differed from the Victorian image of the home as a man's refuge from public life that the woman maintained for that purpose. In Russia, the absence of a public forum in which to discuss social and political issues amplified the significance of the domestic sphere, where ideas that the censorship sought to suppress could find more open discussion and works whose publication would be allowed only in expurgated versions could be read aloud or circulated in their entirety.[36] The very domesticity that sustained the existing order could also shelter ideas that subverted it.[37] This duality is crucial to Pavlova, whose recourse to domesticity in "We are contemporaries" strategically advances the woman poet's cause.

The professed adherence to domestic ideology is striking in light of George Sand's prominence on the Russian cultural scene at the time Pavlova wrote "We are contemporaries."[38] The excitement surrounding Sand is vividly captured by Lesley Singer Herrmann, who writes of this period as a time

> when Dostoevsky suffered from fever all night after reading *L'Uscoque*; when Herzen pleaded for a copy of *Revue des Deux Mondes* containing the ending of *Spiridon*; when Bakunin confessed (àpropos of *Consuelo*) that each time he read Sand he became better and better; when Belinsky called her a contemporary "Joan of Arc" and harangued his friends interminably on her virtues; when lovers memorized passages from her novels and left their spouses to live the "life of the heart"; when Slavophiles and Westernizers alike praised her humanity; when Pauline Viardot, on operatic tour in St. Petersburg, wrote to Sand herself, "you reign over Russia more sovereignly than the tsar."[39]

Beginning in 1832, with the publication of her first novel, *Indiana*, which won her immediate celebrity in Russia, Sand was avidly followed and talked about as a source of the newest thoughts France had to offer. Promoting ideas that the censorship sought to keep out of Russia, Sand's novels undermined domestic ideology and championed the woman's right to love freely. Sand herself dramatized her disregard for conventional gender norms with her much-publicized nom de plume, men's apparel, cigar smoking, and participation in men's drinking parties. Although much of the reading public of the time was still conversant in French, Russian translations of Sand's works followed (often in multiple versions) swiftly on the heels of the originals.

The trajectory of Sand's reception in Russia reflects changes in thinking that her writings helped to bring about. If in the early 1830s Sand was vilified by a Russian press that rushed to defend the norms and values she challenged, by the 1840s leading liberals of the Russian intelligentsia hailed her as a catalyst for social change. What had been regarded in the 1830s as Sand's immoral behavior was construed by liberals of the 1840s in broader, sociopolitical terms as active rebellion against limitations of individual human freedom. Progressive thinkers, notably Belinsky, Chernyshevsky, Herzen, and Druzhinin, took up Sand's novels and the ideas they advanced. Yet even as her writings fed the liberals' urge to disrupt the status quo, Sand herself—in appearance and behavior—provided conservatives with material for warnings against such disruption. Though Sand was hailed as a writer of genius, her flamboyant image left her open to ridicule. Indeed, Sand's writings and her public image often worked at cross-purposes, and not all readers found her persuasive. Leo Tolstoy, for one, remained intransigent in his assessment of Sand as a shameless libertine.[40] Caricatures of Sand and distortions of her ideas accrued to her larger-than-life image, and the influential *zhorzhsandistka* became, among other things, "a comic type of the period."[41]

Significantly, the novels that held particular interest for Russian readers were those dealing with love and the emancipation of women.[42] The woman's freedom of the heart that these novels promoted supplanted earlier models of self-sacrificing matrimonial fidelity. Sand's heroines were held up as examples for flesh-and-blood women and literary heroines alike. Thus, for example, Indiana came to compete with—indeed to eclipse—Pushkin's Tatiana as a literary presence and role model. Juxtaposed to what is habitually read as Tatiana's selfless loyalty to her wedded spouse[43] was Indiana's convention-defying pursuit of emotional fulfillment.[44] Although in his famous ninth article on Pushkin of 1845 Belinsky does not refer to Sand by name, the reproach he levels at Tatiana for failing to break with convention in order to follow the dictates of her heart reflects the extent to which that critic had fallen under the sway of ideas that Sand espoused.[45]

The role that women played in the French Revolution was not yet forgotten, and the threat that Sand's radical departure from the status quo constituted for the existing sociopolitical system in Russia was evident. Nicholas I, like his mother, Empress Maria, before him, held that the stability of Russia's monarchy depended on a social order that was rooted in precisely those values that Sand undermined. Threatened by Sand's defiance of the principles on which his regime and authority rested, Nicholas I was determined to repulse her challenges to existing norms.[46] For the Western-minded Russian intelligentsia of the time, the enlargement of women's compass was ancillary to broader social change rather than an end in itself. Thus it is possible to say, as Herrmann does, that "not all 'zhorzhsandistki' were women" and that prominent liberals, including Alexander Herzen, Mikhail Bakunin, and Alexei Pisemsky, numbered among the George Sandians of the time.[47] Indeed, it is precisely because "Sand's novels linked the repression of women with all social repression"[48] that she held sway among Russian liberals of the 1840s, who could use the situation of women much as Pushkin's generation had used Africans enslaved in America to encode protests against serfdom and the autocracy.

To understand Pavlova's rejection of the *zhorzhsandism* she has Ros-topchina represent in her poem, it is important to bear in mind the significant differences in how men and women in Russian society could act on the ideas embraced by Sand-inspired liberals. If read as bespeaking not forward-looking social reform but immediate emotional (read sexual) gratification— that is to say read not by men confident in their ability to effect social change but by women confined in a system that denied them agency—Sand's novels and the ideas they promoted did not expand possibility. While the super-annuation of an ideal based on self-sacrificial dedication to matrimony and maternity freed the woman from domesticity, it did not yet move her toward self-realization. A chasm remained between the ideas espoused by liberals and the actual situation in which women found themselves.

The problem, as Richard Stites summarizes, stemmed from the fact that there was no concrete, practicable role for the newly envisioned woman in Russian society. To be sure, there was "the programmatic dogma," which Stites describes as promoting "freedom in sexual life, equality in those re-lationships including the right of the woman to retain her own name, the public rearing of children, and a role for woman in the common work of the new society." At the same time, however, there were "the unspoken contra-dictions as well: abolition of marriage and comments on the family almost in the same breath and the absence of any clear idea of how woman will take up her role in society and how much of a role that will be."[49]

Absorbed into broader efforts to effect social and political change, the question of the woman's role in Russian society was concerned less with women themselves than with the leverage their situation could gain pro-gressive thinkers. The erosion of time-honored gender roles became part of the liberals' armamentarium, making the woman more of a political tool wielded by men than a freely acting agent. The degree to which jurisdic-tion over progressive ideas advanced by George Sand remained under male control is vividly exemplified by Aleksandr Druzhinin's *Polin'ka Saks* (1847), one of the many works of the time overtly modeled on Sand's work. In it Saks, a paternalistic husband who educates his child-wife Polin'ka (note the diminutive of her name), has her read Sand's early novels on the assumption that "a woman's genius would be accessible to a woman."[50] This proves not to be the case. The celebrated Sand elicits only yawns from Polin'ka, who casts the books aside in a gesture that relinquishes control over the views they espouse. It falls to her husband to closely monitor and direct the exercise of Sandian freedom of the heart on which Polin'ka unwittingly embarks. The reading of Sand's novels and the realization of the ideas they promote remain, Druzhinin's tale insists, a male prerogative.

For all the politicization of their social and private behavior, women themselves still lacked the means to take independent, purposeful action in the public arena. Leached of their social and political underpinning, Sand's ideas threatened to become little more than a justification for irresponsible, impetuous behavior. Thus Barbara Engel comments on "the phenomenon of noblewomen using the pretext of 'elevated love' in order to deceive their husbands,"[51] and Helena Goscilo notes that Sandism "at the crudest level meant adulterous liaisons contracted under the banner of emancipation."[52] Pavlova was wary of such "emancipations," which increased the tendency to sexualize women and to uphold the ruling prejudice subscribed to by conservatives and liberals alike that women were irresponsible creatures in need of men's guidance.

Cognizant of the inadequacy of the politicized constructs of the woman and of the fluid meanings that accrue to them, Pavlova resists aligning Sandism with the liberation of women and domesticity with their subjugation. In "We are contemporaries," she uses "stumbling blocks"—those "obtrusively enigmatic features" that, as Leo Strauss describes, alert the enlightened reader to meaning concealed from the censor in deeper strata of the text.[53] The most pointed of these is the notable discrepancy between the authored Pavlova and Rostopchina of "We are contemporaries" and the actual poets' circumstances at the time of the poem's composition. Responding to this prompt, I trace the particulars first of Pavlova's and then Rostopchina's situations, which, in the sociocultural context outlined above, lead us to appreciate the multiple layers of meaning in Pavlova's poem. Beyond providing context necessary for understanding the poem, this allows me to enlarge on reader-imposed censorship of women's poems.

In 1835, Pavlova's husband, Nikolai Filippovich Pavlov, earned the double boon of Pushkin's praise and Nicholas I's displeasure with the publication of his *Three Tales* (*Tri povesti*)—stories with a critical edge toward serfdom that brought him acclaim and presaged a bright literary future. After his marriage to Karolina Jaenisch in 1837, Pavlov, who also authored poems and translations, devoted ever less time to writing.[54] A second collection of his stories that came out in 1839 attracted only scant notice. In 1841, a friend of the family's, the poet Aleksei Khomiakov, remarked apropos of Pavlova, "She is annihilating him; soon her poems will be more widely read than his stories."[55] By 1847, the time I am considering here, Pavlova's writings had indeed eclipsed her husband's, and their personal relations were deteriorating rapidly. Describing "We are contemporaries, Countess" as

Pavlova's poetic credo, Rapgof comments, "As for the husband in the role of poetic judge, this hardly corresponds with reality."[56] There is, of course, no reason to expect poems to "correspond with reality." Here, however, the noteworthy discrepancy serves as a stumbling block that urges readers to look more closely at the poem.

When Pavlova penned "We are contemporaries, Countess," she was better established in the literary world than when she wrote "To Countess R" and no longer needed to address her sister poet to draw attention to herself. Rostopchina's career, in contrast, had suffered a serious downturn. The difficulty besetting Rostopchina was the immediate stimulus for Pavlova's composition of "We are contemporaries, Countess." The December 17, 1846, issue of the paper *Northern Bee* (*Severnaia pchela*) carried a series of poems by Rostopchina, among which was a ballad titled "A Forced Marriage" ("Nasil'nyi brak"). The ballad presents a dispute between an old baron and his wife that his "servants and vassals" are summoned to hear out and judge fairly. In the first half of the poem, the all-powerful baron rails against his wife's intractability, ending each of the four stanzas of his plaint with increasingly adverse epithets that underscore his high displeasure and her alleged guilt: (1) "My rebellious wife!" (2) "Ungrateful wife." (3) "My perfidious wife!" (4) "My criminal wife!" The thrust of the baron's argument is that he extended his patronage over his orphaned spouse, provided her with wealth and luxury, and personally stood guard over her to protect her from enemies. In response to these magnanimous gestures, his wife, as he maintains, maligns him far and wide and behaves in a treacherous manner. The baron's enemies, in the meantime, derive pleasure from his discomfiture and egg the wife on to further insubordination.

In the second half of Rostopchina's poem, the wife has her say and complains of the harsh limitations her husband imposes on her. Beginning with the marriage forced on her, she describes herself as a vassal who thirsts for vengeance on the baron, who forbids her the use of her own language, prevents her from taking pride in her ancient lineage, and bars her from observing the rites of her faith. She bemoans the loss of her servants and bridles under the oppression she endures at the hands of the "slaves" set over her by her spouse. Under such circumstances, the wife asserts, she has good cause to complain and can scarcely acquiesce in silence to her lot. The four stanzas of her argument end with self-characterizations that emphasize her plight and offset the accusations the baron levels at her: (1) "I am a prisoner and not a wife!" (2) "I am his enemy and not his wife!" (3) ". . . unfortunate wife." (4) "A wife taken by force."

The ballad could be read variously. Rostopchina's own less than satisfying personal relations with her husband inclined readers to see this poem as airing the poet's personal infelicity. At the same time, the ballad, which appeared at the apogee of Sand's popularity in Russia, could be read more broadly as a protest against the institution of matrimony. There was yet another way in which the poem signified, and Faddei Bulgarin, the founder and editor of the *Northern Bee* who accepted it for publication, found himself in hot water when it won scandalous notice as an allegory of Russia's repressive treatment of Poland. Before submitting her manuscript to Bulgarin, Rostopchina, who was traveling with her family in Europe at the time, removed the subtitle "Allegory" and the overt references to Poland—specifically the note that she had written the poem en route from Cracow to Vienna and the dedication to the Polish Romantic poet Adam Mickiewicz.[57] These deletions, however, could scarcely obviate the political import of the domestic grievance the poem describes.

We may well marvel that Rostopchina had the temerity to submit her provocative poem to the conservative *Northern Bee*, the only paper read at court. We must marvel still more that Bulgarin chose to publish it.[58] The story of this venture is instructive in that beyond explaining Pavlova's poem, it offers striking examples of the subversive potential vested in enactments of conventional femininity and of the superficiality of readings accorded to poems written by women. Here reader-imposed censorship phases into the invisibility of the unthinkable, demonstrating the intransigence of gender stereotypes that prevents readers from perceiving even blatant departures from the norm.

Rostopchina sent the offending "Ballad of Chivalry," as she subtitled "A Forced Marriage," to Bulgarin with several more poems and a letter in which she—in a show of feminine modesty—asked that they be published with no indication of authorship. Preconceived notions about gender, which Rostopchina skillfully exploited, left Bulgarin susceptible to her flattery and blinded him to the seditious aspect of her poem. Gratified by the accolades to the *Northern Bee* and his editorship with which Rostopchina generously interlarded her instructions,[59] Bulgarin, in an episode worthy of a Krylov fable, published the first installment of her poems, together with the letter that accompanied them.[60] He prefaced the publication with his own laudatory remarks, concluding with a paean to

> the lofty talent, the tender feelings, the elevated ideas, the sweet language and the primary property of genius, the key to the human heart, especially to the inscrutable heart of a woman![61] It has been ages and ages since such sweet sounds have been heard in our orphaned Russian poetry. For a long time our poetry has not been warmed by such kindly feelings as are contained in these verses born under the charming sky of Italy! F. B.[62]

Whatever the charms of the "sky of Italy," the sky over Bulgarin's head darkened ominously when Emperor Nicholas was discerned in the "old baron" and Poland in the "wife" of Rostopchina's poem.[63] The tsar's wrath was conveyed to the unhappy editor and his coeditor, Nikolai Grech, by Count Aleksei Orlov, the chief of the Third Section—the secret police. Grech was quick to point out that Bulgarin was the one who agreed to publish the poems and to declare his own distaste for verse—women's verse in particular. He insisted that he took "A Forced Marriage" at face value because he never dreamed that a woman, and especially one of Rostopchina's class, would be capable of such perfidy.[64] Bulgarin, whose position was all the more precarious because he was of Polish extraction, similarly protested his innocence of the poem's political dimension. Offering his own reading, he argued that to see Nicholas in the baron and Poland in the wife was to misread the poem, which, if taken for a political allegory, showed the baron Austria in argument with his wife Italy.[65]

According to various stories spawned by the incident, Bulgarin was interrogated and let off with humiliating but relatively minor chastisement.[66] It could scarcely have been otherwise, for the poem had slipped not only past him but also, as Grech justly notes in his letter to Orlov, past two rounds of government censors.[67] Bolstered by Rostopchina's enactments of conventional femininity, the double unthinkability that a political allegory of such audacity could be penned by a woman and submitted to a conservative paper blinded censors and editors alike to the obvious import of her poem. Publication of the *Northern Bee*, which the tsar threatened to close down, continued after copies carrying the offending poem were seized and destroyed.[68] Bulgarin was "made to be more aware of the presence of government pressure on the editorial policies of his journal."[69] The offending poem enjoyed wide circulation in manuscript and appeared in Russian publications abroad,[70] while loyal subjects of the tsar responded with poems that took unruly wives to task.[71]

Rostopchina's allegory irrevocably impaired her relations with the court. For all the anger the emperor vented on Bulgarin, the brunt of his displeasure fell predictably on the author of "A Forced Marriage" herself. When in 1847, nearly a year after publishing the poem, Rostopchina returned to St. Petersburg from the European voyage on which she embarked with her family in 1845, she was no longer welcome at court and had to remove herself from the capital to Moscow.[72] Thinking to regain admission to the social circles from which she had been expelled, Rostopchina appeared at a Moscow ball given in honor of Nicholas I, only to be shown out.[73] None of the patriotic poems she subsequently penned could reinstate her in the good graces of Nicholas I, and she returned to St. Petersburg only after his death. The intensity of the tsar's displeasure—like the length of royal memory and the thickness of royal blood—are well illustrated by the fact that Rostopchina's request to present her daughters at the court of Nicholas's successor, Alexander II, was denied on the grounds of the trouble she had caused.[74] As Diana Greene cogently summarizes, "Rostopchina made the forbidden connections between the oppression of women, the oppression of Russians, and the oppression of Poles (patriarchy, autocracy, and imperialism) and paid dearly for it."[75]

The consequences of the "Forced Marriage" scandal went well beyond Rostopchina's banishment from court. Writing of the increasingly stringent censorship that set in after the "relatively lenient" years 1846 and 1847, Pedrotti argues persuasively that "the publication of Countess Rostopchina's allegorical ballad in 1846, prompted by the earlier political events in the Cracow area, could have served as the initial reason for this new hard line of Russian censorship."[76] Rostopchina, whose poem naturally offended conservatives, thus came to disaffect liberals as well. In light of the intensified censorship, the publication of "A Forced Marriage," which initially suffused its author in "an aura of martyrdom,"[77] came to look like an impetuous, ill-considered gesture. Even as it demonstrated the power of a woman's pen, the ensuing scandal and its consequences pointed to her willfulness and lack of judgment.

This episode explains Pavlova's otherwise perplexing valorization in "We are contemporaries, Countess" of a domestic ideology to which she did not herself subscribe.[78] Pavlova could not refer to "A Forced Marriage" explicitly, but the fact that "the variant stanzas share lexicon with Rostopchina's poem"[79] shows that she had Rostopchina's allegory in mind when she composed her poem.[80] Like Rostopchina's lyric, Pavlova's "We are contemporaries" infuses a domestic situation with political import. Yet if Rostopchina's is a defiant statement, Pavlova's is a conciliatory one, constructed to distance her from the "Forced Marriage" scandal and to present an alternative image of the woman poet. Although registered obliquely, the position Pavlova assumes is clear: the submissiveness to her spouse that her poem avows extends to the head of all Russia, whose authority Rostopchina challenged.

This raises the question of what, if anything, distinguishes "We are contemporaries, Countess" from the poems professing loyalty to a backward-looking social order that were penned in response to "A Forced Marriage." Beyond reflecting her mindfulness of the government censor, Pavlova's decision to decrease lexical allusions to Rostopchina's poem in the final version of her own suggests that she is not focusing exclusively on "A Forced Marriage" and that her poem absorbs the scandal it precipitated into broader concerns. Considering Pavlova's poem in a wider context shows that, however unlikely it may seem at first glance, in "We are contemporaries, Countess" Pavlova aligns herself with male Romantic poets and inscribes herself into the Pushkinian tradition.

As she penned her missive to Rostopchina in the aftermath of the "Forced Marriage" scandal, Pavlova faced the ticklish situation of having to reassure conservatives and liberals alike that writing women were capable of self-control and responsible action. For conservatives, the scandal provided concrete evidence that the enlargement of the woman's sphere of activity— here specifically writing and publishing—threatened to destabilize the Russian monarchy. Liberals, whose support of Sandism was prompted by a drive toward just such destabilization, deemed women incapable of directing those very emotions to which they urged them to give free rein. Even as they sought to expand women's compass beyond conventional bounds, they assumed that it was for men to determine the nature, scope, and implementation of this expansion. Thus, for all the obvious differences between conservative and progressive thinkers and between the social norms their respective ideologies dictated, both groups operated under the shared assumption that women were to be situated in a society constructed and directed by men.

As she sought recognition in the existing literary tradition, Pavlova worked to naturalize the woman poet in it, establishing ties with poets who were men and emphasizing that she neither deviated from the literary norm nor rebelled against it. Accordingly, in "We are contemporaries," as in other writings, she counters the image of the woman as a disruptive element and shows her working successfully within the established order. Pavlova, whose self-presentations resisted the alignment of creativity with eros, was leery of George Sand's freedom of the heart, which she saw as undermining the individual responsibility and self-command on which she herself predicated women's freedom and agency. For Pavlova, Sandian defiance of established norms was a manifestation of willfulness (*svoevolie*) and not of genuine freedom (*volia*)—of the libertine and not of liberty. Her designation of the *zhorzhsandistka* Rostopchina as "a slave of vanities" (*suet rabynia*) in "We are contemporaries, Countess" rhymes with the "pride of vanities" (*suet gordynia*) of which she accused her in "To Countess R." It was also just such "slaves of noise and vanities" (*rabyni shuma i suet*) that Pavlova invoked in September of 1846, in a poetic dedication that prefaced *A Double Life*, a work that secured her literary fame when it was published in full in 1848.

In that dedication, Pavlova explains that she wrote *A Double Life* for her "mute sisters" (*nemye sestry*).[81] Significantly, this muteness, as Pavlova frames it, is the consequence not of stifling gender norms or a cultural setting inimical to writing women but of women's own unthinking surrender to vacuous social pastimes. This subtle link between the Rostopchina of "We are contemporaries" and the "slaves of noise and vanity" on whose behalf Pavlova claims to write upholds her basic premise that, far from being a source of freedom, a free-wheeling lifestyle prevents the woman poet from connecting with the inner self that Pavlova designates as the locus of creativity. Falling in line with the "retreat from social to interior arenas" that "is marked formally by the emergence of Romantic lyricism" in the aftermath of the French Revolution,[82] Pavlova promotes a responsible selfhood that is not dependent on her surroundings. This dedication to an inner world remains an essential feature of her creative identity and the keystone of her efforts to establish the woman poet in traditionally male-gendered space.

The insistence on the woman's self-command that is a constant in Pavlova's works points beyond the seeming acquiescence of the authored self in "We are contemporaries, Countess." In this light, the dutiful wife of that poem emerges as a feminine variant of the stoic. Described as "the French revolutionaries' primary mode of demonstrating personal autonomy and authenticity," the stoic was a strictly moral being for whom freedom was neither political nor social but individual and hinged not on the contingencies of the surrounding world but on the control exercised over the self. With this model, which was used "to separate self-contained men from emotionally demonstrative women,"[83] Pavlova countered the image of the unbridled woman in need of male control with a potent emblem of self-sufficiency and self-mastery. The wife of "We are contemporaries, Countess" joins the Spartan boy who remains silent while the stolen fox cub gnaws at his entrails, whom Pavlova invokes in her poem "We Came Together Strangely" ("My stranno soshlis'," 1854). The noblewoman she describes in her memoirs who dies of breast cancer, having concealed her pain and the ravages of the disease from those closest to her, is another emblem of the female stoic.[84] The stoic model gains Pavlova another advantage: it allows her to recast the absence of women's voices from the Russian poetic tradition as a silence of self-restraint rather than of a lack of anything to say.

With this liberating turn inward, Pavlova meshed woman and poet in a way that insisted on her autonomy and self-determination. This, in turn, allowed her to supersede the gender binary by absorbing it into the oppositions of responsible/irresponsible and of poet/philistine. This redrawing of boundaries so that the divide falls between poets and nonpoets rather than between men and women enhanced the writing woman's position. The strategic shift of attention from restrictions imposed from without to the self-command maintained from within proved fruitful for subsequent generations of writing women, and the conventionally male-gendered fortitude that Pavlova translates into female-gendered space appears in works of women writing after her. Thus, for example, Marina Tsvetaeva and Sophia Parnok, who cite Pavlova as a literary model, develop the image of the stoic in their self-presentations and invoke her Spartan boy in their verse.[85]

In this context, it is clear that the invented self of "We are contemporaries, Countess," champions not a repressive social order but the ability to sustain creative freedom within it. Opposite the *"zhorzhsandistka"* she makes of Rostopchina, Pavlova presents an authored self who continues to write, unhindered by social and political strictures, just as she is unconstrained by the rules governing her chosen genre and the norms of the poetic tradition. Beneath its seemingly acquiescent surface, the poem manifests Pavlova's capacity to rise above repressive conditions, and this capacity validates her as a poet. This allows Pavlova to inscribe herself into the Pushkinian tradition, whose poets attained creative freedom within the twofold dictates of their chosen genre and a political system that circumscribed their self-expressivity. The analogy between the paterfamilias to whom Pavlova's authored self delivers her poems for judgment and Nicholas I, the father of all Russia who was Pushkin's personal censor, reminds us that some of the greatest works of the Russian canon were written under house arrest.

Rostopchina wrote no poems in direct response to either of Pavlova's missives, but in 1854 she parodied her in "A Song on the Occasion of the Correspondence of a Learned Man and a No Less Learned Woman" ("Pesnia po povodu perepiski uchenogo muzha s ne menee uchenoi zhenoi"). The poem referenced Pavlova's polemics with the editor of *The Contemporary*, Ivan Ivanovich Panaev. Triggered by a negative review of Pavlova's poem "A Conversation in the Kremlin" ("Razgovor v Kremle"), which appeared in 1854, first in the *Northern Bee* and then in a separate edition, these polemics are the butt of Rostopchina's parody. It was now Rostopchina's turn to disassociate herself from a woman poet who had fallen into disfavor. I first sketch Pavlova's circumstances at this time and then consider the terms Rostopchina uses in her parody to describe Pavlova.

When Rostopchina composed "A Song on the Occasion," Pavlova was living in Derpt, separated from her husband and with little left of the literary acclaim she had earned in the latter 1840s. Pavlova had a lot riding on "A Conversation in the Kremlin," which she composed in an effort to improve her standing in Russian literary circles that was compromised by misfortune in her personal life. In 1853, Pavlova's father, Karl Jaenisch, lodged a formal complaint on her behalf against Nikolai Pavlov, who was squandering her estate on cards and a second family and who mortgaged her house to pay off his sizable gambling debts.[86] Zakrevsky, the governor-general of Moscow who was assigned to the case, harbored animosity toward Pavlov, who had authored a widely circulated epigram ridiculing him.[87] Taking this opportunity to retaliate, Zakrevsky ordered a punitive search of Pavlov's study, in the course of which forbidden writings were discovered among his papers.[88] Judged as politically unreliable, he received an eighty-day prison sentence, followed by six months of exile in Perm. Pavlov's irresponsible behavior toward his family met with disapprobation in Moscow society, but the political turn that his wife's quarrel with him unexpectedly took, precipitating his arrest and exile, turned the tide of public opinion against her. The contempt she now faced forced Pavlova to leave the old Russian capital she extolled in her verse to settle—in a reversal of Rostopchina's fate—in St. Petersburg.[89] The fallout of this domestic-quarrel-turned-political is reminiscent of the aftermath of the "Forced Marriage" scandal in that it alienated conservatives and liberals alike and served as evidence of women's inability to act in a politically responsible way.

In the wake of her strife with her husband, Pavlova found herself more sternly judged as both woman and poet and increasingly prey to the sexualization she had taken pains to avoid. Thus, for example, Granovsky alleged that Pavlova complained to him about the fourteen years of marriage she spent "dans un lit virginal," implying that her action against her husband, like her literary activity, was fueled by sexual frustration.[90] Descriptions of Pavlova's appearance as unprepossessing—skinny, bony, and dry, which is to say sexually undesirable—cropped up repeatedly to explain both her failed marriage and her urge to write. Along the same lines, the question arose as to whether Pavlova was capable of experiencing human emotions since only an unfeeling monster would inflict such damage on her husband and the father of her child. When, in her haste to flee cholera-stricken St. Petersburg with her mother, Pavlova did not stay to attend the funeral of her father, who had fallen victim to the disease, her flight was seen not as an attempt to avoid more deaths but as the consequence of an unnatural dedication to poetry that leached her of womanly feelings. The tenacity of such assessments is well illustrated by the fact that when Ivan Aksakov visited Pavlova in Dresden in the early 1860s, he saw not a poet who remained true to her calling or a woman who confronted hardships with stoic determination, but a callous creature who remained unaffected by tragic experiences, and who, worse yet, had become a German writer.[91]

Inspired by the threat of impending war, Pavlova's "A Conversation in the Kremlin" presents a dispute between a Russian, an Englishman, and a Frenchman.[92] The patriotism that figured in "To Countess R" is now part of an urgent effort to reestablish herself in the literary arena from which she had been hounded in the wake of her husband's arrest. Under attack for allegedly failing in her responsibilities as wife, daughter, mother, and loyal Russian subject because of her dedication to writing verse, Pavlova responded with a poem. This revived the question of how someone so heartless toward her family could aspire to the status of genuine poet. The circularity of such allegations left Pavlova little space: she purportedly failed as daughter, wife, and mother precisely because she had assumed the role of poet and yet failed as a poet because of her grave deficiencies as daughter, wife, and mother. "A Conversation in the Kremlin" was an effort on Pavlova's part to repair her image on all these fronts.

To this end, Pavlova presents her poem as an act of maternal solicitude and a patriotic gesture. By dedicating it to her fifteen-year-old son, she de-

fends herself from accusations that writing poetry made her a bad mother
and counters Nikolai Pavlov's complaints that she was a foreigner educat-
ing his son in an alien land.[93] "A Conversation in the Kremlin" champions
Russian culture and destiny as distinct from Europe's. Wherever Pavlova
finds herself, this is the Russia she bears within her and bequeaths to her
son. The poem was noted in major publications of the time,[94] but most of
the responses were unfavorable.[95] The unsigned piece titled "Bibliography"
("Bibliografiia") that appeared in *The Contemporary* and was attributed to
Panaev was the most negative. It pronounced the poem too narrow in compass to accomplish the sweeping historical defense of Russia that Pavlova
undertakes in it, criticizes her rhymes, and brands her as deficient in both
fervor and technique.[96]

The significance Pavlova ascribed to the reception of "A Conversation
in the Kremlin" is evident from a letter of October 21, 1854, that she sent
to Panaev in response to the review. Carefully formulated, Pavlova's letter
balances between self-defense and counterattack, framed by protestations
of feminine modesty.[97] Observing how useless criticism is for a poet, she
explains that "feminine weakness" prompted her to read the review of her
poem that appeared in *The Contemporary*. This in turn, as she explains,
prompted her self-defense. Public recognition, she adds, means nothing to
her. "A Conversation in the Kremlin" was her contribution to the Russian
cause:

> Last spring when we awaited unheard of events, the bombardment of Kron-
> stadt and war in the vicinity of Petersburg, desperate attack and inspired re-
> pulsion, when the entire fatherland responded, when everyone did what he
> could, gave what he had, I, too, gave all that I had—my poem. These stanzas,
> written in the last weeks of great lent, practically created themselves: I assure
> you that I neither invented new rhymes nor sought effects. With Russian sen-
> timent, I wrote this poem in the half-foreign town of Derpt.[98]

A practicing Lutheran living in Derpt when she wrote this poem, Pavlova
invokes the Orthodox calendar and emphasizes her "Russian sentiment" and
the patriotism she felt compelled to express in verse. Panaev, who disclaimed
authorship of the review, responded by publishing her letter in *The Contemporary*, side by side with a derisive reply that belittled her publicly as a
woman, a poet, and a Russian—those very areas that Pavlova hoped to repair
with her poem.[99]

It was at this unhappy juncture of Pavlova's career that Rostopchina
composed her "Song on the Occasion." Siding with the dominant group,
Rostopchina joined those of Pavlova's detractors who ridiculed her displays
of intellect and dedication to poetry. The parody features a "learned man"

who strolls with a "no less learned woman" down an avenue of lindens, an arboreal setting beloved of Romantic poets that Pavlova invoked in her letter to Panaev.[100] Head high and gesticulating dramatically, the "learned woman" treats her interlocutor to recitations of her works before going on, in the second stanza, to read him her Sanskrit translation of a Finnish poem. Here a parenthetical observation informs the reader that the lady in question publishes poems "In Chinese or maybe Japanese" (*Po-kitaiski, ne to po-iaponski / Eta dama stikhi izdaet*).[101]

Even readers who missed the exchange between Panaev and Pavlova on the pages of *The Contemporary* could recognize the "learned woman" of Rostopchina's caricature. Pavlova was frequently criticized for what were regarded as theatrical displays of her multilingualism and her dedication to poetry.[102] In the aftermath of the political problems she inadvertently caused her husband, this criticism grew increasingly strident.[103] In Rostopchina's poem, the "learned woman's" captive auditor, far from appreciating his interlocutor's gifts, is stupefied and can only hiss imprecations through tightly clenched teeth at "All Corinnes, all bluestockings." Although both of these terms were already outmoded when Rostopchina wrote her parody, the sentiment they conveyed remained in force. "Bluestocking," which had taken a derogatory turn some three decades earlier, typified a woman whose dry, intellectual interests leached her of both attractiveness and imaginative faculties. The term insinuated that these women were driven by frustrated sexual needs and did so, moreover, in a way that left the woman nothing of the tragic aura commanded by the unsatisfied desires of a man.

The twofold loss of desirability and creativity translated into failure both in the private and in the public domains. Its threat was held over the woman frequently enough to merit attention here. The double jeopardy found particularly vivid manifestation earlier in the nineteenth century in the fate of Corinne, the eponymous heroine of Germaine de Staël's acclaimed novel, which codified an image of the woman artist that persisted well after de Staël's influence in Russia was eclipsed by George Sand.[104] *Corinne, or Italy* (1807) describes the public glory and private anguish of a woman of genius, who "best exemplifies the woman poet's condition of exile, her dually alienated position as artist and woman."[105] In it, de Staël distinguishes between the conventional and the unprecedented woman and between Corinne's emotional needs and her artistic genius. At the heart of the novel is an insuperable tension between domesticity and a woman's public practice of her art, which culminates in Corinne's tragic failure in both domains.

To summarize briefly, Oswald (Lord Nelville), the man she loves, professes an anti-Enlightenment disapproval of women appearing in the public arena. Though powerfully attracted to Corinne, he is frankly jealous of her acclaim and mindful of his duty to his deceased father, who judged her talents ill-suited for matrimony and maternity.[106] This leaves Corinne in an untenable position between the gift she wishes to exercise and its sacrifice that her beloved exacts. In an excruciating gesture, de Staël's exceptional dark-haired heroine surrenders Oswald to her blond, commonplace half-sister. Oswald, who has no difficult choice to make, fulfills his filial duty and secures happiness with his conventional wife. Corinne's unrequited passion for him overwhelms her artistry, leaving her bereft of both the man she loves and her creative gift.

Notably, as Vincent describes, "Corinne's suffering, rather than her literary glory or passionate love, most directly impressed women readers and informed the work of myriad poets and novelists who followed in her wake."[107] In other words, a novel that highlights the impossible situation of a talented woman was read—even by women—not as a call to support women's creative fulfillment but as a warning against disrupting the status quo that prohibits it. To read the heroine's end as a punishment is to construe Corinne's exercise of her talents as transgressive and deserving of penalty, reaffirming the norms she contravenes rather than challenging them. Given Pavlova's widely publicized rift with her husband, and the denigration she endured of her womanhood and her poetry at this stage in her career, Rostopchina's invocation of de Staël's heroine is particularly hurtful. Pavlova is not Corinne in her glory as an acclaimed poet but the dispossessed woman at the novel's end who finds herself in an alien land bereft of family and voice. Rostopchina gained nothing from this unkind gesture. Both poets fell prey to biases that inhibited a relationship of mutual support, degraded their discord to a manifestation of petty female jealousy, and discounted them as poets.

Women's disagreements, like their poetry, are vulnerable to male condescension and its corrosion of the potential value of their differences. Thus it is clearly prejudice and not serious appraisal that informs Vladislav Khodasevich's dismissive attitude to both poets:

> Unattractive, unloved, closed up inside herself, Pavlova did not lead the life of a woman, and this is probably why she so disliked her more fortunate contemporary and literary competitor, Countess Rostopchina, who was a woman first and foremost, who shone with beauty, combined social successes with poetical ones and lived a fairly turbulent life . . . But fate reconciled them: now Rostopchina is forgotten no less than Karolina Pavlova.[108]

This chapter reconstitutes the significance of Pavlova's 'contretemps with Rostopchina to underscore the importance of the resistance they offered to the perceived incompatibility of woman and poet. Pavlova overrides the gender binary with the overarching dichotomy of poet/philistine. Capitalizing on the essential similarity between the marginalized poet and the marginalized woman, she includes the impediments that women confronted in the broader category of restrictions whose overcoming authorizes the poet. Pavlova holds firmly that adverse conditions are best met not with rebellion or self-abandon but with intensified self-control. Whatever the external circumstances—and these were harsh indeed in the latter years of her life, which found her impoverished in exile—she remains dedicated to an inner creative domain that she sees as the locus of self-determination. Refusing to be either victimized or liberated by social constructs—be they backward-looking or progressive—Pavlova privileges an inner sphere where selfhood and creativity can flourish. This removes the woman poet from passive victimhood and affirms her agency to act in accordance with the precepts of her poetic calling. Rostopchina takes a different course. Under the cover of exaggerated femininity, she subverts gender norms and turns the tables on the male establishment, developing strategies of enablement that I elaborate in the following chapter.

Chapter Two

Evdokiia Rostopchina versus the Male Tradition

> In the evening I read Rostopchina. How I
> marvel at her talent! When I pick up her book,
> it is hard to tear myself away from it. Here is a
> poet not in verse alone. Tell me, how old is she
> and what does she look like?
> —Ia. K. Grot, letter to P. A. Pletnev

> Rostopchina is a major talent, but I love and
> regard Kar[olina] Pavlova more, probably for
> old times' sake, and because her verse is not
> womanish.
> —N. M. Iazykov, letter to A. M. Iazykov

> We remember Rostopchina first and foremost
> as a poetess of the Pushkinian pleiade, as one
> of the first woman writers, who forced us to
> think about "the poetics of a woman's soul."
> —M. Sh. Fainshtein, *Pisatel'nitsy pushkins-*
> *koi pory*

IN A LETTER OF 1854—the year she wrote her parody
of Pavlova—Rostopchina complained to a male correspondent about the in-
equity of men's treatment of women and, echoing the chapter "On Women"
from Germaine de Staël's *On Germany*, maintained, "Women are always
better, that is, kinder, more selfless, more truthful than men."[1] This fundamental belief, Rostopchina explains, informs her own writings and dictates
the hostilities she directs against men: "As a consequence of this conviction
I hold my pen in my hand as the only weapon given us against you."[2] This
combative assertion may seem startling in light of Rostopchina's reputation
as a gracious salon hostess whose successes in poetry equaled those in aristocratic society. Indeed, over the course of her literary career Rostopchina
often enacted a femininity that appeared sooner to accord with prevailing
constructs of gender than to question them.

At the time she composed this letter, Rostopchina had had many opportunities to wield her pen as a weapon of defense and offense. The ideals—poetic and social—of the bygone Pushkinian era, which she continued to defend, fell increasingly into disregard and became targets of progressive critics' attacks. Civic prose had eclipsed lyric verse, and Rostopchina's relations with Westernizers and Slavophiles alike had soured. As the aristocracy ceded dominance over the arts, the growing disaffection with Rostopchina's class joined tenacious gender biases to tarnish her celebrity in the latter part of her career. The cited passage from her letter—written some four years before her death—could be seen as a sign of bitterness brought on by the decline in her literary fortunes. In fact, however, Rostopchina's resistance to the male establishment began much earlier and is evident even at the height of her literary acclaim.

Iurii Lotman observes that the late eighteenth and early nineteenth centuries "were marked essentially by the woman's struggle not to lose the right to be a woman once she had won the right to a place in the culture."[3] This chapter studies Rostopchina in the process of just such a struggle, which persists beyond the time frame of Lotman's study. Looking at illustrative poems, I demonstrate how Rostopchina uses feminine masquerade as she works to win approval from the male establishment whose restrictions on women's self-expressivity she subverts.

Rostopchina's enactments of conventional femininity smoothed her entry into the literary arena and protected her from the type of criticism leveled at Pavlova, whose efforts to sidestep gender were used to devalue her as a woman and a poet. There was another motive behind Rostopchina's feminine self-presentations. Diana Greene notes "a fascinating tension between her exhorting women to be modest and self-sacrificing, on the one hand, and her own very successful literary career on the other."[4] This important observation is the point of departure for the argument I develop in this chapter, which shows that the disjunction between Rostopchina's professed compliance and active insubordination indicates a more complex project than has been recognized. Beyond diverting attention from her transgressive act of writing, the compliant femininity that Rostopchina enacts effectively masks subversive messages in her poems. This strategic recourse to feminine masquerade is important in two ways. First, it shows that Rostopchina related to gender as a social construct, anticipating a line of thinking theorized only in the following century.[5] Second, the tension created by Rostopchina's apparent endorsement of prevailing norms that she in fact contravenes situates her poems among those time-honored encodings that conceal from oppressors what they make legible to enlightened readers. This strategy, which Leo Strauss famously describes in "Persecution and the Art of Writing,"[6] was one that tsarist censorship gave Russian poets ample opportunity to perfect.

Aesopic writing that balanced between concealment and revelation was established practice at the time. Rostopchina adapted it to her sallies against the male establishment.

Rostopchina successfully engaged prevailing gender biases to smuggle "A Forced Marriage" past government censors for the benefit of readers who could apprehend its politically subversive meaning. To subvert gender biases was more difficult and led to an impasse: the gatekeepers of the tradition from whom she veiled the transgressive aspect of her writing were precisely those enlightened readers on whom poets relied to recognize hidden messages in their poems. Taken at face value, Rostopchina's feminine masquerade upheld norms that she in fact contravened and triggered superficial readings of her poems. Readers who failed to distinguish between the poet and her mask (or chose not to) did not recognize the challenges to prevailing constructs of gender in poems like those discussed in this chapter. To recuperate this aspect of Rostopchina's writing, I revisit some of her most frequently anthologized lyrics—three poems to Pushkin and the lyric "How Women Must Write," which gives this book its title. In these poems, Rostopchina engages restrictive gender norms combatively in order to turn the tables on the dominant group only to have her efforts neutralized by reader-imposed censorship. I begin with context that prepares the subsequent discussion of the poems, the messages Rostopchina embeds in them, and the readings that blot them out.

Already an established poet by the end of the 1830s, Rostopchina attained the peak of her literary fame in 1841 with the publication of her first book of verse, *Poems of Countess E. Rostopchina* (*Stikhotvoreniia grafini E. Rostopchinoi*). The lyrics in it, which spanned the decade 1829 to 1839, had already attracted favorable notice when they appeared singly in leading journals of the time. Critics now hailed the collection as a literary event, lavishing praise on Rostopchina's poetic accomplishment and on what were seen as the expressly feminine qualities of her poems. This success marked also the turning point of Rostopchina's poetic career—largely on the strength of a review by Belinsky, who was "the sole literary critic not to offer unqualified praise for Rostopchina."[7] Reflecting on her literary career sixteen years later, Rostopchina wrote, "The first to sting me was Belinsky . . . Instead of growing fearful and entering into close ties with the world that was just coming into being here in Russia, I paid no attention to it."[8] The "sting" in question was that critic's review of her *Poems*. The nascent world she chose to ignore was the new social order shaped by the intelligentsia of mixed ranks that displaced the aristocracy and its authority over Russian culture and society. In earlier reviews, Belinsky had registered his high estimation of Rostopchina, whom he compared favorably with Pushkin, Lermontov, Baratynsky, and other leading poets of the time. Now, however, the critic tempered his praise with reproaches that reflected his changing sociopolitical views and their influence on his reading of her poems.

Belinsky's accolades and his objections to Rostopchina's poetry document closely interrelated views on class and gender in this transitional period. His review pays tribute to Rostopchina's "genuine talent" but counsels that she remain within a circumscribed feminine sphere:

> And yet even so it cannot but be said that her verses would gain more in the poetic [sphere] if they would want to remain poetic revelations of the world of the feminine soul, melodies of the mystery of the feminine heart. Then they would be of greater curiosity for the remaining half of humankind, which heaven knows why, appropriated for itself the right to judge and reward. God save us from the vandal-like thought of limiting the woman's poetic activity solely to the sphere left to her by the barbarism of men, but we think that women who enter those spheres that men have appropriated for themselves by force must be possessed of masculine strength together with feminine grace, like the genius Dudevant [George Sand].[9]

The new image of the woman emblematized by George Sand, in whom the admiring Belinsky perceives "masculine strength," had overshadowed the Pushkinian ideal—vested in his heroine, Tatiana Larina—that the critic once esteemed and to which Rostopchina continued to adhere. This shift in the construct of the woman is directly linked with the waning prestige of the aristocracy and the poetic genre.

Belinsky goes on to assert, "Exclusive service to the 'god of salons' is also not entirely advantageous to Countess Rostopchina's muse. Our salons are excessively dry and infertile soil for verse."[10] The prominent role that literary salons played in the development of the Russian poetic tradition gainsays the aridity that Belinsky alleges. Rostopchina's own salon was instrumental in bringing together the most prominent cultural figures of the time, but as the social class in which salons flourished came under attack, the institution was dismissed as mere frivolity.[11] In short, Belinsky censured Rostopchina both as a woman and as a representative of a social class to which he had little direct access. His explicit feminization of poetry—a grammatically feminine noun in Russian—in the review reflects the concurrent devaluation of the genre: "Poetry is a woman: she does not like to appear in the same garb every day."[12]

Of everything that Belinsky wrote in his review, one rebuke in particular prevailed—this despite its patent unsuitability for characterizing Rostopchina's poetry: "All of Countess Rostopchina's verse is, so to say, chained to the ball."[13] This unjust assessment overlooks the impressive array of genres, moods, themes, and styles of the poems in the volume under review. It also ignores a sizable body of poems denouncing the frivolity of society and ball-room ritual and discounts the epigraphs that testify to the breadth of Ros-topchina's reading in several languages. Finally, it disregards her society tales "Rank and Money" ("Chin i den'gi") and "The Duel" ("Duel'") that appeared in 1838 and her politically seditious poems dedicated to the Decembrists that circulated in manuscript.

Earlier in the century, Pushkin and Ryleev had discussed the ques-tion of whether descriptions of social events—and the ball in particular—had a place in poetry and answered it in the affirmative.[14] But Belinsky was no longer enamored of the culture that nurtured Golden Age poetry and its constructs of womanhood. Not in a position to appreciate the semiotic perspicacity of Rostopchina's poetic accounts of society, the critic feminizes them and dismisses them as shallow.[15] He advises that Rostopchina confine herself to satisfying men's curiosity about women in her verse and denies her right of entry into the male-gendered sphere in which he includes George Sand. By criticizing Rostopchina—an easier target for his attacks on the Golden Age than Pushkin himself—Belinsky promoted a new social order that, although inspired by Sand, continued to be determined by men. Al-though Rostopchina's poetry collection received praise from many critics, and Belinsky continued to include her among prominent poets of the time in subsequent reviews, she never sprang free from the chains with which he fettered her to the ballroom.

Belinsky was not alone in voicing disapproval of the image of the socialite that appears in some of Rostopchina's poems. The religious poet Elisaveta Shakhova similarly objected to what she saw as the frivolousness of individual lyrics. Like other women of the time, she was preoccupied with women poets' self-presentations and their reception. Like Pavlova, Shakhova was wary of objectification and eager that the woman poet be taken seriously. Her "antagonistic exchanges" with Rostopchina, as Judith Vowles summa-rizes, "propound different versions of womanhood."[16] Because women of the time lacked the authority to be critics, Shakhova couched her disapproval in verse. Her image of the pious woman that she counterposed to Rostop-china's society lady also countered notions about women held by Belinsky, who saw love as the definitive feature of a woman's life, only now, under Sand's influence, favoring the gratification rather than suppression of her desires. His review cites in full and lavishly praises Rostopchina's "To the Indifferent One [fem.]" ("Ravnodushnoi"), which she wrote in response to Shakhova. The poem's argument "that giving up love and romance as the stern, cold, and moralistic girl with a religious vocation does . . . is unnatural and unwomanly"[17] was consonant with his constructs of the woman.

Rostopchina was vulnerable to these constructs because, unlike Pav-lova, who downplayed her gender, she embraced it. From the very outset of her career when she signed poems with only her initials, she included the feminine endings of her name that marked her as a woman. In the opening of his review, Belinsky notes that beginning in 1835, major periodicals carried verse with the "mysterious signature 'C-tess E. R-na'" and suggests that the poet used this to attract attention to herself:

> Was it out of modesty, or out of insufficient understanding of the literary arena, or for some other reason? But the poetic "incognito" did not long remain a secret, and all readers pronounced the mysterious letters in definite, clear words: "Countess E. Rostopchina." Genuine talent, especially in light of social and personal importance, is the enemy of all "incognitos." Moreover, people are strange creatures (truly the *offspring of crocodiles*): sometimes they don't know your name precisely because you were in a hurry to say it but struggle to learn it and find out what it is only because you concealed or pretended to conceal it.[18]

Whether or not Belinsky is correct in his conjecture, his observation is—unbeknownst to him—relevant to rehearsals of conventional femininity that appear in some of her best-known poems. Recognizing that gender was a social construct, Rostopchina used it as a mask to stimulate interest in what lay beneath it. This mask highlighted the difference between her social image and her poetic identity and drew attention to the creative individual behind the conventional feminine guise. By analogy, it also indicated the deeper meaning masked by the surface of her poems.

Given the popularity of masquerades in the culture of the time and their characteristic displacement of conventional norms, Rostopchina's strategy was well conceived. It remained vulnerable, however, to her reader's capacity and willingness to distinguish between the mask of feminine compliance and the poet beneath it. The thematization of masks and costumes and the condemnation of false social norms that crop up repeatedly in Rostopchina's poems are her efforts to shore up this weak spot. Both the early "Putting on an Albanian Costume" ("Nadevaiia albanskii kostium," 1835) and the late "Why I Love Masquerades" ("Zachem ia liubliu maskarady," 1850) protest the roles that women play in society. Vowles observes apropos of these poems, "Lies, secrets, dissemblance, and the masks and costumes that women must assume in life become subjects in themselves."[19] At the same time, however, these poems present the donning of fancy dress as an open, forthright masking of the self that stands in contrast to the false, unacknowledged masquerade dictated by social norms. Thus, in the first of these poems, Rostopchina speaks of "shattering the chain of tedious proprieties" (*razbivshi tsep' prilichii skuchnykh*) when she dons her exotic costume. In the second, she embraces the respite from hypocrisy that a literal mask affords her (*Ot litsemeriia pod maskoiu vzdokhnut'*), allowing her to express genuine feelings and to avenge herself on the society that enslaves her:

> Я, жертва общества, раба его,—я рада,
> Что посмеяться раз могу в глаза над ним
> Я смехом искренним и мстительным моим! . .[20]

> I, a victim of society, its slave,—I am glad
> That for once I can laugh in its face
> With my genuine and vengeful laughter! . .

Embracing her frankly admitted disguise, Rostopchina affirms her love not of the masquerade itself but of the freedom she gains by replacing the false mask that society compels her to wear with an actual costume: "Yes, really, I love the freedom of a masquerade" (*Da, tochno, ia liubliu svobodu maskarada*). Significantly, masquerade revels in the difference between the costume and the individual who devised it, between the "I" and the "not I" that it places in enticing tension that is analogous to the tension between the inventing and invented selves of a poem. Arja Rosenholm and Irina Savkina summarize the mask's dual function in these poems:

> On the one hand, it was associated with the motifs of pretence, deception, mimesis, and concealment . . . But on the other hand, the mask can be understood as a means for liberation. The mask does not conceal but, on the contrary, protects the authentic I, it hides all the social roles and statuses inscribed onto the face and body, and when wearing the mask it is possible to be authentically oneself.[21]

Rostopchina's readers, however, consistently neglected to look beyond the mask, reading her poems as praise for shallow social amusements and their author as a flighty society lady.[22]

Rostopchina is not discomfited by what Judith Pascoe describes as "the disjuncture between a theatrical imperative (the need to attract public attention and win public support) and an anti-theatrical anxiety (the result of an equation between performance and falsity)."[23] Indeed, she relies on her readers' recognition of the difference between the social role that she *played* and the poet that she *was*. Speaking of an earlier period in a way that has direct bearing on the time considered here, Lotman observes that "to say that behavior is 'theatrical' does not imply that it is insincere or reprehensible in any way. It simply indicates that behavior has a meaning that extends beyond the everyday. It is the object of attention, valued not for itself but for its symbolic significance."[24] The very theatricality of Rostopchina's gestures marks them as signifiers rather than the signified. Yet, just as they remained on the surface of her poems, readers tended to stop also at her gestures rather than what she meant them to convey. Rostopchina's performances of conventional femininity made it too easy to assume that she was reaffirming the status quo rather than using familiar vocabulary to destabilize it. Rostopchina's enactments—poetic and actual—of the society lady for which Belinsky took her to task indicated a poetic identity that was situated in a private creative sphere well beyond what she repeatedly describes as the false social world. Over the course of her literary career, Rostopchina places ever-greater emphasis on this inner creative sphere which, as she stressed, was hidden from public view. What I term invisibility of the unthinkable and reader-imposed censorship closed down this crucial aspect of Rostopchina's self-fashioning in her writings.

"A Forced Marriage" shows Rostopchina enacting conventional femininity to conceal politically seditious content. Here I focus on how her feminine masquerade veils culturally subversive messages—specifically her claim to ascendancy over Pushkin and Lermontov and her retaliation on the male establishment for restrictions it imposes on women's creative self-expression. I begin with three poems that Rostopchina addressed to Pushkin: "Pushkin's Draft Notebook" ("Chernovaia kniga Pushkina," 1838) and the cycle *Two Meetings* (*Dve vstrechi*, 1838, 1839), which Rostopchina wrote shortly after Pushkin's death when she was at the height of her literary career. Rostopchina had solid grounds on which to invoke the progenitor of the Russian poetic tradition. Leading poets and critics of the time—Iazykov, Zhukovsky, Pletnev, and Belinsky among them—had compared her poems favorably with Pushkin's, and the two poets frequently appeared side by side in prominent literary journals. When Rostopchina's *Poems* came out, Pletnev, who took over the editorship of *The Contemporary* (*Sovremennik*) after Pushkin's death, proclaimed, "She is, without a doubt, now the foremost poet in Russia."[25] Comparisons of Rostopchina and Pushkin came up also in private correspondence of the time.[26] With the rise of the radical critics, Rostopchina's ties to Pushkin and his era became a liability, but initially the invocation of her Golden Age predecessor suggested a means to secure a place in his tradition.[27]

Appealing to Pushkin made sense given his literary stature and because of the attention that he accorded to women's writing in the latter years of his life. Pushkin had initially taken a dim view of writing women, but over time his interest in the possibility of feminine authorship grew. Instrumental in this change, as V. Brio persuasively documents, was Germaine de Staël, whose writings Pushkin studied[28] and "whose name he links in his own reminiscences with his first steps in the area of political education and his first acquaintance with new ideas in literature."[29] Rostopchina had been compared with both de Staël, whom she admired, and her renowned heroine, Corinne. The passage from her letter that opens this chapter echoes lines from the section devoted to women in de Staël's *On Germany*, which Pushkin valued highly. Other stimulants to Pushkin's acceptance of women authors noted by Brio include the cultural importance the poet ascribed to literary salons presided over by women and his recognition of the importance of women readers to the development of Russian letters.[30] Women's claims to the Push-kinian aegis under which all poets sheltered could find additional support in lyrics and letters he wrote to aspiring women writers, his encouragement of Nadezhda Durova, and his own attempts to write from the perspective and in the language of a woman (*A Novel in Letters* [*Roman v pis'makh*, 1829] and *Roslavlev*, 1831). The fact that the last letter Pushkin penned, on January 27, 1837, the day of his fatal duel, was to Aleksandra Ishimova, endowed his praise of her writing with enduring significance for women authors. In the century that followed, Marina Tsvetaeva referred to this letter, claiming that Pushkin's last lines were addressed to her.[31]

Rostopchina could boast, moreover, of personal ties with Pushkin that dated back to March of 1831, when shortly after his marriage he, his wife, Natalia (née Goncharova), and the then Evdokiia Sushkova (she married Count Rostopchin only in 1833) participated in Shrovetide festivities together.[32] Pushkin was among those poets who frequented the salon over which Rostopchina presided in St. Petersburg after her marriage. A habitué of her home, he dined there on the night before his fatal duel, a detail that Rostopchina drew to the attention of her readers. Like other poets of the time, she penned an immediate response to Pushkin's death—the poem "January 20, 1837" ("20 ianvaria 1837 g."), which is lost.[33] Rostopchina maintained her acquaintance with Pushkin's widow and dedicated a number of lyrics to her.

Rostopchina's Pushkin poems provide compelling examples of subversive, self-affirming writing masked in feminine modesty. "Pushkin's Draft Notebook" features a living poet addressing a poet silenced by death and shows Rostopchina—under the cover of the humility expected of women—authorizing herself as Pushkin's heir. *Two Meetings* highlights her own poetic destiny and her close ties with Pushkin in the realm of verse. Balancing compliance and defiance, the poems undermine the cultural biases they invoke. Using to advantage the assumption that women's poems document actual experiences rather than imaginative ventures, Rostopchina uses specific events as points of departure for these poems.

In 1838, Vasilii Zhukovsky presented Rostopchina with a notebook in which Pushkin had planned to write drafts of his poems.[34] The symbolic potency of Pushkin's erstwhile mentor presenting this hallowed notebook to Rostopchina and charging her to fill it in Pushkin's and his own stead was not lost on her. She publicizes this bestowal in the poem "Pushkin's Draft Notebook," which she dedicates to Zhukovsky and publishes in *The Contemporary*, which Pushkin founded in 1836. Rostopchina prefaces her poem with the letter that accompanied Zhukovsky's gift:

> I send you, Countess, as a souvenir, a book that may be of some value to you. It belonged to Pushkin; he prepared it for his new poems and did not have time to write a single one; I received it from the hands of death, I began it, that which you will find in it has not been published anywhere. You will fill and complete this, his book. It has now arrived at its true destination. In the old days, I would have written all this in verse, and the verse would have been good because it would have been about you and your poetry; but poems no longer flow as they once did,—I will conclude simply: do not forget my exhortations; let this year of your solitude be a truly poetical year in your life. Your Zhukovsky. April 25, 1838.[35]

An explanatory footnote that Rostopchina supplies for the poem reads, "Pushkin ordered himself a notebook. After his death, it went to V. A. Zhukovsky, who wrote a few unfinished poems in it and then gave it to me with the injunction that I fill and complete it."[36] This paratextual framing of "Pushkin's Draft Notebook" masks the self-assertiveness of the poem and presents Rostopchina as a poet whom Pushkin's mentor elects to perpetuate the tradition that he himself is no longer able to sustain.

The poem itself opens with reveries that the notebook inspires in Rostopchina and culminates with a proclamation of modesty that is distinctly at variance with her self-promotion in it. Writing about the last two lines, Diana Greene notes "the tension between their apparent humility and the repetition of 'mne' (to me) eight times in the last ten lines of the poem."[37] Rostopchina's project relies precisely on what this tension conveys. To begin with, the energy of her protestations of unworthiness acts sooner to display a vivacity in the face of Pushkin's death and Zhukovsky's failing powers than to exemplify the "humble modesty" she invokes—especially since these protestations are couched in verse, a form that Pushkin and Zhukovsky no longer command. Rostopchina's hyperbolized humility emphasizes that she was chosen to write in the hallowed notebook and is not herself laying claim to the title of Pushkin's heir. At the same time, she offsets her show of humility with a masterful display of her command of the Pushkinian idiom.

Significantly, it is only after she has amply demonstrated this mastery that Rostopchina demurs that, as a woman, she cannot take on the lofty mission that Zhukovsky assigns her. The situation, as she presents it in her poem, is that the (male) Russian poetic tradition, having lost Pushkin to death and Zhukovsky to old age, now turns to her for its perpetuation. In this context, her professed modesty signals not submission but retaliation: the restrictions that the male establishment imposes on women inhibit her from complying with Zhukovsky's plea that she rescue the tradition:

Но не исполнить мне такого назначенья,
Но не достигнуть мне желанной вышины!
Не все источники живого песнопенья,
Не все предметы мне доступны и даны:
Я женщина! . . . Во мне и мысль и вдохновенье
Смиренной скромностью быть скованы должны![38]

But I cannot fulfill such a purpose,
But I cannot attain the desired heights!
Not all sources of living song,
Not all topics are accessible or given me:
I am a woman! . . . In me both thought and inspiration
Must be fettered with humble modesty!

Repeatedly cited out of context, this paroxysm of diffidence is widely touted as Rostopchina's willing embrace of prevailing gender norms in complete disregard of its implicit argument against restricting women's self-expressivity. As in "How Women Must Write," Rostopchina's point in "Pushkin's Draft Notebook" is that inhibiting the woman poet's self-expression is ultimately injurious to the male tradition.

In a review of Stephanie Sandler's *Commemorating Pushkin: Russia's Myth of a National Poet*, David Bethea takes Rostopchina to task for the concluding lines of "Pushkin's Draft Notebook." Calling them "impossibly cloying" and "tasteless," he asks, "What else are we to make of lines like 'I am a woman! . . . In me both thought and inspiration / Must be fettered with humble modesty!' which come off as being the very opposite of what they say they are—thought, inspiration, fettered, humble, and modesty."[39] The question these lines prompt Bethea to ask, like the irritation they elicit from him, reflects their efficacy as a Straussian "stumbling block" that prompts readers to look for underlying meaning.[40] If the stumbling block is ignored, the irony of the poem and the message it conveys fall victim to reader-imposed censorship.

Gender bias, working together with the assumption that dedications to Pushkin inevitably sing his praises, blinds readers to Rostopchina's sabotage of his larger-than-life image. As her protestations of modesty veil but thinly, in "Pushkin's Draft Notebook" she takes the upper hand over him. In it Rostopchina says nothing about the poetry Pushkin left behind. She insists instead on what his death prevents him from accomplishing and emphasizes that his plans for the notebook—in which she presumably writes—remained unrealized. "He did not have time to write a single word" (*On nachertat' ni slova ne uspel*), she laments, subversively echoing the words of Zhukovsky's letter. Rather than praise Pushkin's transcendent verse, Rostopchina describes his death as leaving nothing intact: "And the grave destroyed everything!" (*I grob vse istrebil!*). She also undermines Zhukovsky's standing. Her footnote speaks of a "few unfinished poems" he wrote in the notebook. In fact, it contained eight poems in the *Greek Anthology* style and one poem on Pushkin's death.[41] Rostopchina's penultimate stanza shows Pushkin's mentor musing on his inability to write in response to the "mute behest" (*nemoi zavet*)[42] of the notebook's blank pages. Purporting to transcribe Zhukovsky's own thoughts, Rostopchina has him confess that he can no longer enliven the symbolic notebook with verse, which is to say sustain the Pushkinian tradition:

> Нет! Полно вдаль смотреть! . . . Не под моим пером
> Ты, книга, оживешь духовным бытием!

> No! Enough of looking into the distance! . . . It is not under my pen
> That you, book, will come to life with inner being!

With her burial of Pushkin and emphasis on Zhukovsky's failing powers, Rostopchina does more than position herself in the line of poetic succession. As she presents it, the Russian poetic tradition now depends on her for its continuation. The epigraph that she selects for this poem—Louis XIV's device "Sic transit gloria mundi"—sets the stage for precisely such a reading of her poem, which builds on the passing of Pushkin's and Zhukovsky's glory in favor of her own. In this context, Rostopchina's invocations of the humble modesty demanded of a woman are not acquiescence to the norm but an emphasis on the limits imposed by the male establishment that now turns to her for sustenance. Greene rightly suggests that "perhaps Rostopchina in these last two lines does not so much humbly prescribe and glorify her lesser role as a woman poet as simply note the limitations to which she is subject."[43] Indeed, Rostopchina does more: she shows that gender-determined restrictions are detrimental both to writing women and the Russian poetic tradition. Having drawn on its symbolic significance to advance her own standing and the cause of the writing woman, Rostopchina put the hallowed notebook to subversive political use. Among the poems she recorded in it are forbidden texts that circulated only in manuscript, including a series of Pushkin's epigrams[44] and her own ballad "A Forced Marriage."[45]

The image of blank pages left by a deceased poet for her to fill appears again in the wake of Lermontov's death, to which Rostopchina responded in 1842 with a seven-poem cycle called *The Empty Album* (*Pustoi al'bom*). The album in question, as Rostopchina again uses a footnote to apprise her reader, is one that Lermontov gave her in May of 1841, on the eve of his departure for the Caucasus, where he met his end in a duel. In it, as the note further explains, "he wrote his poem to me: 'I know that you and I were born / Under the same star' ("Ia znaiu, pod odnoi zvezdoiu / My byli s vami rozhdeny").[46] As in "Pushkin's Draft Notebook," in the lyrics of *The Empty Album* Rostopchina places greater emphasis on the loss of the poet than on his legacy and again positions herself—here all the more firmly—as the one destined to continue writing in his stead.

Rostopchina followed "Pushkin's Draft Notebook" with the cycle *Two Meetings*, in which she records direct encounters with Pushkin. Here, too, affectations of modesty veil her self-affirmation, and the poems express not adulation but her ascendancy over Pushkin. Now, however, her poetic status is validated not by an authoritative male poet but by her own precocious, un-mediated contacts with Pushkin and the poems that describe them. Rostopchina sent *Two Meetings* to *The Contemporary* for publication, dedicating it to Pletnev. A member of the Pushkin pleiade and dedicatee of *Eugene One-gin*, Pletnev was favorably disposed toward women's writing.[47] He was also on friendly terms with Rostopchina, whom he hailed as a Muscovite Sappho and whose poetry he praised in the journal. In the letter to him that accom-panied her poems, Rostopchina explained, "*Two Meetings* is a true account of my first two meetings with Pushkin, and I developed this idea specifically for you and *The Contemporary*, knowing how pleasing it is for you to collect in this publication everything relating to the memory of the Unforgettable One."[48] Rostopchina's claim that she writes as a memoirist in order to please Pletnev with her contribution to Pushkin's legacy deflects attention from her self-affirmation at Pushkin's expense in the poems.

Two Meetings opens with an oxymoronic epigraph from Friedrich Bouterwek—"Es gibt im Menschenleben ewige Minuten" (There are in human life eternal moments)—which affirms that the meetings with Pushkin Rostopchina describes endure beyond the time in which they transpired.[49] Accompanying this expansion of temporality is a transformation of the spaces in which the encounters take place, as populated public arenas become loci of Rostopchina's private bonding with a fellow poet. The first of these meet-ings occurs at outdoor Easter festivities in Moscow in the spring of 1827— that is, when Rostopchina was sixteen years old and the nearly twenty-eight-year-old Pushkin was at the height of his fame. Impatient to plunge headlong into life, the youthful self of Rostopchina's poem animatedly responds to a world that is not yet fully accessible to her:

> И с нетерпеньем думы детской
> Желала время ускорить,
> Чтоб видеть, слышать, знать и жить!

> And with the impatience of childish thought
> [I] wanted to speed up time,
> So as to see, to hear, to know and live!

Crucially, the surrounding gaiety does not arrest her attention but serves instead as a catalyst to the imagination:

> Народа волны протекали,
> Одни других они сменяли . . .
> Но я не замечала их,
> Предавшись лету грез своих.

> Waves of people flowed past,
> One following the other . . .
> But I took no notice of them,
> Having surrendered to the flight of my fancy.

When Pushkin appears on the scene at the very center of the poem—the fortieth line of the eighty constituting it—her receptivity is at its peak.

The crowd of revelers suddenly surges forward, and the child is told, "*He°* is coming: / *He*, our poet, *he*, our glory / Everyone's beloved!" (*On° idet*: / *On, nash poet*, on, *nasha slava* / *Liubimets obshchii!*). Lest her reader fail to identify the antecedent of the emphatically articulated pronoun, Rostopchina provides an explanatory footnote to ascertain his identity. With Pushkin's appearance—a moment that is destined, like the one in the epigraph, to endure beyond itself—a new world opens to the girl, who subjects Pushkin to the penetrating reading that the now mature poet Rostopchina documents in this poem. Bypassing the intermediary of the poetic text to enter directly into the world of the poet himself, Rostopchina's recollected self immediately recognizes the stamp of genius on his features and intuitively gains access to his emotions and experiences—all of which are well beyond her own. Pushkin passes swiftly before her penetrating gaze, but his image continues to nurture that quintessentially poetic imaginative realm into which she absorbs him. Even as a girl, Rostopchina demonstrates here, she is already possessed of an inborn sensibility that marks her as a poet. With her precocious reading of Pushkin, she manifests her poetic destiny and claims him as her muse:

> И часто девочке смиренной,
> Сияньем чудным озарен,
> Все представал, все снился *он*!

> And often to the meek girl,
> Illuminated by marvelous radiance,
> *He* repeatedly appeared, repeatedly entered her dreams!

With the pretextual ties to Pushkin that she establishes here, Rostopchina presents herself as a born poet. In 1937, on the centennial of Pushkin's death, Marina Tsvetaeva followed Rostopchina's lead, offering her own pretextual reading of the Golden Age poet to validate herself as a poet in the essay "My Pushkin" ("Moi Pushkin").

The "I remember" (*Ia pomniu*) that opens Rostopchina's poem draws attention to the vantage point of the now mature, celebrated poet who describes her meetings with Pushkin in verse that demonstrates her mastery of his poetic idiom.[50] Pushkin's swift stroll past the reticent girl of whom he naturally takes no notice thus becomes the prelude to the timeless "meeting" that takes place not in the crowd of revelers she describes but in the space of this poem, which realizes the creative promise of the girl it recollects. The ability of the girl who observes Pushkin "to dream a similar future of fame and injury," as Sandler notes,[51] prompts the reader to recognize the renown, and yet also the pain and suffering of the poet who now authors these lines.

Rostopchina's second encounter with Pushkin takes place, like the first, in the midst of a large public gathering—now a ball.[52] Describing the evening, her brother Sergei Sushkov says that, having learned that his sister was a poet, Pushkin sought her out and "became so interested in the passionate, fervent outpourings of his youthful interlocutor that he spent most of the evening with her and afterward immediately made the acquaintance of the Pashkov family."[53] Like the earlier meeting Rostopchina describes, this one antedates her first appearance in print in 1830 with the publication of the poem "Talisman" in *Northern Flowers* (*Severnye tsvety*), famously submitted to the almanac by the poet Viazemsky without her knowledge. (The indignation that her appearance in print aroused in her family inhibited further publications until after Sushkova's marriage to Count Rostopchin in 1833.) With continued emphasis on the perspective from which the now recognized poet recollects her younger self, the poem begins with a twofold iteration of the "I remember" (*Ia pomniu*) with which the first poem opened. Two years have gone by since that first encounter, and the girl whom Rostopchina describes no longer gazes at the renowned poet from afar. She appears instead as his proud partner—in dance and in poetry.

As the first poem of *Two Meetings* demonstrates, a fleeting glimpse of Pushkin in a crowd is enough to gain Rostopchina's recollected self access to his world. The Pushkin of her second meeting apparently lacks a similar facility. Unable to read *her*, he must rely on what she tells him and on the poems that she recites to him in order to enter her world. It falls to her to acquaint him with "The song of a feminine heart, song of feminine suffering" (*Pesn' zhenskogo serdtsa, pesn' zhenskikh stradanii*). Significantly, it is precisely at this point in her poem that Rostopchina describes herself—an eighteen-year-old on the evening of her coming out in society—as a "little girl" (*devochka*). Motivating this not entirely appropriate word choice is an effort to forestall both an eroticized reading of how she and Pushkin relate to each other and a sexualization of the feminine world that she reveals to him.[54] Like the "friendship" (*druzhba*) that she describes Pushkin extending to her earlier in the poem, the girlhood that Rostopchina writes into her account marks an effort to prevent eros from intruding on the creative bond that develops between them as poets. She would have her reader know that Pushkin is attracted not by her feminine charm but by her creative vitality. As they dance, she and Pushkin leave behind the erotically charged contests that characterize balls to enter a transcendent sphere. The differences in their gender, age, and standing—she is a would-be poet, he a celebrated one—disappear. As they move through the socially prescribed movements of the dance, they relate to each other on a higher plane. It is this poetical meeting that the poem describes and not the ball. Rostopchina's coming out in society is superseded by her coming out in poetry.

Unintimidated by her lofty partner, the "little girl" readily opens her heart to him. On the strength of the mutual understanding at which they quickly arrive and that sets them apart from the other guests, she and Pushkin enter into a poetic confederacy, described in terms that further desexualize and equalize the encounter: "In the soul of genius there is a sacred fraternity" (*V dushe genial'noi est' bratstvo sviatoe*). That she declaims her verse "surreptitiously" indicates a departure from ballroom etiquette, while its "artlessness" speaks of an unaffectedness that contrasts sharply with stilted ballroom comportment:

> Под говор му́зыки, украдкой, дрожа
> Стихи без искусства *ему* я шептала
> И взор снисхожденья с восторгом встречала.
>
> To the murmur of music, trembling,
> I surreptitiously, artlessly whispered my poems *to him*
> [I surreptitiously whispered my artless poems *to him*][55]
> And met his condescending gaze with delight.

The "condescension" with which Pushkin listens to her is short-lived, as he soon finds himself inspired by Rostopchina's poetic confession. The poems she recites prompt him to recollect his own spent youth and reinvigorate what Rostopchina describes as his waning powers of the imagination:

> Он пылкостью прежней тогда оживлялся,
> Он к юности знойной своей возвращался,
> О ней говорил мне, ее вспоминал.
> Со мной молодея, *он* снова мечтал.

> *He* then became enlivened with his former ardor,
> *He* returned to his fiery youth,
> Talked to me about it, recollected it.
> With me, growing younger, *he* dreamed again.

Moved by his young interlocutor's creative energy, a world-weary Pushkin expresses his disappointment that he did not meet her sooner and that he is not the object of her passions or the addressee of her poems. This de-eroticizes their relations still further and advances Rostopchina's authored self to a position of superiority over Pushkin, whose litany of regrets culminates with the admission that his life is essentially over and that he lived out his time before she did (*chto ran'she menia / On otzhil*).

Rostopchina presents Pushkin as a poet eclipsed by her creative energy even before she had become a published poet and some seven years before his death at d'Anthès's hand. It is, moreover, in her memory and, implicitly, in the poems that record it that the dead poet lives on:

> Но живо и ныне о *нем* вспоминанье;
> Но речи поэта, его предвещанье
> Я в памяти сердца храню как завет
> И ими горжусь . . . хоть *его* уже нет!

> But my recollections of *him* are alive to this day
> But the speeches of the poet, his portents
> I treasure in the memory of my heart like a testament
> And take pride in them . . . although *he* is no more!

The reverence bordering on deification conveyed by Rostopchina's reluctance to utter her forebear's name can scarcely conceal the advantages she claims over him. Rostopchina underscores that it was *he* who sought her out, *he* who desired access to the feminine creative sphere, *he* who found her inspiring and rejuvenating, and finally that it is *he* who now depends on her for an existence beyond his death. It is, moreover, *she* and not Pushkin who is alive and writing and it is *she* who is now the keeper of his words and practitioner of his art, just as in the earlier poem it was *she* who filled his empty notebook with verse.

In his review of Rostopchina's poetry collection, Belinsky cites this poem in particular to support his characterization of her as a flighty society lady. As he puts it, "Having transpired at a ball, even her meeting and friendship with Pushkin are essentially the description of a ball, which would be better suited to a letter or an article in prose than to rhymes."[56] In fact, however, Rostopchina uses the ballroom setting as a backdrop that accentuates the contrast between the social world and the poetical sphere into which she and Pushkin withdraw together. In his haste to fetter Rostopchina to the ballroom, Belinsky overlooks the point of the poem, in which Rostopchina describes not her public appearance as a debutante but her private poetic debut in the Russian poetic tradition. It is also possible that, sensing what Rostopchina was doing in this poem, Belinsky felt that she had overstepped her bounds and read her back into her place.

Rostopchina's three poems to Pushkin are indicative not of a feminine modesty that situates her at Pushkin's pedestal but of a poetic assertiveness. There is no reason to doubt the sincerity of Rostopchina's admiration of Pushkin, but there is also no reason to doubt her intent to position herself at the head of his tradition. Her recourse to feminine modesty and her invocation of Pushkin make her subversion of gender biases less conspicuous but no less potent. With her strategic self-positioning, Rostopchina claims a place in the male tradition not by rebelling against its norms but by using them punitively against the male establishment. That this has remained unrecognized testifies to the staying power of assumptions that readers bring to her poems. The double unthinkability that verse written by a woman and dedicated to Pushkin could do anything but breathe reverence leaves readers ill prepared to see that Rostopchina is taking the upper hand over the progenitor of the tradition into which she inscribes herself. Without the excision of a single word, reader-imposed censorship—whether inadvertent or intentional—expunges the import of the poems and reaffirms the status quo that the poet disrupts.

In her much-anthologized "How Women Must Write" ("Kak dolzhny pisat' zhenshchiny," 1840, pub. 1841),[57] Rostopchina uses a stratagem like that of "Pushkin's Draft Notebook," for in this poem, too, she turns restrictive gender biases against the male establishment that dictates them. Repeatedly singled out by commentators as Rostopchina's poetic manifesto,[58] the poem is widely seen as setting down guidelines for women's creative self-expression that dictate modesty and reticence in place of untrammeled self-expression. The obvious question of why Rostopchina would promote such instructions has remained unasked, leaving the argument she develops in the poem unappreciated.

"How Women Must Write" opens—significantly—with Rostopchina

casting herself in the role not of a writer but of a reader: "How I love to read others' poems" (*Kak ia liubliu chitat' stikhi chuzhie*). The poems that Rostopchina refers to here are those authored by men, and her designation of them as "others'" (*chuzhie*) invokes the prevailing ideology of separate domains. She proceeds to explain that on the strength of texts authored by men, the reading woman can gain access to men's experience:

Все испытую я; и всей душой моей
Делю восторг певца, дружу с его несчастьем,
Любовию его люблю и верю ей.

I experience everything, and with my entire soul
I share the rapture of the singer, acquaint myself with his misfortune,
I love with his love and believe it.

In the first of her *Two Meetings* poems, Rostopchina gains access to a male domain through her reading of Pushkin. Here she claims a similar prerogative.

Having established women's ability to partake of male experience by reading poems by men, Rostopchina maintains that she finds poems written by women more engaging: "But women's poems appeal to me with particular delight" (*No zhenskie stikhi osobennoi usladoi / Mne privlekatel'ny*). What distinguishes poems written by women, she goes on to explain, is that in them, intense emotions are discreetly veiled and innermost storms and secrets of the heart only hinted at. Assuring her reader that this is precisely the sort of poetry she loves best, Rostopchina devotes the remainder of "How Women Must Write" to praising women's verse and its restraint. The poem ends with what are, together with the lines that conclude "Pushkin's Draft Notebook," the most frequently cited of Rostopchina's oeuvre:

Да, женская душа должна в тени светиться,
Как в урне мраморной лампады скрытой луч,
Как в сумерки луна сквозь оболочку туч,
И, согревая жизнь, незримая, теплиться.

Yes, the feminine soul must glow in shadow,
Like a hidden ray in the urn of a marble lamp,
Like the moon at dusk through a veil of clouds,
And, warming life, glimmer unseen.

Distinctly at variance with her own writing and comportment, this professed endorsement of reticence arouses suspicion. Indeed, the argument behind it is readily discerned: because a woman reader has herself experienced what another woman's poems only hint at, she can fully grasp what the poems intimate. This is something a man (*chuzhoi*) cannot do because he is not privy to the world that women's poems suggest but modestly veil. Thus, while men's immodest texts gain women free access to their experiences, men are barred from similar access to the feminine world by those very prohibitions they impose on women's self-expressivity. The argument is a cogent one. Interest in the woman's sphere was on the rise, and, as reviews of Rostopchina's *Poems* document, women's writing was increasingly seen as a source of information about the their unknown inner world. The mutually exclusive expectations that women's poems be revelatory and yet also modest harbored the expectation that women and their poems reaffirm male constructs of the feminine. If the woman poet deviated from prevailing assumptions, reader-imposed censorship marshaled her back into prescribed, familiar territory.

While the interest that writing women increasingly attracted gained them prominence, it also threatened to reinforce their othering and the assumption that it was for men to dictate the scope of their self-expression. At the height of George Sand's popularity, Belinsky counseled that Rostopchina confine herself to satisfying men's curiosity about the feminine in her poems.[59] Rostopchina takes advantage of such curiosity to argue against the curtailment of the woman poet's self-expressivity by turning the tables on the male establishment. In both "Pushkin's Draft Notebook" and "How Women Must Write," her professions of modesty, like her embrace of the ideology of separate domains, are a masquerade that indicates not submissiveness but subversive intent. Holding two distinct aspects of the writing woman in productive tension—the compliant mask and the enigmatic poet who works beneath it—her poems repeatedly draw attention to a privately sustained inner world that is uniquely the woman's own and that eludes male scrutiny and control. Here Rostopchina comes up against a problem: although the demand is that women write in order to reveal a new world to their male readers, the premium remains on constructs of the feminine that men read into women's poems. Like others of her lyrics, "How Women Must Write" is taken at face value and her feminine mask seen as her own visage. This situation is exacerbated by the repeated citation of lines taken out of context to reaffirm what Rostopchina in fact destabilizes.

Here it is important to draw attention also to the respect that Rostopchina commanded at the turning point of her career when Belinsky chained her to the ball. The delight that reviewers expressed in Rostopchina's ostensibly feminine qualities did not preclude their readiness to accept her as a poet. In a review of Rostopchina's *Poems*, Belinsky's opponent, the conservative poet and historian Shevyrev, praised what he saw as Rostopchina's multifaceted revelations about the woman's sphere, spoke seriously of her verse, and concluded by endorsing Zhukovsky's bestowal of Pushkin's notebook on her.[60] Rostopchina's social class, her success in society, and her lively salon contributed to this success, as did conservatives' growing need for allies at this time. Yet the fact remains that even reviewers who emphasized her gender in stereotypical terms had thoughtful praise for her poetry and welcomed her into the tradition. In his review of Rostopchina's collection, literary historian and government censor A. V. Nikitenko first distinguished Rostopchina from all other contemporary poets and only then situated her at the forefront of women writing at the time.[61] Pletnev, the editor of *The Contemporary* to whom Rostopchina sent *Two Meetings* for publication, also praised her poetry earnestly and in laudatory terms. Commenting on the rich variety of her poems, he spoke of her respectfully as "the author" (grammatically masculine).[62] Even Shevyrev, who wrote of the femininity of Rostopchina's verse, called her a poet and a woman poet (*zhenshchina poet*), never resorting to the deprecatory "poetess."[63] This is not to say that women poets attained parity in the male-dominated literary world or that patently denigrating evaluations of them suddenly vanished, but only to observe that it was in the latter part of the nineteenth century that liberals, who feminized poetry in the course of devaluing it, began to call her a poetess. This unfortunate designation seeped into the twentieth century and was perpetuated by precisely those cultural figures who reestablished the preeminence of poetry and professed interest in women's creativity.[64]

The rise and fall of Rostopchina's career coincided with sociopolitical shifts that brought dramatic changes into the culture of the time and how women were regarded in it. Her literary fortunes were linked with the transition from the poetic ideals of the fading Pushkinian era to the demands for civic-minded prose of the rising progressive movement. Rostopchina's social class, which came under increasing fire, and her staunch loyalty to the Pushkinian era of which she saw herself as the last representative[65] left her out of line with the views promulgated by progressive thinkers and with constructs of the woman informed by George Sand. Rostopchina's poetry and social class had become untenable. Belinsky's review that fettered her to the ballroom referred to her exclusively as countess and never as poet, author, or even poetess. In 1847, the year Rostopchina returned to Russia after a two-year absence to face imperial wrath precipitated by the "Forced Marriage" scandal, the editorship of *The Contemporary* was taken over by Panaev and Nekrasov, who steered the journal in a new direction. Rostopchina had no desire to adjust to these changes, but the new world refused to be ignored. As Rostopchina's celebrity went into decline, she was increasingly mired in bitter polemics and the target of growing attacks.

The poems discussed in this chapter exemplify two interrelated strategies that Rostopchina develops to wield her pen as a weapon against men. Rostopchina presents the restrictions imposed on women's expressivity as the male establishment's self-exclusion from their creative world. At the same time, she uses feminine masquerade to intensify interest in this world and to conceal her bold self-positioning vis-à-vis major poets of the Golden Age. Although well conceived, Rostopchina's calculated emphasis on the feminine increased the vulnerability of her poems to reader-imposed censorship. Though successful in that it did not "disturb the slumber"[66] of the gatekeepers of the tradition on whose approval she depended, Rostopchina's strategy ran aground on the fact that readers were comfortable with the gender norms that she invoked with seditious intent. This compromised their efficacy as "awakening stumbling blocks"[67] and left readers oblivious to the seditious dimension of her poems. Apparently sensible of this Achilles' heel, Rostopchina repeatedly drew attention to the incongruity between the social mask of femininity that she wore and the creative self that sheltered beneath it but could not break through the obduracy of preconceived notions about women and women's writing. Shallow, selective readings and the citation of passages divorced from the contexts in which they signified strengthened the chain with which Belinsky attached her to the ball, and this, in turn, strengthened the tendency to take both the poet and her poems at face value.

Pavlova downplays her gender, minimizing its importance to the poet's creative identity and aligning the marginalized woman with the increasingly marginalized poet. Foregrounding her abiding dedication to the poetic calling, she maintains that the ills of society are detrimental to men and women alike and urges women to assume responsibility for themselves. Rostopchina draws attention to her gender and takes a more combative stance to claim that limits on women's self-expressivity are detrimental to men.[68] Yet Pavlova and Rostopchina have this in common: in responding to gender-determined limitations, both draw on images of feminine compliance to asseverate an unassailable creativity that remains beyond the reach of those who would restrict it. Rostopchina repeatedly indicates a private inner domain that is inaccessible to the male establishment. Pavlova, in "We are contemporaries, Countess," presents a creative self who works undeterred by the house arrest of conventional matrimony. In these variants of the Romantics' turn inward in response to subjugation, Pavlova and Rostopchina concur.

It is not difficult to understand why radical critics of the 1850s and 1860s, following Belinsky's lead, would become increasingly hostile to Rostopchina and what she, as a countess, stood for in their eyes.[69] It is less clear why Rostopchina was not reinstated in the Russian literary pantheon when poetry came into its own again with the advent of the neo-Romantic Symbolists, who professed interest in women's creativity and reconnected with the Pushkinian tradition. Rostopchina, who died in 1858, had not faded from the cultural scene. Even during the reign of prose, her poems continued to be read—largely by women, who were perhaps attuned to the import of her poems—and to be sung as lyrics of romances by major composers.[70] Yet

Rostopchina was not simply ignored by the male establishment in the early twentieth century. She was purposefully belittled.

In an essay of 1908 titled "Countess E. P. Rostopchina: Her Life and Lyrics" ("Grafinia E. P. Rostopchina: Ee zhizn' i lirika"), Khodasevich upholds Belinsky's unjust chaining of Rostopchina to the ball: "The sentence turned out to be the only and the final one. Belinsky's words were repeated and are repeated to this day as incontrovertible truth."[71] Khodasevich, who is not averse to perpetuating this "sentence," says nothing of Rostopchina's active role in the culture of her time and the recognition she attained in it, maintaining only that her poems hold no more meaning than her vacuous social life did.[72] Indeed, he goes so far as to question the intentionality of the political dimension of "A Forced Marriage." Twice asserting that he is unable to determine the true meaning of the ballad, he suggests that Rostopchina was unaware of its subversive political meaning, which, he proposes, was projected onto the poem by her readers.[73] Demonstratively dismissing the woman's creative inner domain that Rostopchina championed, Khodasevich goes out of his way to emphasize his indifference to women's inscrutability.

Khodasevich's attitude reflects a gender-driven anxiety that informs intentional reader-imposed censorship. The tone and content of his entire essay support this proposition. Along the same lines, his review—tellingly titled "One of the Forgotten" ("Odna iz zabytykh")—of Pavlova's collected works that Valerii Briusov brought out in 1915 relegates to oblivion the two leading women poets of the nineteenth century who were promising role models for women writing after them. The next two chapters lead into the time in which Khodasevich wrote this essay: the early years of the twentieth century, when a marked interest in women's creative psychology and the rapidly growing number of women poets triggered efforts to retain control over the writing woman on the part of the male establishment. The focus is on concrete manifestations of such efforts—two "women poets" invented by men in anxious response to the rising tide and growing selfhood of the woman.

PART II

Female Impersonations

Chapter Three

The Cherubina de Gabriak Mystification

I am speaking of the *real*, not of the living
woman.
—Auguste Villiers de L'Isle-Adam, *Tomorrow's Eve*

Women exist to please men and to be
subjugated to them.
—Rousseau, *Émile*

WHEN POETRY REGAINED ITS pride of place at
the turn of the twentieth century, a dramatic rise in the number of women
poets and the expanded opportunities for them to publish ensured their visi-
bility and made it impossible to dismiss feminine authorship.[1] With the move
away from civic-minded prose, the focus on women's sociopolitical role gave
way to speculation about their distinct creative psychology. The Silver Age
was marked by an unprecedented interest in the woman's creative domain[2]—
the site of the woman poet's agency that Pavlova privileged and the terra
incognita that Rostopchina repeatedly invoked in her verse. Symbolists do
not refer to the woman question, and for them the "new woman," as Kirsti
Ekonen summarizes, "functions as the *other*."[3] This othering reflects a palpable undercurrent of male anxiety that manifested itself alongside the curiosity sparked by women's creativity. The male establishment's apprehension
of the unknown feminine terrain and the need to govern it grew in proportion to the rise of women poets. Explorations of women's creative psychology
remained rooted in preconceived notions that reflected the staying power
of gender biases carried over from the previous century. Theorizing about
gender remained in the male domain, and constructs of the woman derived
not from women's self-disclosure but from assumptions and needs that men
projected onto them. As Ekonen describes, women continued to be seen in
relation to men in the roles of muse, wife, or beloved.[4]

Women's authorship did not yet gain liberation from established
norms, and the image of the woman poet remained under male Symbolists'
control.[5] Encouraged to write, women were also encouraged to stay within

the bounds drawn for them by men, who defined what constituted women's unique perspective and its articulation. A steadily mounting number of publications devoted expressly to women's writing provided women poets with venues for their work, but also distanced them from the mainstream.[6] At the same time, male mentors took charge of women poets' expressivity, and fictional heroines from men's works remained more influential than women themselves in shaping constructs of the woman. It was held that women had neither the requisite characteristics nor the authority to be critics, and even the established writers Zinaida Gippius and Sophia Parnok signed their critical articles with male pseudonyms.[7] Men continued to decide which women poets to advance and which to censure or to recast in accordance with their own projects.

With the woman poet's identity not yet under her control, the question remained of how she could embrace gender as a constitutive but not overdetermined aspect of her creative self. Women poets who, like Zinaida Gippius, masked their gender implicitly acknowledged a lack or defect in womanhood. Women poets who, like Mirra Lokhvitskaia, embraced their gender contended with objectification. Though potentially daunting, this challenge energized a wide range of experimental self-presentations that spanned everything from cross-dressing to enactments of the ultrafeminine and ultimately helped to destabilize prevailing constructs of gender and preconceptions about women poets. As the number of recognized women poets grew, more models emerged for women to draw on, strengthening their claims to authorship and self-determination. This gradually gained them greater autonomy from the male establishment and marked an important advance.[8] Initially, however, the authority men exercised over writing women continued to foster competition for male approval, while ties among women that could foster a supportive community threatened to reinforce the gender divide that denied them equal status in the tradition.

There was yet another challenge confronting women poets that extended into the Silver Age. Although their access to publication expanded, reading practices of the previous century remained intact and interfered with full appreciation of their poems. A poem by a woman continued to be seen as a source of information about its author rather than an artifact in its own right. The assumption that women's poems recorded only actual experiences discounted the woman's creative imagination, while the direct equivalence presupposed between her authoring and authored selves closed off possibility for signification that their nonidentity offered. The belief that the woman writing the poems and the woman inhabiting them were identical extended into the notion that the authoring poet must physically resemble the woman that the reader envisioned in her poems. The richly varied personae that Lokhvitskaia devised resisted entrapment in such presuppositions. Indeed, the myriad challenges women poets confronted ultimately fostered growth both of individual poets and of women's poetry as a whole. In part three of this study, I examine enabling opposition to male authority. First, however, I turn to two striking manifestations of this authority: the Cherubina de Gabriak mystification to which the present chapter is devoted and the Nelli mystification that is the focus of the next.

In early September of 1909, an envelope sealed with black wax and bearing the imprint "Vae victis!" arrived at the elegant offices of the newly established Symbolist journal *Apollo* (*Apollon*). Inside was a packet of poems with a cover letter to the editor, Sergei Makovsky, penned in French in a graceful hand on black-bordered paper and signed only with the initial "Ch."[9] This elaborate presentation of the de Gabriak poems deployed an exaggerated femininity in order to enter a male domain and to predispose readers to her works. Like the trappings devised for them, the poems submitted to *Apollo* catered to Symbolist aesthetic sensibilities and underscored feminine authorship.

The exotic image of the woman who emerged from these poems worked together with the staged mystery surrounding their author to command attention. Telephone calls from Cherubina followed, together with more poems, which Makovsky shared with his editorial board and which won unanimous approval for publication. When the first issue of *Apollo* came out in October of 1909, a "Cherubina de Gabriak" figured in its list of contributors, together with Annensky, Bal'mont, Briusov, Voloshin, and Gumilev. Members of the literary circle that formed around the journal were captivated,[10] and even before twelve poems signed by Cherubina de Gabriak appeared in the second issue of *Apollo* the following month, the mysterious unknown woman (*neznakomka*) was basking in celebrity.

Just as readers were discovering this new poet on the pages of *Apollo*, its editor was suffering pangs of loss and his staff discomfiture, having learned that Cherubina de Gabriak was a fiction invented by the poets Maximilian Voloshin and Elizaveta Dmitrieva. The unveiling of the mystification created a stir among those affiliated with the journal and led to a duel between Voloshin and Nikolai Gumilev. In the public domain, however, the hoax remained unadvertised, and Cherubina de Gabriak remained on the list of *Apollo*'s contributors together with her two inventors. The tenth issue of *Apollo*, which appeared on September 15 of the following year (1910), carried thirteen poems signed by de Gabriak, extravagantly and uniquely framed by Evgenii Lansere's graphics.[11] This marked Cherubina de Gabriak's final appearance on the pages of the journal, but by no means her end. In his essay "Women's Poetry" ("Zhenskaia poeziia"), which appeared in *The Morning of Russia* (*Utro Rossii*) on December 11, 1910, Voloshin praised de Gabriak's poems, which found their way from *Apollo* into other journals to win a following among readers who continued to take their author for a flesh-and-blood poet.[12]

The mystification originated in Voloshin's hospitable Crimean home in Koktebel', a veritable writers' colony where artists of all stripes gathered. Among the guests in the spring and summer of 1909, the year of Cherubina's birth, was the aspiring poet Elizaveta Dmitrieva, whom Voloshin drew into the project of inventing and sustaining de Gabriak. Dmitrieva and Voloshin met in St. Petersburg in the spring of 1908, corresponded while he was in Paris, and in 1909, upon his return to Russia, attended meetings of Viacheslav Ivanov's "Poetic Academy" together. A philologist by education, Dmitrieva specialized in medieval history and medieval French literature at the Women's Pedagogical Institute. She also audited courses in Spanish literature and Old French at the University of St. Petersburg and devoted independent study to Sanskrit. In 1907, she visited Paris, where she attended classes on Old French literature at the Sorbonne. Upon completing her degree at the institute, she taught Russian history in a women's *gimnaziia*. All the while, Dmitrieva read avidly, wrote poetry, worked on translations, and actively participated in the literary world of St. Petersburg. Her spiritual searchings connected her to the teachings of theosophists and anthroposophists. Her first publication—a Russian rendering of Saint Teresa of Ávila's "Octave"—appeared in the *Theosophical Herald* in March of 1909 under the pseudonym "E. Li."[13]

Dmitrieva arrived at Koktebel' with the poet Nikolai Gumilev, whom she had met in Paris. Already betrothed to the engineer Vsevolod Vasiliev, who became her husband in May 1911, Dmitrieva formed a close relationship with Gumilev but rejected his proposals of marriage. During their sojourn at Koktebel', Dmitrieva's affections shifted to Voloshin, with whom she also entered into close ties and who also vied, unsuccessfully, for her hand in marriage.[14] Refused as a spouse, Voloshin drew her into his project to create a new woman poet.[15]

Writing about this period, Irina Shevelenko observes that "male writers actively engaged in the formation of the new identity, the *cultural personality* of the woman poetess."[16] Evident in men's controlling mentorship of women, which was seldom free from sexualization, the dynamics and consequences of such formation find vivid instantiation in the Cherubina de Gabriak episode. A culturally and psychologically complex event, the mystification lends itself to many approaches.[17] In the context of the present study, it emerges as a realization of the metaphoric "invention of the poet who makes the poem"—one that documents the construction of de Gabriak from both sides of the divide between the woman poet and her male reader, complicated here by Voloshin's mentorship.[18] From this perspective, the mystification is an illuminating instantiation of the male modernist effort to shape the new woman poet.[19]

Cherubina emerged against the backdrop of a flourishing interest in women that affirmed their otherness and put them in the peculiar state of celebrated marginalization. The male establishment's assumptions about what women could bring to literature corresponded with its own needs and fantasies. Because men controlled instruments of publication, women poets competing for their approval were inclined to comply with male expectations, a tendency to which the initial dearth of feminine role models contributed. Although women poets could knowingly enter into compromise with the dominant group, some remained unconscious of the extent to which they upheld prevailing biases that were detrimental to their advancement. By embracing extant images of the woman in response to the call for self-revelation, the woman poet could enter male-controlled literary space more easily. In so doing, however, she reinforced norms that were retrograde to her self-realization. She also incurred a serious risk: recourse to familiar images of the woman triggered habits of reading that left her poems undervalued.

In the Cherubina de Gabriak mystification, these propensities of the culture of the time and their effect on the woman poet appear in concentrated form. The motivation for inventing Cherubina is generally explained—in terms that Voloshin promoted—as an instance of Symbolist myth- and life-creation that allowed Dmitrieva to realize her creative potential. It has remained largely without comment, however, that this multifaceted project exemplifies a deliberate effort to form a writing woman in accord with male notions just as women were making inroads into the tradition. My purpose here is to study the mystification for what it tells us about this effort. To this end, I attend to the real-life implications and consequences of this imaginative venture, focusing not on the de Gabriak poems but on the invention of their fictional poet by three major players in the episode. I begin with Makovsky, whose response to Cherubina shows tenacious preconceptions of the time in action, determining how he reads the poems and envisions the woman who ostensibly authors them. Next I look at how writing on behalf of Cherubina destabilizes Dmitrieva's creative identity as she confronts a woman poet invented in response to male fantasies rather than her own expressive needs. Finally, I explore the multiple roles that Voloshin assumes in the ruse, which include directing de Gabriak's creation, overseeing what she wrote, manipulating how she was read, and then appropriating the story of the mystification.[20]

At first glance, it seems that the invention of Cherubina de Gabriak created for Dmitrieva a situation that Karolina Pavlova could only dream of—the publication of poems by a woman freed from her body. Such liberation, however, is not easily won, and the physical absence of the poet from the public eye only intensified preoccupation with the body implicit in her texts.

Indeed, the de Gabriak poems came to be valued not in their own right but as a means to reconstruct their absent author, thus shifting attention from the poems created by a woman to the woman created by the readers of her poems. On the strength of her absence, Cherubina commanded attention as a flesh-and-blood woman, while her celebrity derived largely from the active role readers assumed in inventing the woman who authored the poems.

Sergei Makovsky, who recollects the episode in his essay "Cherubina de Gabriak," is a case in point.[21] Never doubting that the woman whom he derived from de Gabriak's poems had an identical real-life counterpart, and believing, too, that the lyrics recorded her actual life experiences and emotions, Makovsky threw himself into discovering who she was. Reading, as he thought, between the lines of the poems to find her out, he saw the lyrics confirming stereotypes and fantasies that he himself projected onto them. Voloshin and Dmitrieva vigorously fueled this propensity. In the time between the submission of the de Gabriak poems to *Apollo* and their publication, they elaborated on the fictional poet. Balancing concrete details with intimations of the ineffable, the two conspirators supplied material—well in excess of what the project demanded—that inspired Makovsky's invention of a Cherubina of his own. The affected presentation of the poems, the elegantly penned French letters, and the dried herbs and flowers that accompanied them worked their magic on the unsuspecting editor, who read these paratextual props, like the poems, for clues to the mysterious woman's identity. From the letters, Makovsky gleaned biographical information: the feminine hand in which Dmitrieva penned them revealed Cherubina's character, while the enclosed herbarium was a language of flowers from which he could derive meaning as he wished. Augmenting this semiotic riot were the telephone calls that Dmitrieva made to him in Cherubina's name. Here is Makovsky's own description of the woman he constructed from this material:

After considerable effort I finally succeed in eliciting something from the "infanta": she really is Spanish by birth, and is, moreover, a fervent Catholic: she is only eighteen years old, was brought up in a convent, has a rather weak chest from birth. Once she also inadvertently said something about embassy receptions at a private residence "on the islands" and about the strictest supervision of her despotic father (her mother died a long time ago) and a certain Jesuit monk, her confessor . . . At the same time the letters accompanying the poems (there were also letters without poems), were permeated with the melancholy of loneliness, the desire to entrust herself to someone, to follow the call of the heart.[22]

Makovsky was soon head over heels in love with a woman he had never laid eyes on. Blind to his own active role in fashioning her, he openly admits that it never occurred to him that de Gabriak might not exist in real life just as he imagined her. "Never until then, it seemed to me," he confesses with disarming candor and solipsism, "had any other woman so fully coincided with my ideal of a woman."[23] Makovsky notes, too, that he was not alone in his adulation: "All the 'Apollonians' to a man fell in love with her, with no one doubting that she was of untold beauty."[24] This collective love[25] for Cherubina guaranteed her celebrity, but, ironically, to the detriment of her verse: "The poems were average . . . But the important thing was that these poems nonetheless harbored the soul of an unusual creature, and it was she who possessed me."[26] A figment of his imagination, Cherubina de Gabriak assumed a presence that was for Makovsky "both ethereal and fully real."[27]

Not all the Apollonians were as credulous as the editor was,[28] but even the skeptics were willing to play along. The mystification persisted until Dmitrieva, overwhelmed by the need to make her authorship known, confided to Johannes von Guenther, a German poet and translator on *Apollo*'s staff, that she was the author of de Gabriak's poems.[29] Von Guenther, who envisioned a very different woman, refused to believe Dmitrieva until she provided tangible proof of her role in the mystification. Gratified to know what so many were eager to learn, von Guenther broke his oath of silence and revealed Dmitrieva's secret to a fellow staff member.[30] The news spread. When Makovsky's close friends Alexei Tolstoi and Mikhail Kuzmin apprised the unsuspecting editor of the deception, they found him loath to accept that there was no Cherubina even though his efforts to catch a glimpse of her had consistently failed. Upon receiving incontrovertible proof that he was indeed the victim of a hoax, Makovsky continued to cling to the hope that the woman who wrote under de Gabriak's name resembled the ideal he saw enshrined in her poetry. His account of the visit that Dmitrieva paid him to apologize for the deception reflects the degree to which he believed in the reality of a woman he helped invent:

> The door opened slowly, very slowly, as it seemed to me, and into the room came, limping heavily, a short, fairly stout dark-haired woman with a large head, an inordinately prominent forehead, and with a sort of truly frightening mouth from which fanglike teeth protruded. She was exceptionally ugly. Or did it only seem that way to me in comparison with that image of beauty that I had been nurturing during those months? I was almost afraid. The wonderful dream suddenly vanished forever; coming into its own was merciless, monstrous, shameful reality. My revulsion brought me to tears, and at the same time, my regret for her, Cherubina, brought me to tears.[31]

Prompted perhaps by her limp, which folklore styles as an attribute of devils and witches, Makovsky's demonization of Dmitrieva conveys the depth of his disillusionment and his conviction that the actual woman who wrote the poems and the woman he read into them were the same. The presupposition of identity between the authored and authoring selves of a woman poet is stretched here into the firm expectation of an identity between the authoring poet and the woman invented by the male reader of her poems.

It would be easy to dismiss Makovsky as naive, but the effect of the mystification's unveiling on assessments of de Gabriak's poetry indicates that although he was perhaps more invested than most in the fictional poet, his reaction was not exceptional. After the unveiling, the poems were more critically evaluated and de Gabriak's erstwhile admirers questioned not their own assumptions and fantasies but the authorship of the poems. Finding the discrepancy between the inventing and the invented poets too difficult to accept, many now insisted that it was Voloshin and not Dmitrieva who wrote Cherubina's poems, and even the duped Makovsky came under suspicion of writing them.[32] The argument that Dmitrieva could not have written the poems because she did not look like Cherubina de Gabriak did not extend to male poets, who resembled her even less. The idea of a man writing in the guise of a beautiful woman was more palatable than of an unbeautiful woman doing so.

Notably, the deception of readers that the mystification presupposed called for verisimilitude that was based on what men thought about how women must write—in both the prescriptive and the speculative meanings of "must." Perversely, the credibility of the woman's inner self that the de Gabriak poems purportedly revealed hinged on how familiar it seemed to her readers. Mysterious in her avoidance of personal public appearances, Cherubina de Gabriak was intimately connected to her readers, each of whom fashioned a privately held image of the enigmatic poet in whose poems they found confirmation of their illusions. A successful ruse followed by its unveiling could potentially awaken readers to their erroneous assumptions about the writing woman. This, however, was neither the goal nor the outcome of the mystification, which banked on gender biases for its success and reflected the degree to which male notions continued to be imprinted onto women's writing.

Makovsky, who soon recovered from his sentimental *mésaventure*, married within a year of the collapse of his dream. Yet though slight, the mark Cherubina de Gabriak left on him was, as he maintained, indelible: "Only over the years did I realize that my passion for a phantom left a trace in me; the scratch never healed completely."[33] The effects of the mystification on Dmitrieva went deeper. The discrepancy between her and the invented woman on whose behalf she had composed poems became a source of guilt and psychological distress that grew in proportion with Cherubina's celebrity. Readers' obdurate expectation of an identity between the authoring and authored selves of a woman's poems overrode the improbability of an identical real-life counterpart to the woman they found in the poems. Interest in this exceptional woman overshadowed interest in her poems, which came to serve not as signifieds in their own right but as signifiers of their absent author. Dmitrieva was left doubly marginalized by an invented poet who overwhelmed not only her author but the very poems that gave rise to the phantom. Ploys intended to shore up the invented poet's credibility exacerbated this situation. Dmitrieva's role-playing in telephone calls to Makovsky and the biting parodies of de Gabriak's poetry[34] that she circulated among the Apollonians enhanced the invented poet's "reality" but further destabilized Dmitrieva's sense of self.

If, with the unmasking of Cherubina, Makovsky lost the woman of his dreams, Dmitrieva lost a good deal more. She appeared before the editor to break the spell just one day after the first installment of de Gabriak's poems appeared in *Apollo*. Her confession, which Makovsky records in his memoirs, reflects the extent to which her creative psychology was tied to a poet whom she neither resembled nor independently invented. Dmitrieva's anxieties were intensified by Makovsky's credulity and by the degree to which she differed from his imagined ideal. Makovsky's rendering of Dmitrieva's apology conveys the guilt and sense of failure that oppressed Dmitrieva:

> You must magnanimously forgive me. If I have caused you pain, then how many times more painful it is for me myself. Only think. I knew who you were, I met you in person, for me you were no fantasy! Only God knows how cruelly I am atoning for my deceit. Today, from the moment I heard from you that everything had been revealed, from that moment I lost myself forever: the unique, invented "I" who over the course of several months had permitted me to feel myself a woman, to live the full life of creativity, love, happiness—died. Having buried Cherubina, I buried myself, never to be resurrected . . .[35]

Dmitrieva's confidence was badly shaken. Even before the second installment of de Gabriak's poems appeared in *Apollo* in September of 1910, she pulled away not just from Voloshin but from the very idea that she was a poet.[36] In a letter to him of November 16 that year, she ruefully confided, "I, the artist, have died. That is not my path."[37] Writing in the guise of a woman who catered to male fantasies smacked more of self-annihilation than of self-expressivity. Precipitated by the nonidentity between herself and de Gabriak that brought opprobrium from her male readers, Dmitrieva's estrangement from the invented poet was magnified by Voloshin's participation in the project. Even before the mystification was unveiled, she faced the question that readers raised in its aftermath: what of Cherubina was really hers? As the mystification unfolded and de Gabriak took on a life of her own, Dmitrieva was effectively closed out of the interaction between the poet and her reader that transpires in the space of a text. A child of Silver Age aesthetics and preconceptions about women, de Gabriak could not accommodate Dmitrieva's individual creativity, even as Dmitrieva herself could not accommodate the fantasies that de Gabriak inspired in her readers. As Dmitrieva saw it, the problem stemmed not from the pressures of the male establishment on the woman poet but from her own inadequacy. Entailed in Cherubina's success was Dmitrieva's own failure. Alienated from and marginalized by the fictional poet into whom Voloshin directed her to channel her creative energy, she emerged from the mystification alternately uncertain and despairing about her own future. She stopped attending literary gatherings, and her relations with Voloshin grew increasingly strained.[38] A letter of December 29, 1909, to a friend who praised de Gabriak's poems reflects Dmitrieva's need to disassociate herself from the fictional poet: "Thank you for Cherubina, but she has already died. And I want to work and then write either *very* well, or to fall silent."[39]

Dmitrieva's situation was all the more difficult because recuperating a creative identity that had become enmeshed with Cherubina de Gabriak demanded a declaration of independence not only from the invented poet but also from the celebrity she enjoyed. In a letter to Voloshin of January 18, 1910, Dmitrieva made it clear that she herself staked no claim to the title of leading Russian woman poet that de Gabriak briefly held. Cut loose from the invention, Dmitrieva doubted her own creative viability. Writing in her letter that she had read Mariia Moravskaia's verse to a delighted Makovsky, who was eager to publish it, Dmitrieva adds, "But I have the feeling that I died, and Moravskaia has come to replace me . . . This makes me feel cold and lifeless."[40]

Dmitrieva's break with poetry proved to be temporary. Her break with de Gabriak proved to be impossible. Seven years after the episode, in a letter to Voloshin of May 26, 1916, she insisted on the importance that Cherubina continued to hold for her. Significantly, she continued to see the situation in terms of a dependency on de Gabriak and her own insufficiency: "I have a strange soul, Max, and no one besides you has ever uncovered it. To you it was given to do so simply because you had the keys: art. 'Cherubina' was *never* a game for me . . . With 'Cherubina' I was truly born: alas, stillborn."[41] Dmitrieva remained invested in a guise of a woman poet that Voloshin conceived and her readers elaborated. She believed, as Voloshin prompted, that the invented poet brought her dormant creative potential to life but that she herself proved unable to sustain it. She doubted not the invention but her own creativity. Hobbled by male constructs of the woman poet, she persisted in her efforts to come to terms with Cherubina as she struggled to regain her selfhood. In 1922, some thirteen years after the mystification, she wrote, again in a letter to Voloshin, "I have begun to think sometimes that I am a poet. They say that I must publish a book. If this transpires, I will remain 'Cherubina' because that is how everyone accepts me and because, after all, my roots in Cherubina are deep."[42]

When Dmitrieva resumed writing poetry in 1915, she signed her poems with the name Cherubina de Gabriak, as she said she would do. With this effort to revitalize the compromised relationship between her authoring and her authored selves, Dmitrieva hoped to establish her creative autonomy. Her new poems differed markedly from those that had appeared in *Apollo*. Dmitrieva now worked in response to her own expressive needs, and the voice of the Apollonian Cherubina no longer resounded in her lyrics. In contradistinction to the earlier de Gabriak, *this* one, as Dmitrieva hoped, would be her own. A passage from her "Autobiography," compiled by her friend Evgenii Arkhipov from letters she wrote him between 1921 and 1927, reflects Dmitrieva's need for a break with Cherubina and yet also for a continuity with her earlier created self:

> Between Cherubina of the years 1909–1910 and that same Cherubina from 1915 on, there lies a very sharp boundary. I don't even know—whether she is one and the same or whether one has died. But I don't abandon this name because I still feel a continuity in my soul, and accepting neither the earlier nor the present Cherubina, I call the future one to account. I do not even know yet whether I am a poet.[43]

Dmitrieva predicated her creative rebirth on a reconciliation of her divided selves—the first Cherubina, who had won success by catering to the male establishment, and the second one, who corresponded to Dmitrieva's own expressive needs and remained uncelebrated. Dmitrieva's story is unique, but her efforts to reconcile these two Cherubinas emblematize women poets' negotiations of their own creative self-expression, the demands and expectations imposed on them by the male establishment, and the gender biases that readers brought to their poems.

While Dmitrieva struggled to free herself from Cherubina de Gabriak, the phantom poet effortlessly disassociated herself from her author and took on a life of her own. Traveling far in time and space, she appeared in Paul Cohen's drama *Cherubina*, which premiered on the stage of the Sanford Meisner Theater in New York on February 1, 2008. She surfaced again the following year in Rusina Volkova's story "Cherubina's Grandchildren" ("Vnuki Cherubiny") of 2009,[44] and, as I write this chapter, is taking on new life in a novel by Karla Huebner.

The events considered thus far took place behind the scenes. I now turn to the multiple roles Voloshin played in the public domain. The twelve poems signed by Cherubina de Gabriak that appeared in *Apollo*, as Marianna Landa catalogues, invoke chivalric love, the Crusades, Spanish Catholicism, prayer, confinement, poor health, Christ, Lucifer, theosophy, mysticism, Rosicrucian and Masonic symbolism, and proclamations of sexual love for Christ.[45] Aptly describing the poems as "rich in an iconography that can be interpreted from a variety of approaches," Groberg notes that they spoke to Symbolist, Decadent, Western, Roman Catholic, and anthroposophical interests of the time.[46] Densely allusive, the poems offered readers a heady mix of ingredients for reconstituting their putative author, assuring de Gabriak's success. "She is imitated, people who have nothing to do with literature know her by heart, while Petersburg poets hate and envy her," Voloshin crowed in a letter of November 29, 1909.[47]

Having worked behind the scenes to bring Cherubina de Gabriak and her poems into being, Voloshin publicly bookended the mystification with his "Horoscope of Cherubina de Gabriak" ("Goroskop Cherubiny de Gabriak") of 1909[48] and "The History of Cherubina de Gabriak" ("Istoriia Cherubiny de Gabriak") of 1930,[49] which I consider in turn. In these markedly different works, Voloshin casts himself in the leading role—first as a critic and then as the inventor of a new woman poet. In the former role, he situates Cherubina de Gabriak in a literary genealogy of fictional heroines of male authors who feature the exceptional woman as posing a serious threat to men. In the second, he describes the part Cherubina allegedly played in Dmitrieva's creative self-realization, producing a legend that departs from actuality in revealing ways. Both works present the discrepancy between Dmitrieva's authoring and authored selves as a disjunction that imperils her, and both demonstrate the degree to which fictional works by men authorize and perpetuate male constructs of the woman and the biases embedded in them. They demonstrate, too, the degree to which the woman in whom male poets of the time express interest is one of their own invention.

When de Gabriak debuted in *Apollo* in the autumn of 1909, Voloshin was on hand to direct the reception of her poems and their putative author. His "Horoscope of Cherubina de Gabriak," which appeared in the same issue of the journal, introduced the new poet to her readers, influencing how they read her poems.[50] The direction this takes is instructive. Voloshin begins by asserting the authority that critics wield over poets, poems, and their readers: "Yet our words have real power. What we say about a poet will be believed. What we cite from a poem is what will be remembered."[51] He proceeds to exercise this authority by situating de Gabriak in a mythical, mystical, fairy-tale sphere and providing an astrological reading of her genealogy, as determined by the ruling planetary configurations of her horoscope. Extravagantly metaphoric and allusive, the essay creates an aura of mystery and otherworldliness heavy with hallmarks of Silver Age aesthetics and anthroposophical references.

Larisa Ageeva describes Voloshin's "Horoscope" as "slightly parodic" and "hinting openly at mystification," but it is not entirely clear that this is the case,[52] for although a modern reader may well deem his "Horoscope" unpersuasive, Voloshin took his studies of the zodiac seriously.[53] Whatever its mix of play and earnestness (and these are not mutually exclusive), the "Horoscope" was designed to influence de Gabriak's reception. The choice of cited passages is governed by the image of Cherubina that the horoscope portends.

Earlier that year Voloshin described his "favorite quality in women" as a "complexity of contradictions,"[54] and it is just such complexity that he underscores in his "Horoscope," where Cherubina de Gabriak is defined by *coincidentia oppositorum*. Alternating between his roles of astrologer and critic, Voloshin foregrounds the erotically charged mysticism of de Gabriak's verse that transports readers to seventeenth-century Spain, "where asceticism and sensuality flow together in one mystical nimbus."[55] He presents de Gabriak as seductive in her religiosity and notes the aura of eros and threat of damnation that waft around her. The incongruous characteristics he singles out in the poems, which he quotes in selective abundance, yield up the image of a beautiful, conflicted woman who perilously spans the erotic and the spiritual, the demonic and the divine. Voloshin draws attention to the confluence of the masculine and the feminine that reflect Symbolist notions about male and female complementarity and accord with Otto Weininger's philosophy. Claiming the prerogative to determine how the new woman poet's defining features are gendered, Voloshin alerts readers to "masculine" characteristics in de Gabriak's verse: "However dubious horoscopes compiled about poets may be, it is certain that the poems of Cherubina de Gabriak harbor in them precious and rare qualities: temperament, character, and passion. We are swept away by Lermontov's passion. We value temperament in Bal'mont and character in Briusov, but we are not accustomed to these features in a woman poet, and they make us a little dizzy."[56]

Rather than inscribe de Gabriak into a feminine lineage,[57] Voloshin chooses to connect her with two French writers in whose work he was absorbed and who were influential in shaping how women were regarded in the culture of the time. "Villiers de L'Isle-Adam, Barbey d'Aurevilly—these are the names that help us determine the sign of the historical Zodiac of Cherubina de Gabriak," he proclaims to his readers.[58] Voloshin, who considered Villiers to be "one of the greatest geniuses to visit the earth,"[59] avidly studied his life and works and devoted two essays to him.[60] At the time of the mystification, Voloshin was working on a translation of *Axel*—justly described as "the epitome of Symbolist drama"[61]—for inclusion in *Apollo*.[62] Known today as the work that gave its title to Edmund Wilson's study of early modernism, Villiers's dramatic prose poem (published posthumously in 1890) was considered the pinnacle of its author's spotty literary career and held in high esteem by French and Russian modernists alike.

Villiers figures with notable frequency in Voloshin's reviews and essays, but his appearance in Cherubina's "Horoscope" is of particular interest here because of the image of the woman it invokes. It has been duly noted that "like his contemporary misogynist Nietzsche, Villiers shows women more formidable than men."[63] In his "Horoscope," Voloshin compares de Gabriak with just such a woman—the seductive heroine of *Axel*, Sara de Maupers:

> Another young woman, also born under the conjunction of Venus and Saturn, the heroine of Villiers de L'Isle-Adam's *Axel*, says about herself, "All the caresses of other women are not worth my cruelties! I am the most disconsolate of young women. I seem to remember how I tempted angels. Alas! Flowers and children die in my shadow. I know pleasures in which all hope perishes."[64]

In a questionnaire of 1909, Voloshin designated Sara as his "favorite heroine from a novel."[65] Endowed with masculine-gendered independence of will and strength of body and possessed of exceptional beauty and intelligence, Sara numbers among the formidable women of Villiers's fictions. At the end of the drama, she joins its eponymous hero in a double suicide in rejection of the illusory substantial world. Though Axel speaks of the lofty male and female union achieved through the nonconsummation of their mutual desire, the roles assigned the hero and his "life-clinging female counterpart"[66] are far from equal. Sara threatens to hinder Axel's transcendence and must be coached by him.[67] Linking Cherubina de Gabriak to Sara, Voloshin puts her in league with the fearsome woman whose exceptionality poses a threat to men, and who must accordingly remain under their control.

Barbey d'Aurevilly, the second writer Voloshin notes in his "Horoscope," creates similarly threatening images of remarkable women. He too was avidly read in Symbolist circles. In 1908, three stories from Barbey's *Les Diaboliques* (1874) featuring tales of women committing horrific criminal acts came out in Aleksandra Chebotarevskaia's Russian translation under Valerii Briusov's editorship as *Liki d'iavola* (*The Devil's Guises*, English translation *The She-Devils*). Included in the volume was a series of Voloshin's studies of Barbey.[68] *Les Diaboliques* and Barbey d'Aurevilly's *Pensées détachées: Fragments sur les femmes* of 1890 were prominent among works that featured terrifying, irrational women.

Linked by Voloshin with dangerous fictional heroines authored by men, de Gabriak is relegated to the sphere of influence of two misogynistic writers, of whom Voloshin writes, "These are two stars of the constellation, which is not rising but setting over the night horizon of European thought and will soon no longer be seen in our expanses."[69] No longer alive at the time of the mystification, Villiers and Barbey preside over the emerging woman poet, who, even as she is welcomed to the pages of the newly established *Apollo*, is relegated to the fin de siècle in what seems to be a denial of her future.

In his role of influential critic, Voloshin proceeds to read Cherubina's poems for information about their author whom he reconstructs on their basis. From her lyrics he gleans information about her temperament, sensibilities, and appearance, making the poems ancillary to the woman he derives from them and promoting precisely the sort of reading from which women poets suffered. Voloshin's "Horoscope of Cherubina de Gabriak" augments the influence he had on the composition of the poems with influence he exerts on their reception.

In the immediate aftermath of the mystification, Voloshin was reticent about his role in it, but in the 1920s he drew up an outline, apparently in preparation for documenting it. Yet although he made at least two starts on the project, the written text he planned did not materialize.[70] Instead, Voloshin's story of the mystification became part of his oral repertoire—a narrative he would recount at preannounced times to audiences gathered in his Koktebel' studio. In the summer of 1930, one of his listeners took down the story in shorthand and produced a typescript, which Voloshin approved, having made some minor corrections.[71] For many years, this was the primary source of information about the mystification in Russia.[72] Voloshin once observed, "A legend about a poet that I create can coincide with reality, but it can also create a new reality."[73] His "History of Cherubina" constitutes such a "new reality." Recent scholarship has led to a more factual version of what transpired,[74] but it yet remains to consider his motivations for recasting the events as he did.

In his private letters Voloshin acknowledged that he was heavily invested in the mystification, but the story he presented in public framed it as a playful, lighthearted episode. In it, an effete, gullible Makovsky acts as an unwitting accomplice in the invention of de Gabriak,[75] while a Cyrano de Bergerac of a Voloshin helps him draft replies to the letters that he, Voloshin, composes on Cherubina's behalf. The comical earnestness of Makovsky's devotion to a figment of his imagination, his hopeless efforts to catch sight of the elusive object of his desire, and Voloshin's and Dmitrieva's loss of control over the rapidly proliferating details relating to Cherubina make for amusing storytelling. But beyond its entertainment value, the way Voloshin styles himself in this account captures the attitude toward aspiring women poets and the pressures brought to bear on them that were characteristic of the period in which de Gabriak appeared.

Making Dmitrieva nineteen rather than the twenty-one that she actually was at the time of the mystification, Voloshin introduces her as an unattractive, impressionable young woman with a grotesque childhood and low self-esteem: "At that time, Lilia was nineteen years old. She was a small young woman with attentive eyes and a bulging forehead. She was lame from birth and accustomed to considering herself a freak. In her childhood, all her toys had one leg broken off because, as her brother and sister would say, 'since you're lame, you have to have toys that are also lame.'"[76] There follows a disturbing account of her childhood, as Voloshin's story slips into the first person of what purports to be Dmitrieva's own voice. Based on Voloshin's diary entry of March 18, 1909, in which he noted what Dmitrieva told him about herself, this account—enclosed in quotation marks in his "History of Cherubina"—describes her prolonged illness, her distant parents, her brother's derangement, and the abuse she suffered at the hands of her siblings.[77] All of this ostensibly contributes to a psychic imbalance of which her limp is an outward manifestation and that cries out for Voloshin's stabilizing mentorship.

Landa notes that at one point in Voloshin's account, "Dmitrieva's 'brokenness' and exceptionality suddenly cross over into a portrait already familiar to us: this is a modest, sweet, simple young girl, a schoolteacher, whose poems are as modest and simple as she is."[78] Pressing on to ask what prompts this transition reveals that it allows Voloshin to set himself up as the one who distinguished the exceptional woman housed in an unprepossessing exterior. This motivates his decision to tap into Dmitrieva's creative potential by inventing a poet whose appearance accords with her inner self. The invention of Cherubina is also Voloshin's reinvention of Dmitrieva. Even as he foregrounds the disjunction between Dmitrieva's inner self and outward semblance, Voloshin has her exaggerated plainness collide with Makovsky's similarly hyperbolized aesthetic sensibilities, exemplified by the editor's idea that the offices of *Apollo* be graced by lovely ladies—preferably from the St. Petersburg corps de ballet. This sets up a dramatic contrast between the limping, singular woman poet Voloshin befriends and the perfectly legged, undifferentiated ballerinas Makovsky favors.

As Voloshin knew from personal experience, which he withholds from his account, Dmitrieva was attractive and generally regarded as intelligent and witty. She was no wallflower and had several suitors, Voloshin among them. Von Guenther calls Dmitrieva "sexy,"[79] and Anna Akhmatova scoffs at the idea of describing her as modest and retiring.[80] Voloshin insists, however, that because Dmitrieva was out of line with the corps de ballet of Makovsky's affected aesthetics, she was barred from publication in his journal: "Lilia— modest, inelegant, and lame, naturally could not satisfy him [Makovsky], and her poems were rejected by the editorial staff."[81] Cherubina de Gabriak emerges as a conveyance better suited than the allegedly mousy Dmitrieva to deliver poems to *Apollo*. Thus, as Voloshin styles it, de Gabriak assumes double duty to ensure poetic success: she is the invented poet who best manifests Dmitrieva's exceptional inner being and the invented woman who best corresponds with Makovsky's ideal. Thanks to the elaborate de Gabriak disguise, as Voloshin would have it, Dmitrieva blossoms as a poet whose verse is readily published in the exclusive journal. These are not the "sweet, simple poems" that he describes her writing in the summer of 1909 but the lyrics of a powerful, captivating poet.[82]

Voloshin's assertion that the mystification was launched for Dmitrieva's benefit fell in both with the reigning beautiful woman aesthetic and with pervasive assumptions about women's dependency on male mentorship for self-realization. Readily believed by his listeners and readers, just as it had been by Dmitrieva herself, his account was accepted and perpetuated in retellings and in scholarship.[83] Recently Voloshin's claim that Dmitrieva could not have her poems published in *Apollo* has been challenged.[84] While a joint translation that he and Dmitrieva delivered to the journal did not make it into print, there is no evidence that Dmitrieva submitted any of her poems to the journal and no reason to assume that they would have been rejected if she had.[85] Beyond the interest in women's writing that improved her chances of publication was the fact that as they vied for Dmitrieva's hand in marriage, Voloshin and Gumilev also vied for the role of mentoring her. Both men had close ties to *Apollo* and influence over Makovsky, whom, if the need arose, they could have persuaded to publish Dmitrieva. Indeed, Gumilev offered to deliver her poems to Makovsky in person.[86] Nor was Dmitrieva necessarily in need of the male mentorship foisted onto her. She was no stranger on the St. Petersburg literary scene. Beginning in 1907 she regularly attended gatherings in Viacheslav Ivanov's famous "Tower," taking part in discussions, lectures, and readings at the Poetic Academy, which met first in Ivanov's apartment and then at the editorial offices of *Apollo*.[87] Dmitrieva presented lectures at these gatherings on rhymes in Spanish romances and on particularities of Old French versification, while a sonnet she recited earned Ivanov's public praise.[88] She was in touch with major poets of the time and was well known to those close to the journal. Although Makovsky had not met Dmitrieva in person, he knew of her and, as he reluctantly admitted, found her biting parodies of Cherubina de Gabriak witty.[89] In short, when Voloshin undertook to transform her into Cherubina, Dmitrieva was already accepted in literary circles, if not yet on the pages of *Apollo*. Moreover, Dmitrieva remained on the list of the journal's contributors even after the mystification was unveiled.

For all Voloshin's assertions that de Gabriak was devised to benefit Dmitrieva, there is much in the "History" that suggests it was less the advancement of her literary career than his control over it that was at stake. Thus, although he insists that Dmitrieva wrote Cherubina's poems, Voloshin claims a major role in their composition for himself: "In Cherubina's verse I played the role of director and censor, suggested themes, expressions, made assignments, but the writing was entirely Lilia's." He goes on to insist, "In the poems I only supplied ideas and took as little part as possible in their realization."[90] Whether or not this is an accurate account of how the poems materialized, the point is that Voloshin presents Dmitrieva as heavily dependent on him, marking an asymmetry in their roles. It was he who had the final say about the poems that he "directed," "censored," and "assigned," and reworked when the need arose. (The phrase "took as little part as possible" indicates that at times he felt compelled to revise Dmitrieva's work.)

Having presented himself as the creator of a poet who enabled Dmitrieva, Voloshin goes on to describe her signal loss of control over the invented poet. To Dmitrieva's twofold disjunction that de Gabriak was purportedly designed to bridge (Dmitrieva's inner and outer selves and her outward appearance and Makovsky's aesthetics), Voloshin adds a third: her break with the invented poet, whom she proves incapable of sustaining and who appears to her as a threatening double. "Lilia, who had always been afraid of ghosts, was horrified. She kept imagining that she would certainly meet the living Cherubina, who would take her to task."[91] This split manifested itself in verse on the pages of *Apollo*, apparently with Voloshin's encouragement. Among the fifteen poems by de Gabriak that appeared in the tenth volume of the journal are two in which the persona describes her fear of an encounter with her double. The first of these, "In the blind nights of the new moon" ("V slepye nochi novolun'ia"), Voloshin maintains, was addressed by Dmitrieva to de Gabriak. The second, "The Double" ("Dvoinik"), he alleges was written by de Gabriak to Dmitrieva. The volume also carries the poem "Meeting" ("Vstrecha"), a poetic dialogue—presumably between her divided selves—signed with Dmitrieva's own name. It is clear that Dmitrieva was dealing not with a childish fear of ghosts but with a psychic unease resulting from expectations projected onto her that she could not satisfy and from ghostwriting for an invented woman unlike herself. Her desire to free herself from de Gabriak is not difficult to fathom. As Voloshin tells it, however, it is not Dmitrieva's untenable situation that made de Gabriak a fearful double.[92] Rather, he maintains, Dmitrieva's faintheartedness was to blame, making her miss the opportunity that Cherubina afforded to come into her own as a poet.

Here it is instructive to observe that the literary phenomenon of the double that entered Russia through the German Romantics and that the Russian neo-Romantic Symbolists took up was a topic of discussion among psychologists of the time. In his influential *Sex and Character* (*Geschlecht und Charakter*, 1880–1903) Otto Weininger notes that "the word doppelganger has only to be mentioned to raise a deep dread in the mind of any man," adding in a footnote, "It is notable that women are devoid of this fear; female doppelgangers are not heard of."[93] Seconding Weininger's assertion was another Otto—Otto Rank, author of *The Double: A Psychoanalytical Study*. Written in 1914 when Rank was still one of Freud's favored disciples, the study echoes Weininger in its assertion that "the double does not appear in the female, but solely in the male form."[94] By invoking the female double— a phenomenon that Weininger and Rank categorically deny—Voloshin replaces the invisible dichotomy between a woman's outer and inner selves with the visible conflicted selves that the double brings out into the open. The resulting knowability alleviates male anxieties relating to the unknown of the woman's creative domain that attracted much attention during this period. At the same time, Voloshin's presentation of Dmitrieva as a woman who is at odds with the invented self of her poems has a cautionary tone: a divergence of the woman poet's authoring and authored selves that men assume are identical is potentially damaging. What is frightening to men is presented as dangerous for women.

There is another reason that led Voloshin to focus so intently on Dmitrieva's disjunctions—one that goes back to Villiers, whom Voloshin invoked in his "Horoscope of Cherubina de Gabriak." Relevant to the mystification, and especially to Voloshin's "History" of it, is another of that author's works: the science fiction novel *L'Ève future*,[95] which, like *Axel*, enjoyed immense popularity at the time. This novel documents an anxious need to demystify and contain the new woman. The lasting impression it made on Voloshin is evident from his 1911 article "The Future Eve and Edison" ("Griadushchaia Eva i Edison"), which he wrote in Paris in the wake of the American inventor's European tour.[96] Though Voloshin makes no mention of it in his accounts of the mystification, it is clear that the substance of this novel informed the invention of Cherubina de Gabriak, her reception, and Voloshin's "History."

Tomorrow's Eve, as one of its English translations styles it,[97] features a Thomas Alva Edison of Menlo Park, New Jersey, in the process of embodying an ideal of womanhood in an android of his own design. Intermingled with the novel's dazzling descriptions of futuristic inventions is an inventory of backward-looking gender stereotypes. As the title of the novel indicates, the guilt-laden Old Testament image of the woman who is a threat to man's well-being persists into the technological age to uphold the deep-seated view that women must remain under male control. The scientific genius of the fictional Edison imparts to the woman a knowability that eliminates the perceived threat posed by her unknown inner self.

Describing the fictional Edison's overall plan, Marie Lathers observes that "the modern couple theorized and fabricated by Edison consists of an artificial female and a human male" and that "Edison explicitly sets out to *replace* the female sex with his manufactured Eves."[98] The reason behind Cherubina de Gabriak's invention coincides with the impetus for Edison's construction of his female androids. This is a confrontation with a woman whose "intimate being was in flat contradiction with the form it inhabited," a woman who "had somehow strayed by accident into this body, which did not belong to her at all."[99] Viewing the female body "as the site of a disturbing and incomprehensible split between inside and out"[100] was neither unique to Villiers de L'Isle-Adam nor new to Russian literature. In Gogol's famous story "Nevsky Prospect," for example, just such an incongruity drives the protagonist to madness after the narrative with which he precariously bridges the disjunction shatters against reality. In *Tomorrow's Eve* a similar disjunction arises, and a perfect female form that harbors deeply flawed content leads Edison's friend and benefactor, Lord Ewald, to contemplate suicide. The perfect body (she is the Venus de Milo incarnate, only with limbs intact) of Miss Alicia Clary, with whom Lord Ewald is hopelessly in love, houses a vacuous mind and shallow being. Edison sets out to save his friend by rectifying this incongruity. Using Miss Clary to create an android possessed of inner qualities that conform to her outward appearance, he brings the divided woman into a unity that renders her knowable to her flesh-and-blood partner, responsive to his needs, and subject to his control. Notably, the actual woman is only the material for the project and not its beneficiary. The android complete, Miss Clary is unceremoniously dismissed.[101]

Edison's previous manufacture of an android provides him with the scientific know-how to help his friend. He readily describes the ingenious mechanisms that make the invented woman tick in a lifelike manner. Light-years ahead of E. T. A. Hoffmann's mechanized Olympia, Edison's first android was inspired by the plight of the upstanding Edward Anderson who was lured by a bewitching woman into infidelity that left his life in ruins. The questing Edison seeks out the temptress, only to discover that her enticements were falsified and guilefully assembled to seduce her male victim. Driven by a need to do away with the false appearances and the deceits inherent in the living woman, Edison creates what he claims is a perfect, more natural woman, which is to say one who poses no threat and brings only contentment to the man in whose control she safely remains.

Opposite the negatively coded woman's self-fashioning is the positively coded male invention of the woman. Lord Ewald struggles with the disturbing rupture between the woman's outward beauty and inner vacuousness. Anderson is undone by a mask of the woman's own design that counterfeits his ideal of beauty. Centering on the unsettling incongruity between women's inward and outward selves and on their duplicitous self-presentations, these complementary narratives of *Tomorrow's Eve* conspire to make women doubly fearsome. In Villiers's novel, the realization of male fantasies attains the status of scientific accomplishment, and the woman of the future remains the product of male inventiveness.

In his "History of Cherubina de Gabriak," Voloshin similarly emerges as a male inventor who reconciles a woman's divided self. If Edison worked to devise an inner being that conformed to the outward beauty of the woman in question, Voloshin worked to promote an outward semblance that accorded with his subject's inward self. The American uses science, the Russian poetic language, but both engage in creating a new, "real" woman who supersedes her living counterpart. Rather than ensure the woman's knowability by lifting limitations imposed on her self-expressivity and enabling her self-revelation, they make the woman knowable by inventing her themselves. The reality that accrues to the woman in the epigraph to this chapter derives from the fact that she is designed in accordance with male needs and expectations to achieve an identity between her outward and inner selves that leaves no hidden recesses of selfhood or agency. The Cherubina de Gabriak mystification as Voloshin relates it in his "History" shows him translating Villiers's ideas into a real-life arena, or more precisely into the domain of Symbolist life-creation, where male fictions and fantasies similarly prevail over flesh-and-blood women. In this light, we see Voloshin enlist Dmitrieva to invent Cherubina de Gabriak much like the Edison of *Tomorrow's Eve* draws on Miss Clary to invent a female android. Like the android, Cherubina takes on greater reality than the living woman from whom she derives—not only for her readers but even for Dmitrieva herself.

Tomorrow's Eve, which informed the mystification, also heightened receptivity to it. Makovsky cites the novel to explain what Cherubina de Gabriak meant to him. "This unusual young woman was becoming for me that very one about whom it is so easy to dream in one's youthful years, she whom Villiers de L'Isle-Adam, then popular in the *Apollo* circle, called l'Ève future in his famous novel."[102] The success that the novel and Cherubina enjoyed is symptomatic of the male establishment's resistance to women's agency and self-realization. The new woman of *Tomorrow's Eve* is tethered to a past that holds her responsible for the fall of man, while her future is co-opted by a conflation of male fantasies and technological advances. Situated by Voloshin between the willful, dangerous Sara who threatens men and the female android constructed to remain under male control, the woman poet Cherubina is not so new.

We cannot know what course Dmitrieva might have taken had there been no Cherubina de Gabriak, but it is not certain that the mystification was essential to her creative development as Voloshin claimed. What is certain is that the mystification enacted deeply engrained gender biases and that writing in the guise of de Gabriak occasioned Dmitrieva psychic distress, engendering insecurities she found difficult to overcome. This makes it all the more curious that despite the deviations from fact now recognized in "The History of Cherubina de Gabriak," Voloshin's claim that the invented poet enabled Dmitrieva to realize her creative potential has remained un-challenged. In her pathbreaking work Landa speaks of the "brilliant myth-creating experiment," whose success she ascribes to the "free choice of a creative 'I' [that] led to the appearance in Russian literature of an actual talented poetess."[103] Groberg and Kelly remark, "What does give Cherub-ina's poetry a more than ephemeral significance is the complex feminine psy-chology which it delineates."[104] Yet Cherubina's "choice of a creative 'I'" was heavily conditioned by male expectations, Symbolist aesthetic sensibilities, and Voloshin's mentoring. In fact, the mystification reveals not a woman's creative psychology but the consequences to that psychology of the male fantasies and expectations projected onto her. Voloshin's tutelage eroded Dmitrieva's agency, destabilized her creative identity, and made her an ac-complice to the endorsement of gender stereotypes and the objectification of women poets that the ruse ultimately upheld. This highlights the manifold pressures brought to bear on women poets in a period of unprecedented interest expressed in them by the male establishment. At the same time, it alerts us to the degree to which the authoritative male voice continues to inform our understanding of the mystification, of its impact on Dmitrieva, indeed of women's writing and its reception in general.

There is nothing in Voloshin's "History" to suggest that the mystifi-cation was connected with his own needs. Yet the fact that he positioned himself as the controlling individual did not preclude dependency. When the mystification ended, he pressed Dmitrieva to choose him over her fiancé, Vsevolod Vasiliev. Dmitrieva refused and urged Voloshin to leave St. Peters-burg, but he postponed his departure for fear that if he left, she would not follow him to Koktebel'. Voloshin's private correspondence shows him ap-prehensive about being alone and concerned about his productivity. Yet even as he acknowledges his need for Dmitrieva, he claims the role of demiurge who brings not just Cherubina de Gabriak but also Dmitrieva herself into being as a poet:

> I am afraid that it may turn out that Lilia won't be able to come to Koktebel' this summer because of that same noble struggle [deciding between him and Vasiliev]. And then I simply don't know what will happen, since all my crea-tive plans are already tied to her and her presence. Maybe this is cowardly fear of being utterly alone, maybe this is even necessary, but I can't overcome it in myself, can't get a grip on myself. And, after all, this is almost certainly a renunciation of creativity for her, too, because her creativity is indissolubly linked with mine and called into being by me.[105]

Dmitrieva did not follow him. Voloshin chose to see this as Dmitrieva's bend-ing to the dictates of honor and duty rather than to her own inclinations, but the need for creative autonomy was surely among the factors that prompted her decision. With Dmitrieva gone, Voloshin turned to Marina Tsvetaeva, reading aloud to her from Villiers de L'Isle-Adam and urging her to join him in inventing poets. Closely guarding her creative identity, Tsvetaeva refused.

Rostopchina's ballroom is far removed from Edison's laboratory, but that poet's affirmations of a woman's hidden creative sphere feeds just the sort of interest and unease that motivate the invention of Edison's android and Voloshin's de Gabriak. The inscrutability of the woman's inward self—that poetic *Innenraum* from which, as Rostopchina notes, men were barred by the limits they themselves imposed on women's self-expressivity—remains a source of male curiosity and anxiety. This unknown suggests promise, but also stimulates an urge to retain command over individual women poets and the unfolding line of women's poetry. Implicit in Rostopchina's poem is a Gordian knot of a proposition: to mitigate the unknowable that threatens their ability to remain in control, men must loosen their hold on women's self-expressivity. Most immediately, a reader-imposed censorship insulated men from the challenge Rostopchina issued in her poems. By the modernist period, however, the growing number of writing women made such challenges increasingly difficult to disregard. The Cherubina de Gabriak mystification considered in this chapter and the Nelli mystification studied in the next showcase male poets who set out—like Villiers's Edison—to access the woman's hidden world by reinventing her in accordance with their own designs. The fear of the unknown in the woman runs deep, but the fear of allowing her the self-expression that would dispel it apparently runs deeper still.

Writing about the mystification some seven years after its unveiling, Voloshin claimed that Cherubina "set the tone for all contemporary women's poetry."[106] She also inspired a series of poets invented by men who purported to write like women, including Khodasevich's Elisaveta Maksheeva, Bagritsky's Nina Voskresenskaia, Nikulin's Anzhelika Saf'ianova, and the subject of the following chapter, Briusov's Nelli.[107] If Voloshin and the fictional Edison give women a part—however unequal—in their projects, Briusov creates a woman poet and writes on her behalf with no female assistance.

Chapter Four

Briusov's Nelli

Nothing brings me back to life like
Bashkirtseva's diary. She is I myself, with all my
thoughts, convictions, and dreams.
—Valerii Briusov, diary entry

I would like not to be "Valerii Briusov."
—Valerii Briusov, "The Tedium of Life" ("Skuka
zhizni")

IN 1913, three years after Cherubina de Gabriak took literary
St. Petersburg by storm, the Moscow publisher Skorpion brought out a slen-
der volume of verse titled *Nelli's Poems* (*Stikhi Nelli*) in a print run of five
hundred sixty copies. Seen widely as yet another "poetess" appearing under
the auspices of Valerii Briusov, the collection marked, in fact, his own debut
as a woman poet. That a poet of Briusov's stature and influence should try
his hand at writing like a woman reflects the degree of interest in women's
authorship at the time but also the efforts of the male establishment to control it. The Nelli poems appeared at an important juncture in a tradition that
sensed a need for creative renewal and looked to women to provide it. As
the otherworldly cast of Symbolism gave way to a poetics that embraced particulars of the concrete everyday world, male poets saw in—or, rather, projected onto—women a capacity to bring the poetic experience back down
to earth. Tied to the quotidien by male constructs, women were to provide
an energizing counterbalance to the rarified abstractions of the enervated
Symbolist movement. The woman's voice gained in prestige,[1] and the growing number of women poets led a critic to remark that "a new and decidedly imposing area appeared in Russian literature—women's poetry."[2] Yet
neither their prestige and number nor the fact that they were to invigorate a
faltering tradition gained women freedom from being defined in accordance
with expectations, theories, and models established by men. Directives for
women continued to appear while gender biases of earlier times persisted
and the ideology of separate domains remained in force. Determining the

woman's creative purview and dictating how she must write was still largely a male prerogative, but one that now met with increasing challenges from women poets. The present chapter studies the Nelli mystification for what it exposes about constructs of the new woman poet and the resistance of the establishment to her autonomy. I begin by contextualizing the mystification in the culture of the time, in Briusov's creative biography, and in his relations with women—both fictional and real. I then turn to *Nelli's Poems* to examine how he frames his fictional woman poet and excludes her from urban modernism.

In the previous century, Pavlova and Rostopchina took advantage of the Romantics' waning vitality to enter the literary arena. In the Silver Age, women again benefited from the weakening of a poetic movement, but with a difference: now women were recruited to invigorate poetry—under the direction of male poets. The woman poet was not yet a free agent. The increasing opportunities for women to appear in print was offset by male mentorship and the control that men retained over a woman's image and creative compass. An additional challenge was the modernists' turn to the city, where women continued to meet with objectification and commodification.

The woman poet Briusov invented and the self she ostensibly revealed in her verse demonstrate the extent to which these conditions disenfranchised writing women. With the Nelli poems, Briusov sought to exhibit his ability to access a creative domain whose emotional and psychological content was posited as uniquely feminine. Briusov claims, in other words, to penetrate that very space from which men were barred by the limitations they imposed on writing women. Nelli does not lift such limitations. She is a disincentive model for women poets that springs from Briusov's resolve to determine women's self-expression. Briusov's arrogation of the woman's creative domain reflects among other things an anxious response to the rising tide of writing women and his own waning authority.

Assessments of how the Nelli mystification figured in Briusov's oeuvre range from dismissals of Nelli as a lark[3] to well-reasoned assertions of her importance.[4] What prompted Briusov—the self-styled Pushkin of the twentieth century and powerful poet and critic—to try to pass himself off as a woman poet has also been explained variously. Schamma Schahadat, who situates the Nelli episode in the broad context of mystification theory, describes the very act of mystification as a hallmark of Briusov's poetic self-fashioning with its heavy reliance on masks and mimicry of other voices. By way of example, she cites the fictitious names (including the feminine Zinaida Fuks) he used to sign poems of his own authorship in his three-volume *Russian Symbolists* (*Russkie simvolisty*, 1894, 1895), which launched that poetic movement. For Schahadat, Briusov's Nelli is an extension of these early poetic inventions and of his subsequent stories featuring female narrators. In this regard, the Nelli poems mark a continuity in Briusov's creative biography and are in keeping with his efforts to retain a position of leadership in the tradition.[5]

Deploring the absence of Nelli's poems from posthumous collections of Briusov's verse, A. V. Lavrov argues for the importance of the mystification in the poet's biography. Presenting the mystification as a sign of Briusov's need for creative reinvigoration,[6] Lavrov explains that already with the completion of the poems of *Stephanos* (1906), Briusov experienced a sense of creative exhaustion that made him seek new directions for his writings.[7] The Nelli poems emerged as both a test of his poetic resources and an effort to revitalize them: "The imitation of a feminine voice was to foster a renewal of Briusov's poetic style, an overcoming in it—through prosaization and psychologization—of the conventions and high rhetoric of 'classic' symbolism."[8] Briusov's position, Lavrov notes, is consonant with the broader cultural agenda of the time. In his article "New Currents in Russian Poetry" ("Novye techeniia v russkoi poezii"), which came out close to the time of Nelli's debut, Briusov wrote, "Of course Russian poetry can expect its renascence only from a new influx of unmediated observations of authentic, real life."[9] It was widely held at the time that women could contribute just such a new perspective, and Briusov set out to demonstrate his own capacity to do so. The Nelli mystification figures in his efforts to this end.

Looking at the Nelli poems in their immediate biographical context, Vladislav Khodasevich ascribes them to Briusov's eagerness to seem younger to his paramour and poetic mentee, Nadezhda L'vova:

> The difference in years between her and Briusov was significant. He awkwardly tried to look younger, sought out the company of young poets. He wrote a book of poems almost in the spirit of Igor Severianin and dedicated it to Nadia [L'vova]. He could not bring himself to publish the book under his own name, and it appeared under the ambiguous title *Nelli's Poems*. With an introductory sonnet by Valerii Briusov.[10]

Whether or not impressing her inspired the composition of *Nelli's Poems*, L'vova herself played a part in upholding the mystification.

The common denominator of Schahadat's, Lavrov's, and Khodasevich's distinct perspectives on Nelli is the importance they ascribe to women in Briusov's personal and creative biography. In the early part of the century Briusov was a powerful and willing patron who prided himself on his discovery of new talent and established himself as mentor to aspiring women poets.[11] In 1915, he brought out a two-volume collection of Karolina Pavlova's works, which he edited and supplied with an introduction. By mentoring up-and-coming women poets and claiming credit for rediscovering

Karolina Pavlova, Briusov took an active role in directing the emergence of women's poetry.

Briusov's promotion of writing women was also a way to bolster his own authority. His protégées, whom he routinely sexualized, often bore the stamp of his controlling, less-than-benevolent tutoring. Bogomolov notes that Briusov's own poetry frequently sprang from his sexual relations with women and that erotic desire was the underpinning of his early Decadent aesthetics.[12] Kirsti Ekonen, who similarly observes that Briusov regarded sexual passion as a means to activate the unconscious and stimulate creativity, adds that he was prepared to sacrifice women to this end. Thus, as Ekonen summarizes, in his relations with Nina Petrovskaia and Nadezhda L'vova, both of whom he mentored and both of whom took their own lives, "passion leads to the creative renewal of the author and the destruction of the woman."[13] Here the use of women as raw material for men's creative projects appears in a tragic tonality.

The degree to which Briusov held sway over emerging writers at the time is seen in Khodasevich's reaction to L'vova's poetry collection *An Old Fairy Tale* (*Staraia skazka*), which came out shortly before *Nelli's Poems*. "To say that Mlle N. L'vova . . . numbers among the poets of the Briusov school would mean to fail to distinguish her in any way from all our poets of the last decade."[14] Khodasevich's remarks appeared in *The Voice of Moscow* (*Golos Moskvy*) on June 4, 1913. On November 24, L'vova killed herself with a revolver given to her by Briusov—that very Browning that some eight years earlier his then paramour Nina Petrovskaia had fired at the writer Andrei Belyi. While mentoring L'vova, Briusov engaged in an affair with her during which, as Khodasevich maintains, "Briusov systematically accustomed her to the thought of death, of suicide."[15] Whether or not this is strictly accurate, the fact remains that Briusov was widely held responsible for his protégée's premature death, and L'vova, whose popularity spiked in the aftermath of her suicide, was seen as the tragic victim not of ill-starred love or creative crisis but of her mentor's envy. The resounding questions Sophia Parnok poses in a poem addressed to Briusov capture this view:

> Кого вы ищете, Сальери?
> Кто среди юных Моцарт ваш?[16]

> Whom do you seek, Salieri?
> Who is your Mozart among the young?

Parnok sidesteps gender to focus instead on what she presents as Briusov's Salieri-like envy and his privileging of technical mastery over inspiration, but the effects of his mentoring also come into question.[17] Briusov's sexualization of women, whom he subordinated to his authority and used for his own ends, ultimately energized resistance. In establishing their poetic identities, some women pointedly disassociated themselves from him and proclaimed independence from his commanding influence. Dmitrieva, for example, cites her disregard for Briusov as a distinctive feature of her creative identity: "I never liked Briusov and never will," she insisted.[18] Parnok similarly distanced herself from this powerful authority figure, while Marina Tsvetaeva defined herself in terms of her demonstrative opposition to Briusov.

For some, Briusov's relations with women undermined his standing as a poet. Recollecting Briusov after his death in 1924, Khodasevich notes Briusov's failure to create any credible women in his poems and ascribes this failure to his inability to relate to women in real life. "The women in Briusov's poems resemble one another like two drops of water: this is because he never loved, distinguished, or came to know a single one of them."[19] Tsvetaeva similarly adduced Briusov's inability to understand women as proof of poetic insufficiency. Notably, such charges responded to Briusov's own claims to have penetrated the woman's inner world. As early as 1908, he had set out to study women's creative psychology, documenting his explorations in the tales and dramatic scenes collected in *Nights and Days* (*Nochi i dni*), which came out in 1913, the year of Nelli's debut. In his brief preface to this collection, Briusov explains that the works in it span the years 1908 to 1912 and that "besides the time and place of action (our days, contemporary Russian society), these tales are united also by a common goal: to scrutinize the particularities of the psychology of the woman's soul."[20]

What Briusov styles as his "scrutiny" is largely a projection of his own notions about women, awash with misogynistic writings of French Decadents, Charcot, Weininger, and Nietzsche, all of whom wielded considerable influence in Russia at the time. The stories of *Nights and Days* center on love presented in terms of emotional and psychological power struggles between men and women. Female sexuality is framed as destructive, and women's irrationality is presented threatening to men. Fabrication outweighs observation, and, as one contemporary critic observes, in these stories Briusov "coldly rummages around in deformities that he himself makes up."[21] Women's defiance of conventional matrimony and their practice of free love figure prominently in the collection. The erotic details with which Briusov modernizes these Sandian themes were relatively new in mainstream Russian literature at that time, but the unhappy outcomes of women's misguided quests for fulfillment were not. The "progressive" content of the stories is offset by rehearsals of women's lack of self-knowledge and inability to act in a socially responsible, self-affirming way. The modern woman depicted in them remains without agency, and her actions, far from liberating her, lead to disastrous consequences.

One tale of *Nights and Days* warrants particular comment: "The Last Pages from a Woman's Diary" ("Poslednie stranitsy iz dnevnika zhenshchiny," 1910), in which Briusov purports to record a woman's intimate thoughts and emotions from her perspective and in her own voice.[22] M. V. Mikhailova writes that while Briusov's studies of female psychology were scarcely original, his method was bold: "He tried to fully transform himself into a woman, choosing the form of a woman's diary as most appropriate for this aspiration and most fully revealing all the nuances of psychological experience."[23] Pushkin had made a comparable experiment in his 1829 *Novel in Letters* (*Roman v pis'makh*) and his 1831 *Roslavlev*, both of which aim to capture a woman's perspective and expressivity. Pushkin's interest in how a woman might record private emotional experiences was similarly part of a quest for new possibility. Such attempts on the part of authoritative men to expand creative opportunity by writing like women draw attention to women's creative potential and can be seen as homage of sorts. At the same time, however, women invented by influential male writers had a normative dimension that reinforced the authority men exercised over women, over their self-expressivity, indeed over their very development.

Also dating to the years of Briusov's exploration of "the psychology of the woman's soul" are pieces dominated by misogynistic sadism and matrophobia. Briusov's unfinished "The Tale of an Obstetrician" ("Rasskaz akushera") offers a first-person account of sadistic pleasures a doctor experiences while observing women in the throes of labor. In "Kind Al'd. The Story of a Female Slave" ("Dobryi Al'd. Rasskaz nevol'nitsy")[24] a white woman tells her story of being sold into slavery in the Congo and enduring eleven years of sexual abuse before regaining her freedom.[25] Both the male narrator of "The Tale of an Obstetrician" and the female narrator of "Kind Al'd" make female physiology and sexuality a spectacle on which a sadistic, misogynous male gaze feasts. The latter story, as the woman telling it explains to the reader, documents in realistic, unembellished, and uncensored detail what she and the women sold with her experienced at the hands of their bestial owners. What she characterizes as her perforce "coarse" and "shameless" account of her trials is a graphic description of the psychosexual abuse that she and the other captive women experienced and that included being tortured while giving birth.[26] Implicit in this self-revelatory tale is that the woman who relates it is the author of her own shame and degradation, which she perpetuates by opening her sexualization and abuse to public view. By framing the narrator's need to tell her story as exhibitionism, Briusov indicates that the woman who relates "The Story of a Female Slave" would have done better to remain silent.

It is against this background that Briusov claims entry into the woman poet's world and mastery of her idiom. Nelli's dependency on the powerful male mentor whose name appears on the cover of her collection situates this purportedly new woman poet in the thick of all-too-familiar gender biases of earlier generations. The absence of the poet's surname is suggestive of the oft-repeated warning that a woman who appears in public does so at the cost of her family ties.[27] The poems that Nelli authors ostensibly document a woman's emotions and experiences, but by making her a courtesan, Briusov has her actively promote her own sexualization in an urban environment that is inimical to women's self-realization. Far from registering protest against this male world that disenfranchises the woman poet, Nelli's poems show her succumbing to it.

Lavrov describes Nelli as a hybrid with direct ties to Briusov's "Last Pages from a Woman's Diary":

> Briusov's Nelli combines traits of the Symbolist image of the woman tradi-
> tional for his poetry—the "priestess of love"—with the psychological type
> of the emancipated woman of the world (perhaps even the demimonde),
> sketched in animated and socially recognizable lines (a few years earlier this
> psychological type was interestingly developed by Briusov in the tale "The
> Last Pages from a Woman's Diary").[28]

Although this is not the point that he wishes to make here, Lavrov's observation corroborates that Nelli derives not from Briusov's study of women but from notions that he projected onto them. Like the women Briusov bent to his will, Nelli is a poet of his own design.

Nelli was the first of three women poets Briusov planned to bring into being in a projected "tale of a woman's soul" (*povest' o zhenskoi dushe*), and his manuscripts document his plans to provide biographies for them.[29] Ultimately, only Nelli materialized as a published author. That Briusov attached considerable importance to her success is evident in the carefully crafted uncertainty of the paratext he devised for her poems. Because the name "Nelli" is not declined in Russian, it remained uncertain as to whether it was in the dative or in the genitive case, which meant that the title of the collection could be read as either *Poems to Nelli* or *Poems of/by Nelli*.[30] Accordingly, the dedication by Briusov touted on the cover could mean either that these were poems he dedicated to one "Nelli" or that he was introducing yet another woman poet to the reading public. Building on this ambiguity, a brief statement appears immediately after the title page: "To Nadezhda Grigor'evna L'vova the author dedicates these poems." Knowing that L'vova was one of Briusov's mentees and lovers,[31] readers could think that these were poems he had written for her. *Nelli's Poems* came out soon after L'vova's first and only poetry collection, *An Old Fairy Tale*, for which Briusov had written the introduction. This led some readers to speculate that the dedication to L'vova in *Nelli's Poems* was intended to conceal the fact that she was the author of the Nelli lyrics as well. On the page immediately after the dedication to L'vova, readers found the dedication by Briusov promised on the cover: a sonnet titled "Nelli." Distinguished in the table of contents from the rest of the poems in the volume, it creates a distance between Briusov and the ostensible author of the subsequent poems and influences readers' reception of the new poet. This elaborate, intentionally disorienting framing reflects Briusov's desire to remain a presence in the collection while masking his authorship and enhancing the credibility of his invented poet. Briusov was in an awkward situation inasmuch as the success of his project depended on two mutually exclusive criteria. His ability to capture the essence of feminine writing would be gauged by the extent to which readers believed that Nelli's poems were indeed composed by a woman. Yet if these poems were to document Briusov's mastery of a feminine poetic idiom, it was necessary that the master wielding the plume be recognized. Briusov wanted it both ways.

Initially Briusov planned to give Nelli's dates as 1879 to 1913 and to present her poems in posthumous publication, thus relieving himself of the need to sustain the fictitious author. In the end, however, he kept Nelli alive and even planned a second collection of her poems.[32] The draft of the introduction for the projected volume shows that three years after *Nelli's Poems* appeared, Briusov was still preoccupied with validating Nelli—which is to say validating his ability to write like a woman. This ability, indeed the value of the project itself, had come under question, for although Briusov's female impersonation persuaded some readers, leading critics of the time recognized him behind the Nelli mask. Sergei Gorodetsky, whose assessment prompted Briusov's public denial of authorship, wrote, "In bookstores it is offered as a book by Briusov, indeed in the very style of the verse the master can be recognized at once . . . The entire book seems like the unnecessary prank of a master."[33] In his review, Gumilev notes that Briusov denied writing Nelli's lyrics but neither challenges that denial nor gives credence to Nelli as a new woman poet. On the strength of the masculine grammatical gender of the noun "poet," Gumilev refers to the author of the Nelli poems as "he" throughout his review.[34]

Khodasevich responded with a tongue-in-cheek review of *Nelli's Poems* in which he pretended to be taken in by the mystification. Spoofing Briusov, he marvels that the new woman poet displays a masculine command of poetic form and power of expression.[35] Khodasevich's only criticism of this new star who outshines her female forebears and contemporaries alike is that her poetry sounds too much like Briusov's. Khodasevich's hyperbolic praise of Nelli's lyrics, like his reproach that her verse is imitative, aims to discredit Briusov's purportedly feminine authorship.

Countess Rostopchina had already demanded that she be compared with women and not with men. Perhaps Nelli, too, as a poetess, would like to be compared with her peers? Why not! Her poems are better than Anna Akhmatova's, because they are written more harmoniously and are more deeply thought through. Her poems are better than N. L'vova's for the same reasons. But in one (and very significant) respect Nelli cedes to both Mlle L'vova and Mlle Akhmatova: in independence. Nelli's voice is louder than their voices, but it is more dependent on outside influence. One can name L'vova's and Akhmatova's teachers, but one cannot indicate a poet whom they imitate as blindly as Nelli imitates Valerii Briusov in everything, beginning with verse form and ending with that feeling of contemporaneity about which we have already spoken.

. . . In Nelli's book, there are more than a few beautiful and genuine content-filled images. Often while reading her one wants to exclaim, "Why, this is no worse than Briusov!" This is, of course, great praise for a beginning poet: "She writes like Briusov." But it is also a great reproach, because, after all, Nelli is not Briusov. If you are Nelli, then be Nelli . . .

In any event, the unarguable and uncommon gift of the poetess permits us to expect with certainty that in her second book she will speak in a distinct voice, characteristic of her and available to her alone.[36]

Khodasevich's review may have sparked Briusov's plans to compose Nelli's second book of poems, but it might also have led him to abandon the challenging project of creating a genuinely new poetic voice for her. Khodasevich was not the only critic to comment on the technical command displayed in Nelli's lyrics, which was noted by those who praised the neophyte for her impressive accomplishment and by those who criticized Briusov for granting his invented poet a proficiency beyond what could be expected of a woman.

The tenacity with which Briusov denied his authorship of Nelli's poems reveals the significance he ascribed to creating a distinct idiom that could pass for a woman's. With the success of his female impersonation, Briusov, that indefatigable student of poetic form, could colonize the woman's creative world and shape it from within. In a letter to the editor he wrote in response to Gorodetsky's review, Briusov insisted, "I find it absolutely necessary to announce that the pseudonym 'Nelli' belongs not to me but to an individual whose wish it is not to reveal the name in print yet."[37] In a draft of his introduction to the projected second volume of Nelli poems Briusov elaborates on this denial.[38]

Briusov's efforts to shore up Nelli's credibility found support in a review titled "The Chill of Morning (A Few Words on Women's Creativity)" ("Kholod utra [Neskol'ko slov o zhenskom tvorchestve]") and signed by Nadezhda L'vova. Published in 1914, a year after her suicide, it speaks of men's superiority in poetry, juxtaposes the irrational, emotional woman to the rational, self-controlled man, and iterates the long-standing bias that "men have the entire world. Women—'only love.'"[39] Featured in this review together with Akhmatova, Tsvetaeva, and Kuz'mina-Karavaeva, Nelli is distinguished as writing verse that is "the most 'feminine,' since she succeeded best of all in finding her own feminine words, her own illumination of a theme common to all [women]."[40] What constitutes the "femininity" of Nelli's words or the "theme" in question remains unexplained, but the assessment proclaims Nelli's success and puts Briusov's female impersonation above leading women poets of the time. As Ekonen summarizes, in Nelli "L'vova finds for herself an acceptable example of the renewal of culture and language in a man's creative work that imitates what is ostensibly a woman's style."[41] The posthumous publication of "The Chill of Morning" with its endorsement of Nelli and Briusov's gender biases raised suspicion that he was responsible for the review. Whether he authored it himself or ventriloquized L'vova to write it, the ideas articulated in "The Chill of Morning" express his own attitude toward women.[42]

Not content with inventing a woman poet, Briusov also directed her readers' reception of her verse along the lines of what Voloshin did with his "Horoscope of Cherubina de Gabriak." His introductory sonnet "Nelli" extends a somber tone over the volume and projects a sense of helplessness onto its purported author. The opening stanza enumerates what the lyrics do not do: they do not capture the sounds of nature; they are not expressive of young, tender love; nor do they present childlike delight in pleasure. With this list of negatives, Briusov frames Nelli's life experiences as burdensome— a loss rather than a gain:

> В твоих стихах—печальный опыт
> Страстей ненужных, ложных слав; (7)

> In your poems is the sad experience
> Of useless passions and false glories;

The sonnet goes on to describe the thickening smoke of the "pyre of love" (koster liubvi) that consumes Nelli and envelops her poems, emphasizing her resignation to an unhappy end with "A last sigh, a hopeless sigh" (Poslednii vzdokh, vzdokh beznadezhnyi). It indicates from the outset that Nelli is destined to remain emotionally and creatively unfulfilled. Hers is a loss of innocence for which there is no recompense. The sense of forfeiture that pervades her lyrics overshadows the sensual pleasures they describe. The reader thus enters what purports to be a uniquely feminine world through the pall that Briusov's introductory sonnet casts over the volume.

The twenty-eight poems it ushers in are divided into four sections:

"From My Observations" ("Iz moikh nabliudenii"), "Pages of a Diary"
("Listki dnevnika"), "The Story of My Love" ("Istoriia moei liubvi"), and
"The Ninth Wave" ("Deviatyi val"). These titles promise unmediated records
of Nelli's personal experiences, which, as the last heading intimates, ultimately overwhelm her. The poems of "Observations" present a nocturnal
urban setting and show Nelli entrapped by the sexualization that she herself
invites by appearing on the city streets—the locus of the modern poet. The
opening poem speaks of her love for the tranquility of evening and her dread
of imminent nightfall that will banish it. It concludes with a description of
night bringing captivating temptations and erotic enticements:

> Будет зыблить блеск многообразный,
> Пряжу отсветов манящих прясть,—
> И над всем живым свои соблазны,
> Словно сеть рыбак, раскинет Страсть. (12)

> A multifaceted glimmer will ripple,
> Will weave strands of enticing reflections,—
> And over all that is living,
> Like a fisherman casting his net,
> Passion will cast its temptations.

Nelli is ensnared in this passion, and the poems of this section speak alternately of her surrender to urban pleasures and her longing to escape
from them.

Set in a concrete, modern world, the poems present heightened sensuality in a Europeanized urban setting. The city is possessed of a seductive,
corrupting power, proffering pleasures to those who can pay, as indicated by
the suggestive rhyming of *vitrinakh* (store windows) with *zmeinykh* (serpent
[13]) later in the poem. The natural light of the stars and moon that inspired
Romantic poets is overwhelmed by artificial illumination that entices, trig-
gers desires, and makes consumption conspicuous. The cover of night no
longer affords privacy, and erotically charged encounters that had heretofore
remained hidden from view are now in the public eye. Images of brightly lit
restaurants and cafés emphasize the spectacle of seduction:

> Но вдалеке разбита тьма
> Горящим взором ресторана. (14)

> But in the distance the darkness is shattered
> By the burning gaze of a restaurant.

References to velocity combine with artificial light to depict an urban setting with a frenzied life of its own. Celebrated by male urbanist poets, this setting dispossesses Nelli of agency. The approach of night portends inescapable self-surrender:

> Опять безвольная душа
> Нисходит в круг ночных безумий. (13)

> Again the will-less soul
> Descends into a circle of nocturnal insanities.

In the three concluding poems of section 1, flights of fancy bring Nelli to the longed-for purity of nature: a beautiful forest to which she offers pagan worship, a pond that takes her back to a happy childhood, and a prelapsarian paradise. Her need to escape underscores her entrapment. A crystal-clear spring day spent far from the city leaves her torn between a longing for innocence and the desires bred by the city. This leaves her questioning her identity:

> Кто я, в этой прелести вешней?
> Не греза ль Мориса Дени? (20)

> Who am I in this springtime delight?
> Am I perhaps a vision of Maurice Denis?

Nelli internalizes the label of fallen woman that alienates her from the Edenic natural world she surveys. Her sense of oppressive guilt pervades the collection, and the escape with which the opening section of *Nelli's Poems* concludes is perforce temporary.

The poems of section 2, "Pages of a Diary," record Nelli's public traversal of urban space. Mikhailova's observation that in "Kind Al'd" "the woman herself gradually begins to relate to herself as to an object at which the male gaze is directed"[43] applies also to this section of *Nelli's Poems*. In it, Nelli appears as a courtesan who works to attract male clients. She and the woman who accompanies her are now themselves temptations that the city offers:

> Плачущие перья зыблются на шляпах,
> Страстно бледны лица, губы—словно кровь.
> Обжигает нервы Lentheric'a запах,
> Мы—само желанье, мы—сама любовь! (25)

Weeping plumes billow on [our] hats,
Passionately pale faces, lips like blood.
The fragrance of Lenthéric scorches the nerves,
We are desire itself, we are love itself!

Trumping the power her sexuality temporarily gains Nelli over the men she entices is the economic power they wield over her. A consumer of urban pleasures, she becomes also one of its commodities. Nelli describes herself admiring a ruby ring given to her by a client whom she will repay with her body:

Блещет обещаньем исхищренной ласки
У меня на пальце пламенный рубин. (25)

The fiery ruby on my finger glimmers
With the promise of refined caresses.

The ending of the poem underscores the commercialism of her exchanges: "The agreement is signed and the trade is completed" (*Dogovor podpisan i zakonchen torg* [26]). There is no room for emotional involvement. She and the friend with whom she traverses the streets pledge,

Обе верны будем строгому служенью:
Расточать соблазны, продавать восторг! (26)

We will both be true to the exacting service:
To disperse temptations, to sell raptures!

A poem titled "At the Skating Rink" ("Na sketinge") underscores that while the courtesan has the power to attract men, it is they who have the power of choice:

Кто-ж из вас наденет мне,
С радостной улыбкой, ролики? (28)

Which of you, with a happy smile,
Will put my roller skates on for me?

Having enticed a male client, she must deliver what he demands. The poem that follows, "Nocturnal Murmur" ("Nochnoi ropot"), depicts the emotional and physical deception entailed in commodified eros:

Тягостно, с дрожью притворной, с волненьем расчитаным,
Мертвые губы к горячим губам прижимать! (29)

It is onerous, with simulated trembling, with calculated agitation,
To press dead lips against hot lips!

The final stanza describes her revulsion:

Влажные руки в истоме прижались мучительно,
Ласки прощальной властительно ищут уста.
О! словно щупальцы спрута сплелись безобразныя;
О! словно я осьминогом на дне обвита! (30)[44]

Damp, languorous hands press against me torturously.
Lips commandingly seek a farewell caress.
Oh! it's as if the hideous tentacles of an octopus intertwined;
Oh! it's as if I am enveloped by an octopus on the bottom [of the sea]!

The end of the "Diary" section speaks again of escape, but in more somber tones. The sense of transgression intensifies guilt and a need for absolution. In the poem "Soraspiatye" ("Cocrucified"), Nelli contrasts her guilt with Christ's innocence, signaling acceptance of the punishment meted out to her and assuming the role of the penitent robber crucified at Christ's right:

И шепчу: «Помяни мя,
Егда будешь в раю!» (32)

And whisper: "Remember me,
When you will be in paradise!"

In the New Testament, these words bring salvation, but on Nelli's lips they underscore resignation to the hopeless inescapability of her situation. Section 2 ends with a poem that registers Nelli's disorientation and increasing alienation from herself and the surrounding world.

Section 3, "The Story of My Love," moves into Nelli's private world to document the emotional consequences of her fall. Its poems describe Nelli's genuine, uncommodified love. The reversal in the erotics of dominance and subordination in this section figures also in Briusov's "Last Pages from a Woman's Diary." Subordinate to the men who purchase her love, Nelli is the dominant partner in her sexual relations with the man she loves. The experience gained in her public role of courtesan invades her private life and precludes an erotics of parallel status with her naive, feminized beloved, whom she instructs in the art of love. The joy of this consummation contrasts sharply with the revulsion occasioned by her professional encounters. Yet the equality precluded in relations with her clients is precluded also in her relationship with her beloved. "At Dawn" ("Na rassvete") opens with a stanza in which the maternal and the erotic commingle, emphasizing the asymmetry in the relationship:

> Мой мальчик, мой милый, мой маленький,
> Как сладко тебя целовать!
> Твой рот, словно розанчик аленький,
> Губами жестокими жать! (45)

> My little boy, my dear, my little one,
> How sweet it is to kiss you!
> To press your mouth like a little red rosebud
> With cruel lips!

Nelli's pleas that her beloved recollect their trysts suggest that all is not well, and in the immediately following poem his love phases into the past tense. This loss of happiness is framed as the consequence of Nelli's loss of innocence in a bleak variation on the oft-rehearsed theme that the pursuit of a public career dooms the woman to misery in her private life. Like de Staël's Corinne, but in a modern setting, Nelli fails to find fulfillment in either her calling or her private emotional sphere.

The poems of "The Ninth Wave," the final section, record a brief, ineffectual protest, followed immediately by surrender to hopelessness. "Shadows of those once loved and damned" ("Teni kogda-to liubimykh i prokliatykh") tries to dispel the specters of paramours who haunt her newfound love. In the third poem, Nelli—using a distinctly Akhmatovian image—describes herself as a carelessly broken statuette to signal her recognition that her beloved will not return. The last three poems of the section show her gradually sinking into a dark sea populated by octopuses and sharks. She expresses a frail hope that she may yet regain her freedom and happiness. Her fantasies, however, describe not freedom but a return to the streets and restaurants, as she torments her beloved with stories of self-destructive exploits with other men:

> Сказкою о моих новых возлюбленных,
> О их ласках, о их глазах, о их уме,
> О ночах, исступленно погубленных
> В ресторанных огнях, в будуарной тьме . . . (57)

A tale of my new lovers,
Of their caresses, of their eyes, of their intelligence,
Of nights, franticly destroyed
In restaurant lights, in boudoir darkness . . .

As this vengeful fantasy passes, Nelli admits that she can neither win the man she loves nor forget him. The concluding poem of the collection, titled like its final section, "The Ninth Wave," shows her abandoning all hope as she describes her silent descent (*bez krika*) into the depths of the sea (59). Resigned to her unhappy fate, she sinks into dark, silent waters, offering one last, lifeless farewell to her now de-eroticized beloved: "My friend, farewell" (*Moi drug, proshchai* [60]). The poems she writes record her despair but do not rescue her from it.

The persona of Nelli's poems succumbs to the role assigned her in a world determined by men. Described from what purports to be the perspective of the woman herself, Nelli's participation in her own sexualization and dependency on love serve to corroborate rather than dispel gender biases that beleaguered women poets. Critics of the day received *Nelli's Poems* in accordance with established norms—that is, in a context that normalized women's sexualization and the untenable position the poems present. Such normalization of the conditions that Nelli's poems project is not confined to her day. Describing the city as Nelli's "own natural element,"[45] Lavrov concurs with a reviewer of Nelli's time, whose words he weaves into his article: "*Nelli's Poems* were perceived, not without reason, as 'the story of the soul of a contemporary courtesan,' told 'in a consecutive series of clear-cut and tender-colored engravings.'"[46] Lavrov goes on to say that in the collection "amorous experiences are the main, if not only, theme."[47] Making no mention of Nelli's entrapment and despair or of the contrast between her commodified and her freely offered love, Lavrov repeats the commonplace that women are preoccupied primarily with love and uncritically accepts Nelli's sexualization and its unhappy consequences as the norm. With the focus falling squarely on the male poet's capture of a woman's perspective and idiom, the deleterious situation that the poems record, like the male conceit of writing like a woman, remains uninterrogated.

Significantly, both those who believed *Nelli's Poems* to be the debut of a new woman poet and those who recognized it as a mystification found the woman who appeared in the poems credible. While the technical mastery of the poems raised eyebrows, the verity of the emotional experiences and the perspective on the surrounding world they recorded were accepted as true to life. This credibility derived largely from the fact that Briusov had folded prevailing biases into his invention so that the poems and the "Nelli" who emerged from them accorded with gender stereotypes readers brought to the poems. "Poetesses," a 1913 essay by the writer and critic Boris Sadovs-koi, unwittingly captures the incongruity of expecting women constructed in keeping with men's biases to bring something new to poetry:

> Seeking the unknown and new angles of vision, if even on old things, con-temporary poetry is now in need of models of women's individualities, which bring with them the new acuity of women's perception. The world of love, eros, impressions of commonplace things perceived from new and unex-pected angles provide noble and interesting material for this poetry.[48]

Notably, Sadovskoi focuses on "models of women's individualities" and not on individual women themselves. With his mentorship and his invention of Nelli, Briusov supplied just such models. The speculative aspect of how women must write modulated yet again into the prescriptive.

Nelli's lyrics advance Briusov's project to shape urban modernism much as he had directed the rise of Symbolism earlier in the century. In particular—and this guides the discussion that follows—*Nelli's Poems* demonstrate the impossibility of a woman's participation in the modernist move to the city. This emerges with particular clarity in the context of that consummate poet of flânerie, Baudelaire, who strongly influenced Briusov and whose flâneur throws into high relief the disenfranchisement of the woman in urban space.

Briusov designated Baudelaire as "the foremost poet of contempora-neity" in an introductory essay to his translations of that poet.[49] Baudelaire's flâneur is a complex image of the urban poet. A connoisseur of "the fugi-tive pleasure of circumstance,"[50] he is a physically idle but perceptually ac-tive reader of myriad, fleeting signs of the bustling city through which he wanders aimlessly, observant of and yet detached from his surroundings. He has the power to attribute meaning to details of the urban spaces he freely traverses. His perceptions are fragmentary, disconnected, and the meanings he ascribes are not subject to verification by any consciousness outside his own. The flâneur enters the public sphere not to seek meaning but to create it. The spectator who brings spectacle into being, he engages public space from within the solitude of his private creative sphere. Baudelaire focuses attention on the peculiarity of the poet's engagement of the public domain, which—in the privacy of his anonymity—he experiences subjectively. As Milica Banjanin summarizes, "The poet transforms the public space into a stage for private experiences, thus transposing the texture of ordinary street life into art."[51] Such destabilization of distinctions between public and private is contingent on his ability to remain "the secret spectator of the spectacle of the spaces and places of the city."[52] Freed from having to pres-ent a purposeful public self and fully possessed of agency, the flâneur has no need to preoccupy himself with how *he* might be read or made a spectacle of and can train his attention exclusively on "the ephemeral, the fugitive, the contingent" in terms of which Baudelaire defines modernity.[53]

The flâneur, whose origins are in nineteenth-century Paris, proved to be a productive model for poetic self-presentations in other times and places as well, as "writers recast the *flâneur* in the image of their own changing conceptions of the social order and their place in it."[54] In post-Symbolist Russia, poets who turned to the here and now of the city could see in this adaptable figure an appealing image of the modern poet. Significantly, this very image problematized the woman poet's situation just as she gained traction in Russian letters. Historically the flâneur is male gendered. "The rejection of female *flâneurs* stems in large part from [the woman's] presumed incapacity for self-sufficiency, from the willingness to join the crowd, to enter into negotiations, and to create relationships in circumstances that the true *flâneur* contemplates from a safe distance."[55] The "presumed incapacity" to remain aloof from her metropolitan surroundings frames the woman as an easily engaged consumer rather than a detached connoisseur. This problem is compounded by the fact that when women "ventured onto the city streets under the conditions necessary to urban strolling and observation, they took on the persona of the fallen woman."[56]

In 1831, George Sand roamed the streets of Paris dressed as a boy to gain freedom of movement and the opportunity to partake of the spectacle of the city without garnering unwanted attention. For all the changes in how women were regarded in the decades intervening between Sand's Parisian romps and Nelli's appearance on the Russian literary scene, Deborah Epstein Nord's question of what "we can say of a distinctly female urban vision" remained problematic even as her answer to that question remained valid. The female urban vision, as Nord describes, "involves a consciousness of transgression and trespassing, of vexed sexuality, of the female body as commodity, of the unreliability of class boundaries, of the need for disguise or some form of incognito, and, most importantly, of the ultimate unavoidability of the primacy of the male gaze and its power to objectify and eroticize."[57] Seen as a consumer and yet also herself commodified, the woman was doubly barred from flânerie, for if "Baudelaire's *flâneur*, caught between creativity and commodification . . . remains, by definition, and impediments notwithstanding, an artist, in other words, a producer,"[58] the woman is objectified and denied such agency.

Feminist art historians have shown the extent to which the structuring of social space is bound up with the ideology of separate gendered spheres.[59] As noted, the woman is left in a double bind by the roles assigned her in the city. She is left in a similarly untenable position by the way the flâneur redraws social space. It would seem that the destabilization of boundaries between self and others, between the private and the public, and between the domestic and the urban could also destabilize constructs of gender. This, however, did not prove to be the case. Situating the modern poet in an urban setting entailed the denigration of conventionally feminine-gendered domestic space. As Baudelaire stresses in "The Painter of Modern Life," the flâneur feels himself truly at home only in the city streets:

> For the perfect *flâneur*, for the passionate spectator, it is an immense joy to set up house in the heart of the multitude, amid the ebb and flow of movement, in the midst of the fugitive and the infinite. To be away from home and yet to feel oneself everywhere at home; to see the world, to be at the centre of the world, and yet to remain hidden from the world—such are a few of the slightest pleasures of those independent, passionate, impartial natures which the tongue can but clumsily define. The spectator is a *prince* who everywhere rejoices in his incognito. The lover of life makes the whole world his family, just like the lover of the fair sex who builds up his family from all the beautiful women that he has ever found.[60]

The flâneur has no need for the shelter and security of private domestic space, which he easily rejects, proclaiming his independence of home, construed as a fixed abode, in order to claim residence wherever he may be at any given moment. Thus to say that "Baudelaire's poet is a man who is driven out of the private and into the public by his own search for meaning"[61] is not entirely accurate, for, having detached the private from the domestic, this poet is free to fashion the public areas he traverses into private space. What can be said, however, is that "he is the man who is only at home existentially when he is not at home physically."[62] Situating his home in the city streets that are inhospitable to women, he removes himself from the female-gendered domestic sphere to inhabit a domicile of his own making. Domestic ideology is undone and the woman's matrimonial and maternal roles are dismissed. Yet with no new place allowed her in the city, where she remains both a consumer and a commodity, the woman experiences not liberation from stultifying norms but intensified marginalization and meaninglessness. For all its sociological promise to disrupt the status quo and expand the purview of art, the modernist move to the city left the woman doubly dispossessed.

This vexing situation is inscribed in the lyrics Briusov writes in the guise of a woman. Like the flâneur, Nelli destabilizes the boundaries between her public and domestic spheres. Unlike the flâneur, however, she gains nothing from this destabilization. Indeed, the hopelessness of her situation derives from her twofold disenfranchisement in an urban space that is determined by men and a domestic sphere that is dismissed as irrelevant by the modern poet. By casting the persona of his invented woman poet as a courtesan, Briusov foregrounds her unsuitability for the role of flâneur. Nelli is perforce an astute reader of signs who is keenly aware of how others read her and of how she can manipulate these readings to advance her own commodification. Documented in her poems are not the flâneur's detached, subjective observations of a city and its inhabitants but the courtesan's self-conscious projection of signs that invite erotic relations and her readings of signaled responses to them. The aimlessness of the flâneur is replaced with a commercial purposefulness that destroys Nelli's private felicity. A series of oppositions reflects the tensions to which she ultimately succumbs. She ineffectually invokes nature as an antidote to the man-made urban setting, fantasizes about flight from the city, underscores her own languor and list-lessness against the background of the fast pace of urban life, and repeatedly juxtaposes the counterfeit of purchased love to genuine love that is freely bestowed. Nelli's accounts of relations with men show her playing the double role of a woman who victimizes men by seducing them and yet herself remains the victim of their sexual desires. A captive of the city, Nelli is an object it acts on and alters. Her relations with paying customers elicit revulsion and a sense of entrapment heightened by the claustrophobic images pervading the lyrics and leading to the despair with which the collection ends. The poems express a desire to escape but offer no protest against this situation. The emphasis falls squarely on the high price exacted for Nelli's traversal of the streets.

The "new" woman Briusov models in the Nelli poems continues to be sexualized and commodified, only now she is an active participant in this process. The poems she writes situate her between the privileged male-gendered urban space where she is eroticized and the denigrated female-gendered private sphere from which she is alienated by her sallies into the streets. The enablement inherent in her mastery of poetic form is offset by her entrapment in untenable conditions. The lyrics, as Briusov's introductory sonnet intimates, are not manifestations of a woman's selfhood but warn-ings against its exercise. The poet Nelli does not fare much better than the courtesan of her poems. The hackneyed parallel between the woman's appearance on the street and her appearance in print implicit in *Nelli's Poems* is supported by Briusov's widely known sexual dominance over the women poets he mentored. Does Briusov allow Nelli a creative act any more liber-ating for her than the sexual? Nelli's poems document her sensuality, her ultimately isolating traversals of city streets, her unfulfilled emotions, her sense of guilt, and the attendant alienation from herself. Far from helping her spring free of limitations imposed by prevailing constructs of gender, the poems argue for the inescapability of their strictures.

Briusov's Nelli mystification responds to the rise of women poets and the interest in women's creativity that peaked in the wake of the Symbolist period. His female impersonation acknowledges the inroads women were making into the tradition and reflects his desire to both influence and contain that very phenomenon that was hailed as a potential source of renewal. Loath to countenance a self-sufficient woman poet on a par with her male counterparts, Briusov seeks to direct the development of the new woman poet and the emerging feminine line of poetry. With his numerous introductions to women's poetry collections, it is he who raises the curtain on the woman's unique creative world. With his mentoring, he continues to objectify women and direct their self-expressivity. With Nelli he colonizes the woman's creative sphere and, showcasing her unsuitability for the urban modernist project, warns the woman of the negative consequences of entering a man's world.

In her essay "The Invisible *Flâneuse*" Janet Wolff remarks on "an apparently common assumption that women who participate in 'the public' on anything like the same terms as men somehow manifest masculine traits."[63] In 1913, the year of Nelli's debut, Aleksandra Kollontai earnestly promoted an image of the "new woman," "walking the streets with a businesslike, masculine tread in search of work."[64] Such masculinization took the woman out of the role of prostitute to that of productive citizen, but only if she surrendered her gender identity. In other words, adjustment was demanded not from the masculine gendering of urban space but from the woman who entered it.

In the context of cultural and sociopolitical changes that subsequently altered the significance of the city and stressed social commitment, engagement, and cooperation, the flâneur was destined to fade out of existence. Although the gender ideology of which he was both a product and a representative lingered on, this ideology was increasingly challenged by women who began "taking control of instruments of cultural expression" and insistently exploring new possibilities for self-realization.[65] Indeed, Nelli is symptomatic of Briusov's attempt to ward off such challenges. Just at the time of Nelli's debut, Marina Tsvetaeva, energized by his authoritarianism, launched an attack on Briusov. Anna Akhmatova, already an acclaimed poet, maintained that with his female impersonation, Briusov was trying to tap into the celebrity she enjoyed at the time.[66]

PART III

Resistance

Chapter Five

Marina Tsvetaeva versus Male Authority

Lord, send me a shore to push away from, a
shoal to cast off from, and a squall to withstand!
—Marina Tsvetaeva, "Natal'ia Goncharova"

I write my autobiography through others.
—Marina Tsvetaeva, letter to A. S. Iashchenko

THE CHERUBINA DE GABRIAK and Nelli mystifications reflect the extent to which the rising interest in women poets in the early years of the twentieth century remained tied to the pervasive assumption that it was for men to define and direct women's newly acknowledged creativity. As in the sociopolitical arena, so too in the cultural domain the advancement of women still depended on norms and constructs that women themselves had unequal voice in establishing. Philosophies and aesthetic platforms that treated gender and sexuality issued from a predominantly male world, and even programs that upheld social change and promoted women's rights often rehearsed notions about gender that impinged on women's agency and self-realization. Weininger's notion of the complementarity of the feminine and the masculine relegated women to a passive state and assigned an active role to men. Women could appear in print with unprecedented ease, but the authority of male critics and the male control over publication perpetuated women's dependency on men and the competition for their approval. The objectification of women and the expectations projected onto them naturally influenced how women saw and presented themselves. It also continued to affect how their poems were read.

This chapter examines how Marina Tsvetaeva reacts against these conditions early in her poetic career and how she subsequently frames her reaction in the retrospective essays "A Hero of Labor" ("Geroi truda," 1925) and "The Living about the Living" ("Zhivoe o zhivom," 1932), devoted to Valerii Briusov and Maximilian Voloshin respectively.[1] I look first at Tsvetaeva's literary debut with *Evening Album* (*Vechernii al'bom*) and how it was received, considering reviews by Briusov and Voloshin and Tsvetaeva's reaction to them. This leads into an examination of the creative self she projects in her essays to Briusov and Voloshin, which feature a viable model of how women poets can establish selfhood.

Together with the problems that continued to beset aspiring women poets, Tsvetaeva inherited also the strategies of enablement that Pavlova and Rostopchina developed in the previous century. Like these two poets, whose lives and works she knew and admired, Tsvetaeva was interested not in overthrowing the tradition but in enlarging it to make it hospitable to women. Accordingly, she works to establish herself as a poet and to show the way for other women to do the same. Like Pavlova, in whom she finds a sustaining role model, Tsvetaeva argues against granting gender a constitutive role in a poet's creative identity, neither masking her gender nor problematizing it. Cognizant that gender would continue to inform how her poems are read, Tsvetaeva also works to elevate the status of women poets, building on Rostopchina's assertion that women are by their very nature closer than men to poetry. Tsvetaeva's embrace of the divergent strategies that precipitated discord between Pavlova and Rostopchina enlarged her compass. No self-contradiction, her multifaceted response to challenges facing women poets is consistent with the all-inclusiveness she privileges, overriding binaries in the name of deeper and broader comprehension.

Tsvetaeva's prose augments the rebellion against feminine stereotypes that is characteristic of her verse[2] with an emphasis on the woman as a penetrating reader who apprehends deeper meaning beyond surface appearances. As I discuss in this chapter and the next, Tsvetaeva's demonstrations of how *she* reads instruct readers in how they should read her. The retrospective readings of her own poetic becoming that she presents in her essays are geared, among other things, to enhance her reader's receptivity. Notably, such readings include not only the written word but also details of the surrounding world and those who people it. This exceptional semiotic reach marks the true poet. In essays dedicated to other poets—written most often in immediate response to their deaths—Tsvetaeva demonstrates a creative capacity to revivify her subjects with her idiosyncratic readings of their lives, their works, and their deaths. Her creative identity emerges from these readings, which accentuate her subjectivity and the unique perceptual and interpretive capacities that she engages to advance the woman poet's cause.

Like all of Tsvetaeva's essays, "A Hero of Labor" and "The Living about the Living" are intricate works in which she interweaves an astonishing range of ideas, observations, and arguments. The polyvalence and polyfunctionality of repeated images, motifs, and tropes endow these seemingly rambling essays with rich texture and density of meaning. Here I follow only selected strands that exemplify how Tsvetaeva, in the course of charting her own poetic development, undermines gender biases and promotes writerly and social behaviors that enable women poets.

Tsvetaeva does not intend "A Hero of Labor" and "The Living about the Living" as accurate accounts, and my point here is not to distinguish fact from fiction but to apprehend what the essays convey. The subjectivity that they prominently feature is an essential component of a self-affirmation that promotes the writing woman from object to subject, directing attention away from the dictates of a male culture and toward the responses that a woman can offer it. This pronounced subjectivity has another function: it shifts the focus from events and circumstances themselves to the poet's idiosyncratic readings of them. Tsvetaeva's reader comes to know who she is by witnessing the richness of meaning she derives from signs. Having the reader look *with* her rather than *at* her is a powerful way to forestall objectification and to instruct the reader in the art of poetic apprehension. With the reading that she advocates, Tsvetaeva productively replaces the reader's gender-driven invention of the writing woman with a cooperative venture in which the poet and her reader enrich each other and the text.

Tsvetaeva appeared on the literary stage in October of 1910 with *Evening Album*, a collection of one hundred eleven poems dedicated to Maria Bashkirtseva. As Irina Shevelenko describes, to begin with the fait accompli of an entire book of verse marked a break with the conventional ritual of debut.[3] Eschewing the male mentor who habitually escorted women into the poetic arena and choosing not to present herself gradually with publications of individual poems in the periodic press, Tsvetaeva declared independence from established practice.[4] She appeared as the self-sufficient author of an entire volume of well-wrought verse that centered uniquely and unabashedly on her own youthful emotions, aspirations, and experiences in a private, domestic setting.

The period in which Tsvetaeva began her literary career and that, echoing Voloshin, she subsequently referred to as the epoch of Cherubina (*epokha Cherubiny*)[5] was one in which, as Shevelenko summarizes,

> Men litterateurs actively occupied themselves with forming the new identity, the *cultural personality* of the woman poetess. The most famous experiment of this sort was the Cherubina de Gabriak mystification, directed by M. Voloshin. It showed how strong the hunger for "enigmatic" Unknown Women [*Neznakomok*] was in the current literary situation, a hunger for whose satisfaction the exceptional personality was far more important than the talent of the texts she created.[6]

With her unconventional debut, Tsvetaeva tapped into this appetite for the exceptional woman, while her verse veered away from Symbolist aesthetics. The poems of *Evening Album* document details of her immediate surroundings and direct experiences. Their author, as references to her youthfulness and the nursery underscored, was a child who eluded sexualization. There was no trace of exoticism, and her exceptionality rested on her command of the poetic idiom and the world of the girl child that the poems recorded. The right to her own subject matter, poetic voice, and self-fashioning that Tsvetaeva claimed in her autonomously published collection declared the independence that remained a constant in her creative autobiography and a model for other women to emulate.

Flanking Tsvetaeva's debut were those of Voloshin's Cherubina de Gabriak and Briusov's Nelli. In "A Hero of Labor" and "The Living about the Living," which describe her lasting hostilities with Briusov and her lasting friendship with Voloshin, Tsvetaeva folds her responses to these mystifications into her self-presentations. The positions she assumes vis-à-vis Briusov and Voloshin inform two complementary paradigms of the poetic enterprise that Tsvetaeva defined. The first is the process of individuation, which demands pushing away from a resisting force to gain creative momentum and determine selfhood. The second is an assimilative process. This is the concept of "confluence" (*sliianie*) of the individual poet with all poets and poetry in a transcendent realm that knows neither spatial or temporal bounds nor those of the individual ego.[7] "A Hero of Labor" presents Briusov as a catalyst for individuation. Tsvetaeva's relations with Voloshin, as described in "The Living about the Living," exemplify poetic confluence.

Briusov and Voloshin were the first to review *Evening Album*. Before examining the essays devoted to them, it is helpful to look briefly at their reviews and Tsvetaeva's responses to them. Although in "A Hero of Labor" she was to claim otherwise, Tsvetaeva sent Briusov a copy of *Evening Album* with the breezy request that he "look through it." Briusov may have remembered Tsvetaeva as the author of a letter she sent him earlier that year that took him to task for not appreciating Rostand as she did (6:37–38). Tsvetaeva was undaunted by Briusov's dismissal of the French writer she revered. The volume of verse she now sent him opened with an epigraph from Rostand.

Tsvetaeva's defiant attitude notwithstanding, Briusov was important to her at this time. As she worked on the poems of *Evening Album*, Tsvetaeva was engrossed in his three-volume collection *Roads and Crossroads* (*Puti i pereput'ia*) of 1909. The essay "Enchantment in Briusov's Poems" ("Volshebstvo v stikhakh Briusova")—her first known work in this genre—documents the remarkable self-assurance with which she appraised the don of Russian poetry. "Enchantment," which was published only in 1979 and remained unknown to Tsvetaeva's contemporaries, provides insight into how she positioned herself vis-à-vis Briusov.

As in her letter to Briusov, in this essay, also of 1910, Tsvetaeva expresses certainty that she has something to offer Briusov, whom she addresses not as a neophyte writing to a powerful potential mentor but as an equal. The "enchantment" of the essay's title alludes to what Tsvetaeva describes as the rare instantiations of Briusov's muse in the guise a young woman (*devushka muza* [5:227]), which she discerns in his poems and urges him to develop further, presumably under her tutelage. The essay concludes with a list of Briusov's failings, which, as Tsvetaeva opines, are redeemed by the enchantment that appears in some of his poems: "Betrayal of Romanticism; affront to youth with intentionally careless criticism of young poets; the complete lack of talent in the psychodrama *The Wayfarer*,—may this all be forgiven Briusov for the fact that in his hands, too, there sparkled at times the multifaceted diamond of enchantment" (5:229). Tsvetaeva assesses Briusov on her own terrain—that feminine domain that he approaches tentatively with invocations of a feminine muse that she singles out for praise. This leaves the Briusov of Tsvetaeva's early essay doubly dependent on the audacious novice who aligns herself with the "young woman muse" who inspires his poems but positions herself also as the reader and critic who magnaniously forgives his poetic shortcomings.

Given that the literary world she entered was thick with newly minted poets, that Tsvetaeva had given no prior notice of herself, and that the print run of *Evening Album* was a mere five hundred copies, the critical attention the volume attracted is notable. The first review to appear was by Voloshin, whose de Gabriak mystification was just ending, and the second by Valerii Briusov, who would shortly launch his own debut as a woman poet with *Nelli's Poems*. These reviews were followed by positive assessments of *Evening Album* by Nikolai Gumilev and Marietta Shaginian.[8] All four reviewers recognized Tsvetaeva's talent, noting the youthfulness of her poems and the intimacy that characterizes them. The reviews reflect their authors' own literary preoccupations at the time. Shaginian discusses Tsvetaeva's collection as representative of women's poetry.[9] Voloshin compares Tsvetaeva to Cherubina de Gabriak. The Acmeist poet Gumilev praises Tsvetaeva's new "unmediated, thoughtless delight in the trifles of life."[10] Briusov the Symbolist is less sanguine about the concrete details of the author's personal world in the poems. Although he concedes that the self-proclaimed youth of the poet is disarming, he has only reproach for the intimacy that Gumilev finds new and bold, that Voloshin sees as naive and sincere, and that Shaginian describes as refreshing.[11]

The fact that Briusov selected *Evening Album* from among a prodigious number of books for inclusion in his survey was a mark of distinction.[12] Tsvetaeva, however, found his appraisal disappointing and more in line with the "affront to youth with intentionally careless criticism of young poets" with which she reproached Briusov in her "Enchantment" essay. As Tsvetaeva was to describe in "A Hero of Labor," this review provoked her to declare war against Briusov, just as in "The Living about the Living" she maintains that Voloshin's review initiated her lasting friendship with him.

Tsvetaeva presented Voloshin with a copy of *Evening Album* on December 1, 1910, at a literary gathering at the publishing house Musaget. Her inscription invokes a writer who influenced Voloshin's invention of Cherubina de Gabriak: "With gratitude for the excellent reading of Villiers de L'Isle-Adam."[13] Voloshin responded with the poem "My soul is so joyously drawn to you" ("K Vam dusha tak radostno vlekoma"). His review, "Women's Poetry" ("Zhenskaia poeziia"), followed on December 11 in *The Morning of Russia* (*Utro Rossii*). Gratified by Voloshin's assessment of her work, Tsvetaeva thanked him in a letter of December 23, in which she wrote, "Accept my sincere gratitude for your sincere words about my book. You approached it like life and forgave life that which is not forgiven literature" (6:39).

Voloshin situates Tsvetaeva's collection in the efflorescence of women's poetry in France and Russia at the time. As Shevelenko justly notes, notions about gender in his review are a "creative reworking" of ideas advanced in Otto Weininger's *Sex and Character* (*Geschlecht und Charakter*),[14] a best seller throughout the first two decades of the twentieth century in Russia, where it appeared in multiple editions and in large print runs. Weininger—who exerted greater influence in Russia than did Freud—situated creativity in the male domain, which, as he claimed, was accessible exclusively to women with a pronounced masculine streak. We have only to recall how Pavlova and Rostopchina were received to recognize that Weininger's ideas accorded with long-standing biases. Indeed, his popularity stemmed at least in part from the fact that his ideas upheld views that had already gained traction in Russia and normalized men's presumptuous mentorship and inventions of women poets.

In his review, Voloshin observes that, like France, Russia could now boast a plethora of new women poets. Noting Liubov' Stolitsa, Adelaida Gertsyk, and Margarita Sabashnikova by way of example, he adds, "In *Apollo* this year two cycles of poetry were published by the very interesting poet Cherubina de Gabriak, and just now Marina Tsvetaeva's book *Evening Album* appeared, about which we would like to speak."[15] At this point, only those close to *Apollo* were privy to Cherubina's identity. A second installment of poems signed by her appeared in the journal on September 15, 1910, leaving the reading public to believe that she was an actual poet. Tsvetaeva, whose *Evening Album* followed in October of that year, could thus have known of de Gabriak but not yet of the mystification or Voloshin's role in it. In the early stages of their friendship, Voloshin related his fictionalized account of the ruse to Tsvetaeva and her sister Anastasia.[16] Tsvetaeva subsequently included the story in "The Living about the Living," recast in a way that dignified the woman poet and her inventor.

When she read his review of *Evening Album*, however, Tsvetaeva did not know that Voloshin had put a woman poet invented in accord with male fantasies on equal footing with her and had done so at what he himself described as a crucial juncture in women's writing. In the immediately preceding generation, Voloshin explains in his review, prominent Russian women poets like Gippius and Solov'eva "preferred a male costume in their poems and wrote about themselves in masculine gender" (319). Now, however, in both France and Russia, women poets speak of themselves as women and relate their personal experiences (319). Emphasizing the sincerity and naïveté of Tsvetaeva's poems, Voloshin calls *Evening Album* a diary that reveals intimate details of the woman's heretofore undescribed transition from childhood to girlhood. Tsvetaeva's command of the poetic idiom, her keen observations of the surrounding world, and her "impressionistic ability to fix the current moment" (320) give the volume, as he maintains, a "*documentary* significance" (320; emphasis in the original). Voloshin praises Tsvetaeva for the "new, as yet untold image of femininity" (322) that she reveals in her poems. This praise reflects the interest in women's creativity at the time, but the insistence on Tsvetaeva's naïveté implies her lack of conscious awareness of what her verse discloses and the male poet and critic recognizes. Voloshin's explanation of how Tsvetaeva's poems are to be understood is an interpretive gesture that plays a normative function. To characterize Tsvetaeva herself, Voloshin cites lines from her poem "In Luxembourg Garden," which reject "an untold image of femininity" to embrace a conventional one: "I love women who showed no fear in battle, who could hold a sword and a spear, but I know that only in the captivity of a cradle is my commonplace, woman's happiness" (*Ia zhenshchin liubliu, chto v boiu ne robeli, umevshikh i shpagu derzhat' i kop'e,—no znaiu, chto tol'ko v plenu kolybeli obychnoe, zhenskoe schast'e moe* [322]).[17]

S. Iu. Kornienko argues that Voloshin's delight in Tsvetaeva's childlike perspective amounts to the woman poet's infantilization of the kind he advanced in his "Horoscope of Cherubina de Gabriak" and other essays published in *Apollo*.[18] Kornienko suggests that in her relations with Voloshin Tsvetaeva falls in with this infantilization, consciously affecting the privileged role of a child vis-à-vis her more experienced critic.[19] The argument is plausible, but Tsvetaeva's emphasis on her youthfulness also indicates a desire to circumvent sexualization, as Rostopchina did, for example, in the second poem of *Two Meetings*, which describes her interactions with Pushkin at a ball. In any event, this still leaves the woman poet between the untenable options of infantilization or sexualization.

Voloshin concludes his review with claims about the woman poet that again derive from Weininger. Describing women as incapable of creating a new poetic language but capable of using the extant idiom in a more nuanced way than men, he denies the woman poet individuality and describes her in generalized terms as representing her entire sex.

> Women's poetry is deeper. But it is less individualistic. It is much more the poetry of a type and not the poetry of an individual. The significance of the poetesses I cite derives from the fact that each of them speaks not only for herself but for a large number of women as well, each is the voice of one of the subaquatic currents that animate the natural phenomenon of the woman with a voice of feminine depth. (322)

Although Tsvetaeva expressed gratitude for Voloshin's review when it first appeared and again in "The Living about the Living," she devoted considerable energy to destabilizing precisely those categories of gender that it mapped onto her collection.

Briusov's appraisal of *Evening Album*, which soon followed in the popular *Russian Thought* (*Russkaia mysl'*), differed sharply from Voloshin's. Observing that the points of departure for Tsvetaeva's poems are concrete facts, details, and circumstances, Briusov also notes the intimacy of Tsvetaeva's verse. Unlike Voloshin, however, he sees it as a negative feature and calls it horrifying (*zhutkaia*) and embarrassing. "When you read her book, at times you feel discomfited, as if you had glanced through a half-closed window and observed a scene that an outsider ought not to have seen."[20] Briusov's review came in the thick of his explorations of the "psychology of the feminine soul" and works that included "Kind Al'd. The Story of a Female Slave" ("Dobryi Al'd. Rasskaz nevol'nitsy," 1906–10), stories and dramatic sketches of *Nights and Days* (*Nochi i dni*, 1908–12, pub. 1913), and "The Tale of an Obstetrician" ("Rasskaz akushera," 1909–10). Why the author of these voyeuristic, luridly misogynous works would find the childlike revelations of *Evening Album* discomfiting is not immediately apparent.

Briusov also sees the youthful quality of Tsvetaeva's verse that delighted Voloshin as a negative feature and decries the attention to detail that pleased Gumilev as a lapse into "some sort of 'household stuff'" (*v kakuiu-to "domashnost'"*).[21] The result, as Briusov opines, is "already not poetic creations . . . but simply the pages of a personal diary and fairly bland pages at that."[22] Briusov's "Last Pages from a Woman's Diary" ("Poslednie stranitsy iz dnevnika zhenshchiny") of the same year is unarguably spicier. It is perhaps the distance between his own French Decadence–inspired fictional women and the young, openhearted self-presentations in *Evening Album* that he finds difficult to bridge. "Disarmed" by Tsvetaeva's acknowledgments of her youth, Briusov registers the stern expectation that the details that she includes in her poems will become synthetic images, symbols common to all mankind, and not simply fleeting portraits of relatives and friends and recollections of her own apartment. We also expect that the poet will find in her soul feelings more sharp than those sweet trifles that take up so much space in *Evening Album* and thoughts more useful than the repetition of age-old truths.[23]

The review closes with words of warning: "Undoubtedly talented, Marina Tsvetaeva can give us genuine poetry of intimate life or can, given the ease with which she, as it seems, writes verse, squander her gift on unnecessary, albeit elegant trifles."[24]

The independence that Tsvetaeva demonstrated from the outset of her poetic career became a source of Briusov's unwavering antagonism toward her. In his memoirs, Khodasevich has this to say of the powerful poet and critic: "To manifest independence meant to gain an enemy once and for all in Briusov. A young poet who did not come to Briusov for evaluation and approval could be certain that Briusov would never forgive this. An example is Marina Tsvetaeva."[25] Briusov was not prepared to countenance Tsvetaeva's self-sufficiency. Tsvetaeva was not prepared to bow to his authority. If Voloshin's review fostered cordial relations between them, Briusov's raised her ire and prompted her to fire back with the poem "To V. Ia. Briusov" ("V. Ia. Briusovu"), which she included in her second collection, *Magic Lantern* (*Volshebnyi fonar'*, 1912). In "A Hero of Labor" Tsvetaeva described this poetic gesture in militant terms: "In a word, troops crossed the boundary. On such and such a date of such and such a year, I, a nobody, opened military action against Briusov" (4:24). Sarcastically repeating selected words and phrases from Briusov's review in her poem, Tsvetaeva publicly defies Briusov's weighty authority and mocks his injunctions. Moreover, she rejects the Symbolism over which he presided, ironizing its dark, theurgist vision.

> В. Я. Брюсову
>
> Улыбнись в мое «окно»,
> Иль к шутам меня причисли,—
> Не изменишь, всё равно!
> «Острых чувств» и «нужных мыслей»
> Мне от Бога не дано!
>
> Нужно петь, что все темно,
> Что над миром сны нависли . . .
> —Так теперь заведено.—
> Этих чувств и этих мыслей
> Мне от Бога не дано! (1:147)

To Briusov

Smile through my "window,"
Or count me among the jesters,—
You won't change me anyway!
"Sharp feelings" and "necessary thoughts"
Are not given me by God!

It is compulsory to sing that all is dark
That dreams threaten the world . . .
—That's how it's done now.—
These feelings and these thoughts
Are not given me by God!

In "A Hero of Labor" Tsvetaeva would write dismissively of this poem, choosing to focus on the response it elicited from Briusov (4:25). The lyric is important, however, because underpinning its declaration of war on Briusov is a subtextual tie with Karolina Pavlova's poem "Laterna magica" that gives Tsvetaeva the title of the collection in which her attack appeared—*Magic Lantern*.[26] Tsvetaeva was alive to biographical and literary affinities between herself and Pavlova, who, as Venclova insightfully describes, was particularly well suited to satisfy Tsvetaeva's need for "an authoritative model according to which she could compose the biography and image of a woman poet."[27] Pavlova remained important for Tsvetaeva for the duration of her poetic career. Indeed, as Venclova reminds us, Tsvetaeva "experienced such unabated interest in very few poets of the nineteenth century."[28] Tsvetaeva's protracted contentions with Briusov included challenges to the authority over Pavlova he established in an early essay devoted to her (1902), his publication of a two-volume edition of her works (1915), and his repeated citations of the lines

Моя напасть! мое богатство!
Мое святое ремесло!

My misfortune! my treasure!
My sacred craft!

from her poem "You, who have survived in my destitute heart" ("Ty, ut-selevshii v serdtse nishchem"). Tsvetaeva's choice of title for her 1923 poetry collection, *Craft* (*Remeslo*), is, among other things, a reclamation of these lines.[29]

Briusov's review of *Magic Lantern* was distinctly cooler than that of

Evening Album. Tsvetaeva, as he writes, persists in taking her themes "from the domain of narrowly intimate personal life," which makes her poems uninteresting to all but her closest friends.[30] He now faults her also for the alleged "carelessness of her verse."[31] Tsvetaeva fired back with a second poem titled "To V. Ia. Briusov," which she included in her third poetry collection, *From Two Books* (*Iz dvukh knig*) that came out in 1913, the year of Nelli's debut.

В. Я. Брюсову

Я забыла, что сердце в Вас—только ночник,
Не звезда! Я забыла об этом!
Что поэзия ваша из книг
И из зависти—критика. Ранний старик,
Вы опять мне на миг
Показались великим поэтом. (1:175)

To Briusov

I forgot that your heart is only a night-light,
Not a star! I forgot about that!
That your poetry comes from books
And your criticism from envy. Prematurely old man,
For a moment you again
Seemed like a great poet to me.

Briusov's harsh criticism of aspiring poets sparked accusations of the envy that Tsvetaeva invoked in this poem and that came to a full blaze in the aftermath of Nadezhda L'vova's suicide in 1913. Tsvetaeva's poem hit its mark. In the opening paragraph of a defensive essay titled "On the Treatment of Young Poets" ("Ob otnoshenii k molodym poetam"), written between July and November of 1913, Briusov refers to Tsvetaeva, without naming her: "One poetess even wrote that all my poetry comes / from books / And criticism from envy" (*Odna poetessa dazhe tak i napisala, chto vsia moia poeziia sozdana / iz knig / Da iz zavisti kritika*).[32]

The review essay "The Chill of Morning (A Few Words on Women's Creativity)" ("Kholod utra [Neskol'ko slov o zhenskom tvorchestve]"), which L'vova purportedly authored and which articulates ideas that coincide with Briusov's own, echoes his comments about *Evening Album*: "In most instances women's poetry does not succeed in attaining that boundary where the personal becomes universal, where the great Synthesis of experiences arises; in most cases the verse of nearly all the poets under consideration is so narrowly personal that one wants to repeat Briusov's harsh words: 'Her poems are interesting only to her good friends.'"[33]

The criticism that "The Chill of Morning" directs specifically at Tsvetaeva iterates also Briusov's reaction to *Magic Lantern*: "And the only thing that hinders Tsvetaeva is her incoherence, her disjointed feelings and sensations, the absence of that depth that we saw in Nelli and Akhmatova."[34] Regardless of who actually wrote it, "The Chill of Morning" shored up the credibility of the woman poet Briusov invented and the authority of his attack on Tsvetaeva by presenting Nelli, together with Akhmatova, as positive counterexamples to Tsvetaeva.[35] In his responses to Tsvetaeva's subsequent collections, Briusov continued to embed grudging praise in stern commentary on what her poetry lacks.

Her counterattacks on Briusov notwithstanding, Tsvetaeva took note of the criticism he leveled against her. Although perhaps he overstates his point, Bogomolov has reason to observe that "Briusov's opinion exerted serious influence on [Tsvetaeva's] entire subsequent evolution as a poet" and that "she feared above all to justify his prophecy about the possibility that she could 'squander her entire gift on unnecessary albeit elegant trifles.'"[36] Critical responses that noted a lack of growth in Tsvetaeva's second and third collections warranted concern. Here it is important to recall that at this time Briusov evinced a growing insecurity about his public image and the power he wielded in the literary arena. His efforts to maintain authority over a swiftly changing cultural landscape included exerting control over women's poetry, which manifested itself in his misogynistic writings, sexualizing mentorship of women poets, and in his invention of Nelli, which Akhmatova later described as Briusov's attempt to capitalize on the celebrity she (Akhmatova) had won with her early poetry.

In "A Hero of Labor," an essay that appears relatively early in her development as a prose writer, Tsvetaeva presents Briusov's criticism as energizing. Her rebellion against his authority features prominently in the self-image she projects in it. At the time of its composition, Tsvetaeva was at a crisis point,[37] and the essay, as Shevelenko describes, "was an effort to delineate her own early literary biography and to explain the particularities of her path in literature and her aesthetic position."[38] Countering Briusov, Tsvetaeva defines herself and her art in terms of a rebellion against a powerful authority figure. Bogomolov maintains that Tsvetaeva exaggerates Briusov's hostility to establish herself as that poet's equal.[39] The point is well taken. Indeed Tsvetaeva does more than this. To begin with, her essay manifests precisely that ability to create the "synthetic images, symbols common to all mankind, and not simply fleeting portraits of relatives and friends" that Briusov claimed were missing from her early verse.[40] More relevant to this study is that Tsvetaeva defines herself in terms of her resistance to an influential poet and critic who emblematizes the impediments women poets confront in their drive for creative self-realization and an equal place in the tradition.[41]

"A Hero of Labor" chronicles Tsvetaeva's actual, epistolary, and poetic contacts with Briusov. The six sections of part 1, "The Poet," describe her poetic beginnings, marked by her mounting opposition to Briusov's authority and his mounting hostility toward her. Part 2, "Revolution," jumps from 1912 to 1920, when Tsvetaeva is already an established poet. The title of the section refers to the political overthrow of the tsarist regime but also to Tsvetaeva's poetical overthrow of male authority, which she urges other women poets to emulate.

Tsvetaeva opens "A Hero of Labor" with the statement, "I loved Briusov's poems from the age of 16 to 17 with a passionate, brief love" (4:12). Despite the brevity of her infatuation, Briusov remained a consequential presence in her poetic self-invention and development. The essay casts him in the role of a stimulating source of contention—an incarnation of views on poetry and gender that are retrograde to her own. Situating herself beyond the mentorship that he extended to so many poetesses, Tsvetaeva challenges his authority over women's poetry and, more broadly, over the Pushkinian tradition as a whole. As is characteristic of Tsvetaeva's prose, "A Hero of Labor" features scrupulously chosen details and vignettes that are ever more meaningfully interconnected over the course of the essay. The discussion that follows centers on sections from both parts of the essay, selected to showcase strategies that Tsvetaeva develops to define herself and to enable women poets. I first look briefly at "Two Trifling Verses" ("Dva stishka"), which describes the start of Tsvetaeva's poetic career and her stand against Briusov. I then look more closely at "An Evening of Poetesses" ("Vecher poetess"), which repudiates Briusov's notions about gender and demonstrates that women poets have the option to refuse objectification. I close with a brief discussion of the last two sections of the essay. The slight inaccuracies in passages from poems that Tsvetaeva cites show that she is quoting from memory.[42] Her conscious modifications of facts shape the message she wishes to convey.

In "Two Trifling Verses" Tsvetaeva traces her early relations with Briusov, beginning with an account of her poetic debut that emphasizes how young she was at the time and how easy it was to publish a book in those days. Her claim that she did not send out any review copies of *Evening Album* is a prevarication intended to signal her lack of practical experience and her independence from outside guidance. It also makes the recognition she received from established poets of the time more remarkable. Tsvetaeva notes three of the four major reviews of her collection: Voloshin's "big article" (*bol'shaia stat'ia*), Marietta Shaginian's "article" (*stat'ia*), and

Briusov's "remark" (*zametka* [4:24]). Fifteen years intervened between the publication of Briusov's review and the composition of "A Hero of Labor," but Tsvetaeva captures the import and the tone of his criticism. This attests to the staying power of Briusov's pronouncement, which she renders in her essay as, "Mlle. Tsvetaeva's poems are possessed of a kind of terrifying intimacy, which at times makes one uncomfortable, as if one had inadvertently looked into the window of someone else's apartment" (4:24).

As noted, Briusov's reviews of her first two collections prompted her to respond with a pair of mocking poems—both titled "To V. Ia. Briusov"—which she published in her second and third collections, respectively, *Magic Lantern* and *From Two Books*. The title "Two Trifling Verses" refers to these mocking lyric rejoinders to Briusov's reviews of her first two poetry collections. Now—as she writes this essay—she sees her poetic volleys against Briusov as artistically negligible and freely acknowledges how much more meaningful the exchange was for her than for her antagonist. In the long final paragraph of this brief section of the essay, she emphasizes the asymmetry of their mutual hostility: "I did not like Briusov, he did not like someone from among the young poets who was, to boot, a woman, all of whom he disdained. This is not something I felt toward him—disdain, neither then at the height of his glory nor subsequently under its rubble" (4:24). Presenting the situation from Briusov's point of view, the now mature Tsvetaeva introduces a theme that she unfolds in part 2: Briusov's deep-seated contempt for women, which she features as symptomatic of his limitations as a poet.

In "Revolution," the influence that Briusov wields in Soviet Russia compromises him as a poet. Briusov now sides with the Bolsheviks, deriving authority and personal advantage from doing so but also revealing the shallowness of his commitment to poetic ideals he had previously espoused.[43] At this stage in the essay, Tsvetaeva has already come into her own. The neophyte's confrontational relations with Briusov now give way to the reflections of a mature, recognized poet for whom he is no longer an energizing adversary but a declining poet who has compromised himself. In the first section of part 2, the reader sees Briusov bar the destitute Tsvetaeva from publication that would have provided her family with scant but desperately needed sustenance in a demonstration of the power that Briusov gains by supporting the new regime and the price that Tsvetaeva pays for preserving her poetic integrity.[44] In the second section, Tsvetaeva reproduces what she insists is the unedited text of Ariadna ("Alia") Efron's diary entry. Her precocious seven-year-old daughter's account of a poetry reading in which Tsvetaeva and Briusov participated describes how the child, upon recognizing Briusov, immediately begins to recite those very poems with which her seventeen-year-old mother had challenged his authority. This interpolated passage carries a characteristically rich polyfunctionality in Tsvetaeva's essay. Alia's rebelliousness, her incisive descriptions of Briusov, and the wariness with which Briusov skirts the disconcerting child capture in miniature Tsvetaeva's relations with him: "Telle mère, telle fille" (4:34). In Alia, Tsvetaeva sees her own temperament and values perpetuated: "But there was in this challenge, besides revenge for me, something that she inherited from me and that I immediately recognized—*the love of enmity*" (4:35, emphasis in the original). This is one of the many examples of how Tsvetaeva accentuates matrilineal ties to counterbalance the paternalistic tradition. Her daughter's challenge to Briusov is also Tsvetaeva's challenge to the matrophobia of Symbolist philosophers and of Briusov himself. Like her description of holding her daughter while waiting onstage to read her poems, Tsvetaeva's embrace of her daughter's text in her own marks her defiance of the tenacious prejudice that creativity and maternity are mutually exclusive. At the same time, this demonstrative maternity counters sexualization and establishes a bond among women.

This brings "A Hero of Labor" to a section titled "An Evening of Poetesses," in which, as Alexandra Smith summarizes, Tsvetaeva "actively rises up against the criteria of creativity artificially foisted onto women writers."[45] The evening in question was a poetry reading by nine women poets organized and headed by Briusov on December 11, 1920, at the Polytechnic Museum in Moscow. Tsvetaeva, who is now above rebelling against him, presents details that expose his weaknesses and discredit his views on women. Carefully prepared by the sections leading up to it, this part of Tsvetaeva's essay promotes women poets' selfhood and shows by example how to establish it. The goal is not to incite women to rebel but to raise their conscious awareness of the situation and how they can resist it. Having thrown doubt on Briusov's poetic acumen in earlier sections of her essay, Tsvetaeva continues to undercut the authority that he wields and that, as she accentuates, women themselves voluntarily uphold.

Tsvetaeva's account of the events relating to the "Evening of Poetesses" urges women to push past the normalized suppression of their creative self-realization and promotes their advancement from muses to active poets. Eschewing abstraction and generalization, the detailed scenes she provides also enhance her readers' awareness. Thus, for example, the invitation to participate in the "Evening of Poetesses" is brought to Tsvetaeva by a woman who introduces herself as Adalis.[46] The brief and seemingly insignificant conversation between them that Tsvetaeva records speaks volumes. Seeing that her name means nothing to Tsvetaeva, Adalis explains that all of Moscow has heard of her and offers a revealing self-identification: "Adalis, with whom—who . . . I am the one to whom all of Valerii Iakovlevich's [Briusov's] latest poems are dedicated" (4:36). Registered here is an alienation from the literary mainstream that gains Tsvetaeva the perspective of a detached observer who is better prepared to recognize what others routinely accept. More importantly, the fact that Adalis chooses to define herself—however euphemistically—as Briusov's current paramour registers the voluntary surrender of her creative identity to Briusov's mentorship and concomitant sexualization. It is this surrender, as the reader can infer, that prompts Tsvetaeva to speak of Adalis as a poetess and not a poet. Opposite the poetess who subjects herself to Briusov stands the poet who defies him.

Significantly, Tsvetaeva does not pass judgment on Adalis and remains well disposed toward her and her poetry, thus dispelling the tension that threatens to arise between women vying for the attention of authoritative male figures. In any event, Briusov's animosity toward Tsvetaeva obviates such competition and fosters friendly ties between the two women. "He cannot stand you," Adalis twice insists (4:36). Framed by these iterations of Briusov's enmity toward Tsvetaeva is a brief, meaningful dialogue from which it emerges that Tsvetaeva prefers to live in extreme poverty rather than court political favor. She does not bend her art to the service of the state for personal gain, as had Briusov, who joined the Party in 1920 and organized the literary division of the Soviet Ministry of Education (*Narkompros*). The promise of remuneration that induces her to accept Adalis's invitation to read at the projected "Evening of Poetesses" is a gesture of maternal self-sacrifice exacted by her role of breadwinner for the family. Responsible action and the material unprofitability of the practice of her art combine to create the image of a woman who sacrifices herself to the demands of her art and the needs of her child.

In the opening section of part 2 Tsvetaeva describes Briusov wielding his power in the new regime to bar a manuscript that, in her desperate need for money, she submitted to him for publication. It now emerges that Adalis was present when Briusov received the manuscript in question. "I regard her highly as a poet," she quotes him as saying, "but I cannot stand her as a woman, and I will never let her get through!" (4:36). Whether or not this is what Briusov actually said or Adalis reported to Tsvetaeva is immaterial here. What matters is that Tsvetaeva is setting up her quarrel with Briusov on the question of gender. "But it was a poet who offered the poems and not a woman!" she protests to Adalis, who immediately agrees and asks what happened between them. Tsvetaeva fills her in: "I relate, laughing, what the reader already knows" (4:36).

This brings us to another crucial facet of Tsvetaeva's project—the conspiratorial relationship she establishes with her reader, who is, after all, the primary target of her persuasion. At this point in the essay, the reader, who knows more than Adalis, is prompted to think back to what Tsvetaeva related in part 1. The laughter that now accompanies Tsvetaeva's account to Adalis shows that her youthful antagonism toward Briusov has shed its significance. Briusov, on the other hand, proves incapable of getting past his antipathy toward the woman Tsvetaeva to publish the poet he grudgingly acknowledges in her. Briusov as he is now—a vindictive servant of the state—justifies Tsvetaeva's instinctual antipathy toward him at the start of her poetic career. This discredits him and authorizes her as a poet.

Their brief conversation draws Adalis and Tsvetaeva together. Anticipating Adalis's complaint that everyone assumes Briusov edits her poems, Tsvetaeva commends her creative individuality: "And the poems are good, not at all Briusovian" (4:37). This is important. Tsvetaeva, who has already established her independence from Briusov's authority, underscores that Adalis has a unique poetic voice of her own. She has no need of male mentorship but, like other women poets who appear in Tsvetaeva's essay, has yet to realize this. Tsvetaeva urges women poets to claim independence of male authority and to move beyond the enmity and atomization spawned in paternalistic environments to enter into supportive sororal ties with one another. Briusov's relations with Adalis emblematize the sexualization attendant on the male mentor's dominant role, but Tsvetaeva's focus here is less on Briusov's culpability than on Adalis's unquestioning acceptance of this situation, shown in her voluntary self-identification not as a poet in her own right but in terms of her subordinate position vis-à-vis Briusov. With this shift of attention from the male establishment to the woman poet's unthinking support of its deleterious norms, Tsvetaeva urges the woman poet to take responsible action to effect positive change.

The seemingly artless conversation with Adalis that Tsvetaeva records lays the groundwork for putting the woman poet on equal footing with men. The account of the "Evening of Poetesses" develops this further. Between the conversation with Adalis, who delivers the invitation, and the evening itself Tsvetaeva interjects her own powerful statement on gender, folding it into a far-reaching repudiation of all divisions and binaries. This allows her to absorb questions of gender into her definition of poetry as an all-encompassing phenomenon that demands an all-embracing wholeness of vision from the poet. Recalling her refusal to participate in another women's poetry reading of the sort to which Adalis invites her, Tsvetaeva explains,

> I had already refused one such "woman's inspection" in 1916, believing that in poetry there are more essential indicators of demarcation than belonging to either the male or the female sex and disdaining from birth everything that smacked of women's (mass) separateness, like: women's courses, suffragism, feminism, Salvation Army, the whole renowned woman's question. (4:38)

In the context of the expansive sweep of Tsvetaeva's pronouncement, Briusov's penchant for categorization is strikingly limited and limiting:

But Briusov, this man in poetry par excellence, this lover of sex apart from the human, this nonlover of souls, this: right-left, black-white, man-woman, was naturally tempted by such divisions and effects. We have only to remember *Nelli's Poems*—his anonymous book in the name of a woman, which betrayed its author precisely by its soullessness, and the—amazing in its impoverishment of feeling—introduction to the poems of Karolina Pavlova. And he was tempted not only by the division man-woman but by all divisions, delimitations, splits, by everything that is subject to numeral and graph. (4:38)

Rather than enter into contest with Briusov, as she had earlier in her career, Tsvetaeva discounts him. Briusov's efforts to penetrate women's creative space document his shortcomings as a poet—not because he fails to write like a woman but because the very idea of doing so stems from an emphatically unpoetical predilection for binaries. This informs her denunciation of Briusov's othering of the woman:

His entire life Briusov was curious about women. He was drawn to them, was curious about them and did not love them. And the secret of his striking lack of success in anything that concerns the feminine Psyche lies precisely in this excessive curiosity, in this further splitting off of something already tragically split, in the excision of the woman from the human sphere, in this artificial isolation, in her bewitched circle that he himself created. (4:39)

Tsvetaeva's judgment of Briusov conveys her own position on gender and poetry. As she zooms out from the particulars of her conversation with Adalis, she prompts her reader to reflect more broadly on what those details convey. Earlier in the essay Tsvetaeva had indicated that Briusov's response to her early verse betrayed a flaw in his poetic acumen. She now indicts Briusov for his proclivity for binaries that cuts him off from women and excludes him from the all-encompassing realm of genuine poetry.

Tsvetaeva's objections to Briusov expand steadily over the course of the essay, moving from her personal relations with him to challenge his authority over women's writing, over the literary arena, and, more broadly still, over the Pushkinian tradition. Yet to deny Briusov authority is not yet to gain the woman poet agency. Tsvetaeva persists in her two-pronged strategy, subverting the gender binary and urging women to deny male poets dominance over their creativity. The essay now moves from Adalis's uncritical acceptance of Briusov's sexualization in private conversation to a public spectacle in which women poets willingly participate in their own objectification. In Tsvetaeva's description of the poetry reading, which she calls an exhibition (*vystavka* [4:40]), the word "poetess" appears with marked frequency in various grammatical forms. Tsvetaeva applies it specifically to women who court the male gaze with their attire, which is inappropriate for the bitter cold of the un-heated auditorium and lavish by the standards of economically impoverished Soviet Russia of the 1920s. The women, among whom is "a beauty with no poems at all" (4:41), gather onstage and readily exhibit themselves before an unruly audience of young military men. "I look at the poetesses: they are blue. The hall is three degrees below freezing, and not one throws on a coat. Here it is, the heroism of beauty" (4:41–42).

Tsvetaeva's own heroism is of a different order. She stands apart from the prettified women who crowd the stage. Clad in a shapeless green gar-ment cinched tightly at the waist with a military belt, a military binocular case slung over her shoulder, she defies sexualization and issues a sartorial challenge to the gender binary:

> My legs in gray felt boots, though not men's and well fitted, surrounded by little patent leather pumps, looked like the pillars of an elephant. My whole attire, on the strength of its very monstrosity, removed any suspicion of inten-tionality ("ne peut pas qui veut"). They praised the slenderness of my waist, remained silent about the belt. On the whole, I would say that in the world of narcotic poetry professionals [fem.] that was alien to me, I was met with kind-ness. Women are, on the whole, kinder. Men forgive neither the hungry chil-dren nor the felt boots. (4:40)

Even as Tsvetaeva distinguishes herself from the other women in the group, she insists on the kindness that they, in contradistinction to men, extend to her. As in her earlier conversation with Adalis, she sets herself apart but avoids adversarial relations with other women. The goal is not to condemn "poetesses" but to show them how to become poets.

Tsvetaeva's stylized, parodic version of Briusov's introductory remarks to the crowd, which has come not to listen to poetry but to gape at the women onstage, foregrounds a tenacious gender bias that she determines to dispel. Three words dominate in Briusov's speech as Tsvetaeva presents it, reflecting the narrow creative zone that he demarcates for women and his deindividuation of women poets:

> Woman. Love. Passion. Woman, from the beginning of time, knew how to sing only of love and passion. The only passion of a woman is love. Every love of a woman is passion. Outside of love, a woman is nothing in art. Take pas-sion away from a woman . . . Woman . . . Love . . . Passion . . .[47]
> And now, comrades, you will hear nine Russian poetesses, differing per-haps in tone, but in essence the same, for, I repeat, the woman is not yet able to sing about anything but love and passion. The performances will be in al-phabetical order (4:42, 43).

The poems read that evening prove Briusov wrong. Tsvetaeva's are about the White Guard, Adalis's are descriptive, other women read poems about machines and nature. But Briusov's authority is undermined already before the reading begins. Upon completing his introduction, he finds himself in an awkward situation as one woman after another refuses to read first. Just before he turns to her, Tsvetaeva volunteers to begin. Relieved, the discomfited master of ceremonies announces, "Comrades, the first to perform (an emphatic pause) is the *poet* Tsvetaeva" (4:43, emphasis in the original). Here Tsvetaeva has Briusov himself distinguish her as a poet. This stands out with exceptional force in light of his antagonism toward Tsvetaeva, his refusal to publish her verse, and his iterations of the word "poetess," which he applies even to Akhmatova (4:42). Most immediately, this mark of distinction shows his gratitude to Tsvetaeva for rescuing him from an awkward situation. In the larger scheme of things, it shows the immediate success of Tsvetaeva's refusal to court objectification and to act shy. The underlying message is straightforward: to advance to the status of poet, the woman has only to refuse to play the role of "poetess."

The restless audience that Briusov proved unable to quiet immediately falls silent when Tsvetaeva takes the stage. Determined to disprove Briusov's characterization of women poets, she defiantly reads her cycle extolling the White Army *The River Don* (*Don*, 1912) to the Red Army soldiers who fill the auditorium. The pronoun "I," as Tsvetaeva apprises her reader, like the words "love" and "passion," is conspicuously absent from the seven poems she chooses to read. Tsvetaeva enfolds this sabotage of Briusov's gender bias in what she describes as a *debt of honor* (*dolg chesti* [4:44; emphasis in the original]) that prompts her to sing the defeated cause to which her husband—then missing in action—devoted himself. The rebelliousness and disruptiveness that Tsvetaeva sees as essential to the poet's constitution are in full evidence here, spanning gender and politics alike.[48]

Tsvetaeva closes with the poem "Placing My Hand on My Heart" ("Ruku ná serdtse polozha"), whose exclamations "Yes, hurrah!—For the tsar!—Hurrah" (4:44), make it a daring choice to recite before her audience of Red soldiers. The triumph of Tsvetaeva's reading and of the poetic precepts she advances in the essay comes in the form of the tumultuous applause with which her unlikely auditors respond to the poem. This reaction is proof positive of the power of poetry to overarch all divisions. "In this poem was my union with the auditorium, with all auditoriums and squares of the world, my ultimate trust covering all differences, the upward flight of all caps—whether Phrygian or familial—above all fortresses and prisons—I myself—the very I" (4:45). Poet and poetry transcend all boundaries and divisions. Tsvetaeva's enactment of her creative selfhood and the poetic principles from which it stems overarches all binaries.

At this point, the discomfited Briusov tells Tsvetaeva that she has read enough and invites Adalis to take the stage. Referring to Adalis as "comrade," Briusov underscores his own political allegiance as distinct from Tsvetaeva's and pulls back from his sexualizing mentorship of Adalis, whose appearance at the podium exemplifies yet another sort of heroism. Frankly pregnant with Briusov's child, Adalis defies the smirks and guffaws that her figure provokes in the audience. As she reads, the crowd's attention turns from her body to her verse in another demonstration of poetry overcoming mere surface appearances. Adalis's pregnancy, her assertion upon finishing her reading that "it is beginning" (4:46), and Briusov's refusal to believe that she is going into labor are lightly sketched in Tsvetaeva's essay, but the underlying import runs deep. Symbolist philosophers' insistence on the mutual exclusivity of creativity and birthing exacerbated the long-standing bias that women's creative self-realization was incompatible with maternity. The presence of Tsvetaeva's daughter in "A Hero of Labor"—both in her mother's description and in the excerpt from her diary that appears in the essay—is augmented here by the image of Adalis, who, on the verge of giving birth, overcomes the mockery of her untutored male audience with her poems. Even as she upholds the contested compatibility of mother and poet, Tsvetaeva shifts the emphasis from gender to the power of poetry to override it.

Tsvetaeva closes "An Evening of Poetesses" with a formulation of her attitude to Briusov that highlights her own span of antinomies: "And in the sincere guise of hatred, I simply loved Briusov, only in that form of love (repulsion) more strongly than I would have loved him in its simplest form of attraction" (4:54). As Tsvetaeva knew when she was writing "A Hero of Labor," the evening her essay describes took place on the eve of attacks that, beginning in 1922, the Soviet press launched against women poets, and (male) poets she admired—Mayakovsky and Mandel'shtam among them— joined vituperative critics to condemn her verse. Tsvetaeva was reviled as a woman, as the wife of a White Army officer, and—after she left Russia that year—as an émigré. Repercussions of the wave of government-sponsored misogyny reached her even abroad.

Two more sections follow "An Evening of Poetesses" in the essay, which gradually zooms out to offer an expansive perspective. In "Briusov and Bal'mont," Tsvetaeva continues her defense of maternity by responding to Briusov's matrophobic poem "The Woman" ("Zhenshchina," 1901),[49] which presents birthing in negative images and describes the mother turning into a beast. This, as the poem sternly presages, is the fate in store for the young ladies who now grace the ballroom like butterflies, but who are destined to become animals. In her early essay "Enchantment in Briusov's Poems," Tsvetaeva noted the comparison of young women with butterflies in this poem with pleasure and made no mention of the harshly drawn birthing in it. She now rises to defend maternity and to discredit Briusov—both as an individual and as an emblem of male authority.

Citing offensive passages in Briusov's poem, Tsvetaeva counters them with a single exclamation of disbelief: "This about motherhood, which *cleanses* everything!" (4:54; emphasis in the original). With this affirmation of the transcendent power of maternity, Tsvetaeva complements her earlier affirmation of the transcendent power of poetry illustrated by the pregnant Adalis overcoming the ridicule of her male audience with her verse. Motherhood serves a triple purpose in Tsvetaeva's essay in that it (1) highlights the falseness of Briusov's notions about women, (2) defies the claim that birthing and creativity are mutually exclusive, and (3) shows maternity elevating the woman above sexualization and aligning her with poetry itself. Beyond undermining Briusov's authority, Tsvetaeva transforms maternity, which was used to denigrate the woman poet, into a banner of her ascendancy.

Tsvetaeva's juxtaposition of Briusov's willfulness and somberness with Bal'mont's abandon and playfulness in this section of "A Hero of Labor" reinforces the Pushkinian theme that courses through her commemoration of the self-styled Pushkin of the twentieth century. Invoking the contrast between Salieri, the determined dissector of music, and the all-embracing Mozart of Pushkin's "Little Tragedy," Tsvetaeva builds on the comparisons of Briusov to Salieri that arose in the wake of Nadezhda L'vova's suicide.[50] Bringing the grave side of Briusov's trivial penchant for division and demarcation to the fore, Tsvetaeva counters Briusov's destructivity with her own creativity.[51] In "Final Words" ("Poslednie slova"), the concluding section of the essay, she displaces Briusov and claims the title of Pushkin for herself: "Briusov will remain in the world, but not as a poet, rather as the hero of a long poem. Just as Salieri remained on the strength of Pushkin's creative will" (4:62). Not simply the Mozart to Briusov's Salieri, Tsvetaeva is the Pushkin who authors him.

Tsvetaeva's fierce individuality makes it clear that her definition of poetry as all-encompassing does not involve the loss or devaluation of distinctive features and particularity. The created self who emerges from "A Hero of Labor" is unique and complex: poet, self-sacrificing mother, sartorial androgyne, loyal wife, and political dissident whose multifaceted constitution documents her determination to act in accordance with her own ideals and not expectations that are projected onto her. Tsvetaeva derives support for her position from Pavlova and Rostopchina, whose dissimilar strategies of enablement she absorbs productively into her own. She embraces Pavlova's resistance to categorizing poets by gender and her insistence that women assume responsibility for themselves. She echoes Rostopchina's defiant assertion that women are superior to men and by their very nature closer to the phenomenon of poetry. These strategies appear in various guises throughout

Tsvetaeva's mature work. They appear in another, markedly different instantiation in her commemoration of Maximilian Voloshin.

Tsvetaeva, who was in French emigration when news of Voloshin's death reached her, responded with the essay "The Living about the Living" ("Zhivoe o zhivom," 1932). The Voloshin who emerges from this essay differs dramatically from the Briusov of "A Hero of Labor." In contrast to Briusov, with his penchant for divisions and categorizations, his inability to comprehend women, and his poetic failings, Voloshin is a larger-than-life, all-embracing androgynous poet. He is a friend to women writers, and his relations with them are free from objectification inasmuch as he penetrates outward appearances to apprehend the woman's creative inner self. Having pushed away from Briusov, Tsvetaeva shows herself and Voloshin in a capacious, mutually reinforcing embrace that effaces nothing of either his distinctiveness or her own.

For all the dissimilarities between her portraits of her first two reviewers, there is a clear continuity in the creative self that Tsvetaeva presents in these essays, in the defense of women and women's poetry she advances in them, and in the active engagement with her text in which she tutors her reader. Characteristically, "The Living about the Living" does not unfold in linear fashion. Harnessing the power of context to shape and reshape meaning, Tsvetaeva offers her reader not static, individual snapshots but dynamic intercontextualizations of the material from which her ideas and arguments develop. With the mutability of signification that this reflects, she leads her reader to expanded ways of seeing and reading signs. In place of clearly demarcated stages of a logical argument crowned with unambiguous results, Tsvetaeva gives a nuanced demonstration of shifting perspectives and fluidity of meaning that celebrates complexity and enlarges understanding. As in "A Hero of Labor," in "The Living about the Living" she builds her essay around personal interactions with her subject. She is again an astute reader of signs who captures seemingly insignificant, random details of the surrounding world and traces their far-reaching ramifications. The defense of maternity, the erosion of the gender binary, and the reenvisioning of women that Tsvetaeva advances in her essay to Briusov are integral also to "The Living about the Living." The basic premise remains that poet and poetry are all-embracing. Voloshin, who embodies hallmarks of the genuine poet, stands as a positive counterexample to Briusov, who receives passing mention in "The Living about the Living." Seven years intervene between the compositions of the two essays, yet her first two reviewers remained linked in Tsvetaeva's memory. The discussion that follows traces prominent themes from "A Hero of Labor" that figure—now in new guises—in the essay to Voloshin.

"The Living about the Living" opens with vigorous, mythologizing images of Voloshin and the poet who authors him. Noting the appropriateness of the time (midday) and place (the ancient Koktebel') of Voloshin's death, Tsvetaeva situates him in "Magic, mythics, and mysticism of the earth itself, of the earth's very components" (4:160). She shows herself striding at his side over Koktebelian mountaintops under the blazing Crimean sun—Voloshin's equal and equally at home in the mythic landscape he traverses. Having established their parity, Tsvetaeva goes back in time to describe the start of their friendship when he was an established poet and she a neophyte.

In "A Hero of Labor" Tsvetaeva claims that she sent out no review copies of *Evening Album*. In "The Living about the Living," she similarly makes Voloshin's discovery of her verse appear unassisted by neglecting to mention the copy she gave him. As she describes it, Voloshin appears unexpectedly in her home with his review, which had appeared a month earlier but which she had not seen. Like others of Tsvetaeva's deviations from fact, these are purposeful. That she knows nothing of Voloshin's unsolicited review underscores her distance from the literary mainstream and her independence from it. Tsvetaeva now folds Voloshin's review, "Women's Poetry," into the affirmation of women's creative agency that figures prominently in her essay. Her self-presentation is, again, highly individualistic and yet also illustrative of the possibility available to all women. Tsvetaeva rejects objectifying male mentorship in favor of a gender-neutral friendship of equals. The differences in their years and gender do not presuppose an inequality in poetic status. A defense of infusing the tradition with new blood is part of the picture, and the fact that Voloshin is older and already established gains him no advantage over Tsvetaeva. She has much to offer her fellow poet. Like Rostopchina's poems to Pushkin, Tsvetaeva's essay to Voloshin frames her youth and inexperience as an asset. Indeed, if Pavlova offers Tsvetaeva a model of individual responsibility and stoicism, Rostopchina offers a precedent for a woman poet to claim equality and even ascendancy in the tradition.

The motifs of myth, male mentorship, and women's writing that Tsvetaeva interweaves in "The Living about the Living" come together in her account of the Cherubina de Gabriak mystification, the story of which Voloshin recounted to Tsvetaeva and her sister Anastasia early in their friendship. In contradistinction to Briusov's Nelli, whom she pointedly shrugs off, de Gabriak attracts Tsvetaeva's serious attention. Sibelan Forrester perceptively distinguishes three roles that Tsvetaeva assigns to the interpolated story of Cherubina in the essay: "It memorializes the recently deceased Voloshin and his support for women poets as well as his own love of pretense, it recovers Cherubina de Gabriak from oblivion, and it sets up Tsvetaeva's resemblance to and difference from Cherubina."[52] These three functions inform the following discussion.

Tsvetaeva responds to the mystification with praise that upholds her characterization of Voloshin as an insightful, supportive friend to women poets. Situating Cherubina amid characters from works with which Voloshin acquainted her, Tsvetaeva speaks of her as a fictional poetess rather than a poet: "Another gift from Max, besides Consuela, Joseph Balsamo, and the Misérables—not to forget the delightful woman's book *The Tragic Zoo* and the excellent Axël—was the gift to me of the living heroine of a living poet, the heroine of her own poem: the poetess Cherubina de Gabriak" (4:169). In her brief summary of the mystification, Tsvetaeva isolates details of Voloshin's account and imbues the story with significance of her own. Thus she repeats Voloshin's description of Dmitrieva as an unprepossessing schoolteacher with a limp but trains attention on the rebelliousness that she conveys to her charges, who declare Grishka Otrep'ev, the false pretender to Boris Godunov's throne, as their favorite tsar.[53] Voloshin's account of Dmitrieva's growing fear of her dissimilar double attracts Tsvetaeva's particular attention. Crediting Voloshin with understanding the tragic rupture between Dmitrieva's exceptional poetic gift and her unexceptional appearance, Tsvetaeva elaborates on this unfortunate situation. Positioning Dmitrieva among distinguished women writers of various nationalities, she underscores the universality of the problem:

First and foremost, he understood that schoolteacher so-and-so and her poems—steeds, cloaks, swords,—did not coincide and would never coincide. That the gods who gave her her essence, gave her the opposite of this essence: her face and life. That here, before him was the always tragic, and here even catastrophic union of soul and body. Not a union, but a rupture. A rupture of which she cannot but be conscious and from which she cannot but suffer, as ceaselessly suffered: George Eliot, Charlotte Brontë, Julie de Lespinasse, Mary Webb, and other, and other, and other unbeautiful women beloved of the gods. The unbeautifulness of the face and life, which cannot but impede her in her gift: in the free self-revelation of her soul . . . I cannot love a self like that, I cannot live with a self like that. *This* I is not I. (4:169–70; emphasis in the original)

With her praise of Voloshin for acknowledging the unjust demand that the writing woman be beautiful, Tsvetaeva lodges her own protest against such demands:

Maximilian Voloshin knew people; that is, he knew their complete mercilessness, that—human—and especially male—completely unjustified demandingness, that most cruel injustice of not seeking soul in a beauty but inevitably demanding beauty from a clever woman,—intelligent and dull witted, old and young, handsome and ugly—but demanding nothing from a woman except beauty. And beauty inescapably. Beautiful women are loved, unbeautiful women are not loved. (4:170)

Tsvetaeva trusts Voloshin's good intentions but subtly rejects the mystification, which caters to this injustice. She credits him with inventing a guise for Dmitrieva that is in keeping with her poetic gift but does so against the backdrop of her own comportment that appears earlier in the essay. In "A Hero of Labor," Tsvetaeva's attire differentiates her from the poetesses at the "Evening of Poetry" who court objectification to secure male approval. In "The Living about the Living," she similarly distinguishes herself from the Dmitrieva of Voloshin's story who caters to male expectations to the detriment of her selfhood. In the account of her first meeting with Voloshin, Tsvetaeva describes herself wearing glasses and a cap that covers her shaved head. Making no effort to appeal to the male eye, the youthful self that Tsvetaeva presents to her reader instinctively eludes objectification. She experiences neither the tension between her creative self and outward appearance that inspires the exotic Cherubina de Gabriak and her extravagant poems nor the split that shatters Dmitrieva. This wholeness authorizes Tsvetaeva as a genuine poet. The seemingly inconsequential details of how she looked when she first met Voloshin is a self-affirmation that obviates the need to falsify her identity. Significantly—and this is to Voloshin's credit—Tsvetaeva's refusal to court the male gaze is the foundation of their poetic friendship. As in "A Hero of Labor," in "The Living about the Living," Tsvetaeva urges women to disregard expectations imposed on them, to remain true to their creative selves, and to trust in the power of poetry to transcend mere surface appearances. As she explains in "A Hero of Labor,"

There is no woman's question in art: there are women's answers to the human questions, like: Sappho, Joan of Arc, Saint Teresa, Bettina Brentano. There are delightful women's outcries (*Lettres de M-elle Lespinasse*), there is women's thought (Maria Bashkirtseva), there is the woman's brush (Rosa Bonheur), *but these are all individuals who did not even suspect that there was a woman's question and were destroying it (destroyed it) with this non-suspicion* (4:38; emphasis added).

In "The Living about the Living," the mature Tsvetaeva presents the budding author of *Evening Album* as similarly unsuspecting of the woman's question, which is to say innocent of prevailing constructs of gender and subject only to the dictates of her art.

In keeping with her self-definition as a born poet, Tsvetaeva shows her young self instinctually enacting ideals that she subsequently manifests in her poetry and explicates in her prose. She shows, too, how over the years these instinctual gestures develop into conscious choices. As in "A Hero of Labor," in "The Living about the Living," Tsvetaeva enjoins women to disregard societal norms, melding this exhortation with the responsibility she assigns all poets to remain impervious to external demands on their art. Unlike Dmitrieva, who agrees to masquerade as Cherubina de Gabriak and to assume a forged identity that responds to male fantasies rather than to her own creative needs, Tsvetaeva holds to her own world. Voloshin is her friend, not her mentor, and when he invites her to create new mystifications with him, she adamantly refuses. Implicit in "The Living about the Living" is the suggestion that Dmitrieva might have channeled the rebelliousness that Tsvetaeva approvingly registers into resisting the beautiful woman aesthetic to which she capitulates. Significantly, Tsvetaeva does not condemn Dmitrieva for participating in the mystification any more than she does Voloshin for instigating it. Instead, she provides an enabling rereading of Voloshin's story, acknowledging the pressures imposed on writing women and his good intentions. She then proceeds to use the mystification to advance the claim that women are better than men as de Staël and Rostopchina had before her.

"And so began the epoch of Cherubina de Gabriak" (4:172), Tsvetaeva summarizes. This "epoch" runs aground on the callousness of the surrounding world and proves to be short-lived. In her retelling, the mystification emerges as a cautionary tale: the guise invented for Dmitrieva's benefit ultimately destroys her. Not content with the image of the beautiful, exotic woman that the poems call up in their imaginations, Cherubina's readers succumb to an overwhelming need to see her in the flesh. This leads the love-smitten staff of *Apollo* to find Dmitrieva out—with disastrous consequences for her:

> They wanted to see, she—to hide. And so—they saw, that is tracked her down, that is exposed her. Called her like a sleepwalker and with this call threw her from the tower of her own Cherubinian castle—onto the pavement of her former everyday life against which she shattered. (4:172)

As Tsvetaeva goes on to describe in keeping with Voloshin's version of the story, "This was the end of Cherubina. She did not write anymore. Maybe she wrote, but no one read her anymore, no one heard her voice anymore. But I know that her friendship with M. V. had no end" (4:172). Tsvetaeva distinguishes Voloshin, that "impeccable friend of so many women's souls" (4:168), from the Apollonians, whose desire to see Cherubina destroys Dmitrieva. In Tsvetaeva's account, the androgynous Voloshin's feminine characteristics allow him to penetrate the woman's soul, to recognize Dmitrieva's creative gift, and to be a true friend rather than a sexualizing mentor. But she also makes it clear that the mystification in which he involved Dmitrieva is ultimately detrimental.

Rather than repudiate the beautiful woman aesthetic that fueled the mystification and was in turn upheld by it, Tsvetaeva adduces it as proof that women are poets by nature. Because they penetrate surface appearances, her argument runs, women neither objectify those around them nor require physical proof of the intangible, as men do. In "A Hero of Labor," Tsvetaeva notes how kindly the prettified poetesses whom she does not in the least resemble treat her in contrast to the men, who, as she puts it, forgive neither her felt boots nor her hungry child. Here in "The Living about the Living," where men do not forgive Dmitrieva her homeliness and humble profession, Tsvetaeva develops her argument more forcefully:

> Can E. I. D. [herself] hope for the love that her soul and gift perforce elicit? Would those who love the latter love the former? To that I will answer: yes. Women and great, really great poets, well and—great poets!—let us recall Pushkin, who loved an inanimate object—Goncharova. So, then, only women. (4:170)

Free from the propensity to objectify that Tsvetaeva observes even in Pushkin, women rise above the greatest of all Russian poets. Presupposed in this argument is also its converse: by objectifying women, men devalue themselves.

Tsvetaeva ascribes the difference in how men and women relate to the surrounding world to the tyranny of the visual in men's comprehension, which arrests their attention on the merely apparent to the detriment of the essential that women readily apprehend. According to Tsvetaeva, "Women—in whom vision does not predominate over the other senses as it does in men—move freely beyond the visible into the visionary."[54] This makes them more penetrating readers of literary texts, people, and the world around them. With her emphasis in her writings on her poor eyesight and her alleged lack of interest in the visual arts, Tsvetaeva situates herself in this privileged category.[55]

Having presented women as superior to men, Tsvetaeva poses questions that indicate also what they lack, prompting them to rectify this deficiency: "But does a girl think of women's friendship when she thinks of love, and does the girl think of anything but love?" (4:170). With these questions, Tsvetaeva directs women away from fulfilling men's expectations, courting sexualization, and competing for male approval toward establishing supportive relationships among themselves. Rather than perpetuate conditions that are inhospitable to their creative self-realization, women can come together in the poetic domain that is rightfully theirs.

Tsvetaeva devotes a sizable portion of "The Living about the Living" to the Cherubina de Gabriak mystification. The homage she pays Voloshin in this context presents him as a model for how poets who are men should relate to poets who are women. If Briusov's incapacity to understand women is proof of his poetical failings, Voloshin's embrace of the feminine validates him as a true poet. His sensitive relations with women are a positive counterexample to Briusov's tyrannical, sexualizing mentorship, a point that Tsvetaeva foregrounds with her explanation of why she dwells on the mystification:

> To present Max in his true sphere of feminine and poetic souls and fates. Max in the life of women and poets was *providentiel*, when, as in the case of Cherubina, Adelaida Gertsyk, and me, it turned out that the woman was a poet, or, what is more accurate, the poet was a woman, there was no end to his friendship, solicitude, patience, attentiveness, devotion, and cocreation. (4:173)

Poetry overarches gender. Opposite Briusov's penchant for binaries and boundaries is Voloshin's all-embracing wholeness—"That unity that contained everything and that everything that was unity" (4:174).

In "A Hero of Labor," Tsvetaeva upheld Adalis's authorship by assuring her that her poems sound nothing like Briusov's. In "The Living about the Living," she refutes the notion that Voloshin authored Cherubina's verse: "There are no poems more dissimilar than Voloshin's and Cherubina's. For he, so feminine in life, is in his poetry—entirely masculine" (4:174). Tsvetaeva's enabling rereading of the Cherubina de Gabriak mystification appears in a context rich with details and images that subvert conventional categories of gender. Voloshin's "feminine" appearance and "masculine" poetry easily coexist, exemplifying a quintessentially poetical androgyny.[56]

Maternity also figures in her account. Voloshin's father is not in evidence, and the poet's dual nature derives entirely from his extraordinary mother, to whom Tsvetaeva devotes a full ten pages of her essay. Deemed irrelevant by editors, who cut this section from the first publication of "The Living about the Living," Tsvetaeva's account of Elena Ottobal'dovna exemplifies a compelling simultaneity of a disruption of the gender binary and the privileging of women. Voloshin's mother is repeatedly mistaken first for a boy and later in life for a man. She is a matriarch, an Amazon, a female androgyne who complements the male androgyny of the poet she births.[57] The paternalistic gives way to the matrilineal and, by analogy, advocates for the recognition of a line of women embedded in the Russian poetic tradition.

The responses to challenges confronting women poets that Tsvetaeva weaves into her essays commemorating Briusov and Voloshin manifest a consistent approach to the vexing problem of gender that appears in various instantiations throughout her writing. How she positions herself vis-à-vis these two poets is integral to the affirmation of her creative selfhood and to her advocacy on behalf of women poets. At the same time, by choosing to present her arguments not logically but analogically, Tsvetaeva draws her reader into actively working through the material she provides toward the conclusions she reaches. This guides her readers into the art of poetic apprehension and introduces correctives into how they relate to the text and the woman who authors it. The next chapter enlarges on an important aspect of Tsvetaeva's self-presentation that, again, extends to the status of writing women. Its focus is on Tsvetaeva's persistent efforts to define how she relates to Akhmatova in a way that champions their distinct creative personalities and yet also protects them from the injurious pitting of one woman poet against another on the part of readers and critics. Broadly stated, the chapter studies Tsvetaeva's efforts to normalize relations among women poets that the male establishment problematizes together with Akhmatova's responses to her sister poet.

Chapter Six

Marina Tsvetaeva and Anna Akhmatova

> Akhmatova! The word has been uttered. With
> all my being, I sense the tense—inevitable—at
> every one of my lines—comparison (with some
> pitting us against one another).
> —Marina Tsvetaeva, "An Otherworldly Evening"

> And there is no reason to juxtapose me to
> Marina. This is not productive.
> —Anna Akhmatova, *Notebooks*

OVER THE COURSE OF THIS BOOK, I examine
case studies that exemplify causes and consequences of strategies that
women poets develop to resist deleterious constructs of gender and to gain
recognition in the Russian poetic tradition. At stake here was more than securing occasional male-sanctioned publication. In order to claim the agency
that would allow them to evade control and the objectification that accompanied it, women poets had to stand up to male authority. They also had to
refute the notion that they were aberrations and to naturalize their entry
into poetry. This chapter elaborates on these efforts and the conditions that
necessitated them, attending now to the isolation of women poets from one
another that deprived them of a supportive community and an authoritative
cohort that would help establish parity with men. Specifically, I explore the
resistance Marina Tsvetaeva mounted against the pervasive pitting of women
poets against one another and the antagonism it breeds between them, as
exemplified by the discord between Pavlova and Rostopchina. The focus
here is on the two leading women poets of the twentieth century who, more
than any others, were (and continue to be) juxtaposed to each other: Marina
Tsvetaeva and Anna Akhmatova. I am interested in the relationship between
these two poets not as commentators frame it but as it emerges specifically
in what they write to and about each other. Noting circumstances motivating
their exchanges, the contexts in which they arose, and their broader implications for writing women, I consider the poets' letters, poems, and prose,
giving particular attention to Tsvetaeva's essay "An Otherworldly Evening"

("Nezdeshnii vecher"). The essay is important to this study because in it Tsvetaeva projects an ideal relationship between herself and Akhmatova in support of a plurality of women's voices and as a model for other women poets. Moreover, "An Otherworldly Evening" provides examples of strategies Tsvetaeva develops to enhance her readers' receptivity to arguments she advances in her essay.

The interactions of the two poets were asymmetrical, with Tsvetaeva initiating the exchange and contributing the lion's share to it. Akhmatova's initial replies were appreciative but scant, and it is only her later responses that make it possible to speak of a relationship between them. To set the scene, I open with a brief overview of the poets' exchanges. I then sketch Akhmatova's debut in the context of how the woman poet was figured in the culture of the time. This leads to a discussion of how Tsvetaeva positioned herself vis-à-vis Akhmatova and the complex image she develops of her sister poet in poems addressed to her and especially in "An Otherworldly Evening." The chapter concludes with Akhmatova's belated responses—those addressed directly to Tsvetaeva and those that react to her writings.

Tsvetaeva recognized that the woman poet's selfhood and her advancement from occasional guest to full-fledged member in the tradition demanded that she reject controlling male mentorship to claim agency. Obviating competition for male authorization that alienated women poets from one another would allow them to establish sororal ties enhancing their confidence and their authority in the tradition. In her own work Tsvetaeva presents herself as equal—or even superior—to male peers and forebears alike. She also establishes ties with Pavlova and Rostopchina, deriving creative sustenance from their writings, their biographies, and strategies of enablement they developed. This reach into the past provided a vital source of sustenance, but a need for reassuring ties with contemporary women poets in the present remained. Initially, Tsvetaeva addressed Akhmatova to tap into her celebrity, much as Pavlova did when she first addressed Rostopchina in verse. Tsvetaeva understood the risks entailed in prompting comparisons with Akhmatova, whose verse and self-presentations were as markedly different from hers as Rostopchina's were from Pavlova's. Accordingly, she cultivates mutually supportive ties with Akhmatova and frames their relationship as embracing reciprocally enriching differences.

Tsvetaeva's efforts were well advised. Her pairing with Akhmatova by critics of the early 1920s who praised the breadth and variety of Russian poetry soon changed into contrasts used to advocate for the preeminence of one over the other.[1] Beyond fueling adversarial relations that it was in women poets' best interest to avoid, such juxtapositions spawned generalizing binaries that reduced the poets' individual creative identities to vague abstractions and political emblems that had little to do with their verse. The embrace of differences that Tsvetaeva insistently promoted overrode just such tendencies, giving freer range to self-presentations women poets could develop and broadening the variety of role models available to them.

Initiated by Tsvetaeva, the exchanges between the two poets, like their scattered references to each other, are complex and polyvalent. These exchanges reflect their distinctive creative temperaments, the changing sociopolitical contexts in which they regard each other, and a mutual respect tinged, at times, with rivalry that Tsvetaeva works earnestly to prevent from becoming antagonistic or being perceived as such. Their relations are additionally complicated by spatial and temporal disjunctions that delay mutual understanding. Initially, Tsvetaeva and Akhmatova had ready access to each other's poetry and the reviews it elicited, but their standing in the literary world was asymmetrical. When she first addressed Akhmatova in a poem of 1915, Tsvetaeva, who received recognition for her first collection *Evening Album* in 1910, was still regarded as showing promise that was not yet fully realized. Akhmatova, who was already known in literary circles when her first collection *Evening (Vecher)* appeared in 1912, had won celebrity with her second book *Rosary (Chetki)* of 1914, which came out in nine editions. Tsvetaeva had something to gain from aligning herself with an acclaimed woman poet whose work she admired. Akhmatova did not need Tsvetaeva's endorsement and was not moved to respond to the poet who demanded her attention in exuberant poems and letters of self-assertive praise. The three lyrics and the eleven-poem cycle that Tsvetaeva addressed to Akhmatova before emigrating in 1922 were left without return in kind, as were Tsvetaeva's dedications to her of the collection *Mileposts (Versty)* and the long poem *On a Red Steed (Na krasnom kone)*.[2] What survives of their correspondence shows it to be similarly asymmetrical, with Tsvetaeva writing longer letters and clamoring for replies. Beyond this tangible imbalance, however, were cordiality and mutual respect. What letters Akhmatova did send, like her inscriptions for Tsvetaeva in three volumes of her verse, convey genuine warmth and appreciation.

In the early 1920s, the two poets were lumped together in the Soviet press as targets of misogynous attacks fueled by a change in policy that decreed the advancement of women as irrelevant to the needs of the new state.[3] Tsvetaeva's emigration in 1922 created a gulf between her and Akhmatova. If earlier the two poets were aligned with Moscow and St. Petersburg—two cities with a history of vying for cultural and political primacy—they now found themselves on either side of a politically determined, rapidly widening cultural divide. The question "There or Here?" ("Tam ili zdes'?"), which Khodasevich took as the title of an essay of 1925, was one that figured prominently in émigré debates about the future of Russian letters.[4]

Akhmatova's early verse came into vogue among Russian émigrés in

Paris[5] just as Tsvetaeva's mature poetry was putting ever-greater demands on her reader. This left her in awkward competition with Akhmatova's earlier creative self, just when she—Tsvetaeva—was compelled to defend changes in her own verse that marked her growth as a poet. At the same time, the adamant refusal to abandon her ailing homeland that Akhmatova proclaimed in verse and incorporated into her creative identity led her to disparage writers who left Russia, enlarging the distance between them. Kornilov plausibly suggests that Tsvetaeva removed her dedication to Akhmatova from *On a Red Steed* after reading—and taking personally—Akhmatova's lyric "I am not with those who abandoned their land for the enemy to tear to pieces" ("Ne s temi ia kto brosil zemliu na rasterzanie vragam").[6] Meanwhile, Soviet propaganda imprinted an image of émigrés as traitors enjoying the good life in Parisian cafés, which even Tsvetaeva's repeated emphasis on her poverty could not dislodge.

For her part, Tsvetaeva did not fully appreciate the inner emigration into which Akhmatova was driven or the toll that Soviet censorship took on her. Upon reading what she did not realize was a heavily expurgated *From Six Books* (*Iz shesti knig*) in 1940, the year after her repatriation, Tsvetaeva expressed disappointment that Akhmatova had not grown as a poet. In March of that year, Akhmatova composed the only poem that she overtly addressed to Tsvetaeva—"A Belated Reply" ("Pozdnii otvet")—but refrained from sharing it with her. Akhmatova dedicated no more poems exclusively to Tsvetaeva, but Tsvetaeva has a palpable subtextual presence in her *Poem without a Hero* (*Poema bez geroia*), begun that same year (1940),[7] as she does also in Akhmatova's later poetry.[8] Early in June of 1941, Tsvetaeva and Akhmatova met in person on two consecutive days for the first and last times. Both were denied publication, both had relatives who suffered arrest, and both were under surveillance. Although conducted in private, their conversation and exchange of poems were clouded by fear and could scarcely bridge the chasm left by intervening time and unread works. On August 31, Tsvetaeva hanged herself. Deeply affected by the suicide, Akhmatova inscribed Tsvetaeva into the list of tragic victims of the regime, attempted to help Tsvetaeva's son, Georgii Efron,[9] and referred to her often in her notebooks and in conversations with Lydia Chukovskaia and Isaiah Berlin. In 1942, Akhmatova likened her own impending fate with Tsvetaeva's in the poem "That's How I Am" ("Kakaia est'").[10] In 1957, Akhmatova met Tsvetaeva's daughter Ariadna Efron and described the meeting with her mother to her.

Some seventeen years after her suicide, Tsvetaeva attracted a burst of interest when Khrushchev's Thaw lifted the ban on her, and the illegal trickle of her works into the Soviet Union was enlarged with selective, officially sanctioned publications. Besides works that circulated in manuscript and typescript, Akhmatova already had access to the collection *Prose* (*Proza*), brought out by the Chekhov Publishing House in New York in 1953. In 1961, after Tsvetaeva's *Selected Works* (*Izbrannoe*) appeared in Moscow, Akhmatova wrote the poem "There Are Four of Us" ("Nas chetvero"), in which Tsvetaeva appears—together with Mandel'shtam and Pasternak—as a treasured poet. The Poet's Library (*Biblioteka poeta*) edition of Tsvetaeva's selected verse that followed in 1965 expanded Akhmatova's access to what Tsvetaeva had written in emigration, deepening her appreciation of her poetry. As Kornilov describes it, "Akhmatova ruled on the all-Russian throne only until Tsvetaeva's poems began to appear in the country (first in manuscript and, decades later, also in books)."[11] The rivalry imposed on Tsvetaeva and Akhmatova extends across time, sociopolitical and cultural boundaries, and even the border between the living and the dead. Akhmatova subsumes it by absorbing Tsvetaeva's poetry into her own later verse,[12] just as earlier Tsvetaeva drew her (Akhmatova's) lyrics into her own writing.

The brief overview of Tsvetaeva's and Akhmatova's interactions now complete, I return to the early years of their poetic careers. Unlike Tsvetaeva's departure from the established ritual of debut with her eschewal of male mentorship and independent publication of a poetry collection, Akhmatova's appearance on the literary arena conformed to established practice. Her first publication was the poem "On his hand are many sparkling rings" ("Na ruke ego mnogo blestiashchikh kolets"), signed "Anna G." It came out in 1907, in the short-lived Russian weekly *Sirius*, edited by her soon-to-be husband, Nikolai Gumilev, who had no qualms about editing it. "An Old Portrait" ("Staryi portret"), of 1911, was the first poem Akhmatova published in Russia and signed with her pseudonym.[13]

Like Tsvetaeva, Akhmatova reached out to Briusov in 1910 but did so in the more conventional tone of a novice anxious for approval and uncertain about her future. The letter that accompanied the four poems she sent him ends diffidently: "I would be endlessly grateful to you if you would write me, whether or not I should engage in poetry. Forgive me for disturbing you. Anna Akhmatova" (1:155). Briusov responded favorably and praised Akhmatova's early publications. In "The Future of Russian Poetry" ("Budushchee russkoi poezii"), his 1911 review of a new poetry anthology, he expressed disappointment that neither Akhmatova nor Cherubina de Gabriak were represented in it.[14] He spoke highly of Akhmatova's *Evening*, and in his 1913 essay "New Trends in Russian Poetry" ("Novye techeniia v russkoi poezii") lauded her verse for the very characteristic that he found lacking in Tsvetaeva's *Evening Album*: "The poems of Mlle. Akhmatova are very precious to us for their remarkable sharpness."[15]

Akhmatova's esteem for Briusov ran aground on Nadezhda L'vova's suicide in 1913, for which many held him responsible. His refusal to support the emerging Acmeist movement and his attacks on Gumilev's manifesto "The Inheritance of Symbolism and Acmeism" ("Nasledie simvolizma i akmeizm") intensified the disaffection. Briusov reined in his commendations of Akhmatova, and in his review of *Rosary*, her second, highly acclaimed poetry collection, he expressed apprehension—just as he had in his review of Tsvetaeva's *Magic Lantern*—that her verse would remain limited.[16] The Revolution gave Briusov an opportunity to bolster his waning authority. He supported the Bolsheviks and served in the cultural ministry of the Soviet state, which gave him power over writers of the time. His 1922 review essay "Yesterday, Today, and Tomorrow of Russian Poetry" ("Vchera, segodnia i zavtra russkoi poezii") dismissed Akhmatova's *At the Very Edge of the Sea* (*U samogo moria*), *Plantain* (*Podorozhnik*), and *Anno Domini MCMXXI* as "feeble efforts" and described her poems as something "a pupil of any practical studio would be ashamed of."[17] Tsvetaeva, whose 1921 collection *Mileposts* dedicated to Akhmatova receives mention in the same essay, is listed among poets who, as Briusov opines, "provided nothing original either in content or in form."[18]

Much later in her career, Akhmatova described Briusov as "understanding nothing at all."[19] Branding him an imitator and opportunist, she included herself among the poets he imitated in his drive for celebrity and described *Nelli's Poems* as "Briusov's reaction to the success of my early poems."[20] After reading the essay "A Hero of Labor" ("Geroi truda") in 1959, Akhmatova noted only that Tsvetaeva was too easy on him. "She does not disparage him enough, she imagines him as learned, but he was an ignoramus. She rebels against his power, but he no longer had any power."[21] I elaborate on Akhmatova's reactions to Tsvetaeva's essays below but return here to the early years of Akhmatova's career.

Akhmatova's celebrity mounted swiftly. When her verse appeared in *Apollo*[22] in 1911, in the wake of de Gabriak's stardom, the aura of the invented poet colored her image and her reception.[23] The elegant dark-haired woman in a mysterious natural setting featured on the cover of her first collection *Evening* (1912) was the work of Evgenii Lansere, whose graphics had framed the second installment of de Gabriak's verse in *Apollo*. The beautiful woman aesthetic, which fueled Cherubina's invention and success, persisted in the journal. Among its early manifestations was an exhibition of women's portraits by male artists of the day organized in 1910 in the journal's editorial offices.[24] The exhibition sparked debates in the press about the real image of a woman. The real woman did not enter into the picture.

In January of 1912, Akhmatova read her poems with resounding success at the Stray Dog (*Brodiachaia sobaka*) cabaret. March of that year brought favorable reception of *Evening*. Akhmatova's poems were seen as offering a new feminine aesthetic that attracted positive attention, while she herself satisfied the demand for beauty. The photographs, sketches, paintings, sculptures, and poetic dedications that she inspired proliferated from the outset of her career, furthering the success she enjoyed in the heady atmosphere of the Stray Dog, where she numbered among "the beauties of 1913."[25] As Veronika Losskaia observes, "in the last prewar years in Petersburg Akhmatova was in fashion."[26]

Akhmatova's celebrity came on the heels of Cherubina de Gabriak's and left her subject to similar invention by her readers. The legends that grew up around Akhmatova spawned a variety of images—in the visual and verbal arts and in readers' imaginations—that diverged in varying degrees from the poet herself. Apropos of one of the best-known paintings of her—Nathan Al'tman's 1914 portrait that was reproduced in *Apollo* in 1916—Akhmatova observes, "Al'tman's portrait has no pretensions to resemblance: an obvious stylization, compare it with my photographs of that time." She adds that "like any stylization in art," she finds the portrait displeasing.[27] That Akhmatova's proliferating images had an enduring effect on how women poets were envisioned is well illustrated in Evgenii Tager's recollections of his first meeting with Tsvetaeva in December of 1939: "I had never seen either Tsvetaeva or her portraits, photographs. And my imagination—quite naive, as I understand now—painted an exquisitely refined image, possibly by association with Al'tman's portrait of Akhmatova. It turned out that it was nothing of the kind."[28]

Tsvetaeva apparently came to know Akhmatova after that poet's collection *Evening* appeared in 1912. In his introduction to that collection, the poet Mikhail Kuzmin mentions Tsvetaeva, together with Mandel'shtam and Erenburg, to situate Akhmatova.[29] However gratifying this might have been for Tsvetaeva, at this point she lagged behind Akhmatova in recognition. Her second collection, *Magic Lantern*, which also came out in 1912, met with relatively cool critical response. Indeed, as chance would have it, number 5 of *Apollo* of that year carried a glowing review by Valerian Chudovsky of Akhmatova's book side by side with a negative one of Tsvetaeva's by Gumilev, who had praised her first collection.[30] The year 1912, during which Tsvetaeva wrote only two poems, marked a creative crisis in Tsvetaeva's development.[31] Her third collection, *From Two Books* (*Iz dvukh knig*, 1913), was, as its title indicates, a selection of previously published poems. (Only the second of her two poems addressed to Briusov was new.) Khodasevich, who had high praise for Akhmatova's *Rosary*, which came out in 1914, responded negatively to Tsvetaeva's *Magic Lantern*, which he reviewed the same year.[32]

Seeing no signs of development in Tsvetaeva's verse, critics were reserved in their assessments and in 1915 still spoke of her as a promising beginner whose literary reputation depended on her subsequent poetry.[33]

The 1915 poem "To Anna Akhmatova" ("Anne Akhmatovoi") was the first that Tsvetaeva addressed to her sister poet. She had just returned from Petrograd, where she met with leading poets of the time and an enthusiastic welcome. After debuting in the northern capital with her reading at an evening of poetry, Tsvetaeva drew Moscow into her poetic identity, composing cycles of poems about "her" Moscow and addressing verse to Petersburg poets—specifically Blok, Mandel'shtam, and Akhmatova.[34] Tsvetaeva's birthplace became an integral part of her creative identity, bringing something new to her own work and to the literary world of the northern capital.

Tsvetaeva's identification with Moscow, which took her into a new stage of growth,[35] figured prominently in her writings and was taken up by critics and commentators. In the previous century, Karolina Pavlova invoked Moscow to distinguish herself from Rostopchina, with Moscow emblematizing traditional Russian values and St. Petersburg progressive European ideas. When Tsvetaeva claimed Moscow for her own, this familiar cultural divide had acquired an additional layer of meaning. Writing in 1929 of Tsvetaeva's reading in Paris of poems from her early Moscow cycle, the critic Georgii Adamovich recollects,

> If memory serves me right, they appeared in *Northern Annals* [*Severnye zapiski*] in the spring of 1917.[36] I remember the impression they made—especially in Petersburg. The competition that had already begun between the two cities as to which would or would not be the capital likely played a role in this. In Petersburg everyone sensed painfully that "the end had come to the imperial period"—independently, of course, of any political sympathies and feelings—and with jealous wariness kept glancing at Moscow. The Petersburg poets were awed by Tsvetaeva's cycle—its charm, the unexpectedness of her Moscow.[37]

Akhmatova was not in Petrograd during Tsvetaeva's visit. The image with which Tsvetaeva's first poem to her opens comes from the widely circulating postcards of Al'tman's painting that celebrated Akhmatova's elegant slenderness and showed her in a shawl slipping from her shoulders.

> Узкий, нерусский стан—
> Над фолиантами.
> Шаль из турецких стран
> Пала как мантия. (1:234)

> Narrow, un-Russian figure—
> Over the folios.
> A shawl from Turkish lands
> Fell like a mantle.

Tsvetaeva goes on to read characteristic features of Akhmatova's biography and verse for the future they encode. Maintaining a reverent distance, she positions herself among those at whose hearts, as she describes it, Akhmatova's lyrics are aimed. Tsvetaeva closes the poem with a stanza proclaiming her love in uncharacteristically subdued, down-to-earth terms:

> В утренний сонный час,
> —Кажется, четверть пятого,—
> Я полюбила Вас,
> Анна Ахматова. (1:235)

> In a drowsy morning hour,
> —Four fifteen, I think,—
> I came to love you,
> Anna Akhmatova.

As understated and suggestive as details in Akhmatova's own poems, these particulars point to the naturalness and inevitability of Tsvetaeva's love, which results, as the reader is left to surmise, from her having stayed up all night reading Akhmatova's verse. Tsvetaeva's self-portrait in this poem is as yet lightly sketched, and her selfhood is conveyed obliquely through her penetrating reading of Akhmatova's poems and of the poet herself.

In the cycle *To Akhmatova* (*Akhmatovoi*) that followed in 1916,[38] Tsvetaeva continues to laud her addressee, now demonstrating her own command of that poet's stylistics, imagery, and diction.[39] This cycle, together with one to Blok written earlier that year, marks the first time that Tsvetaeva consciously and systematically used other poets' texts as her "building material."[40] In the poems to Akhmatova, which materialized in less than a month, Akhmatova's name, details of her appearance, her personality, representations of her by other artists, and the powerful effect that her verse has on readers signify variously as Tsvetaeva conjoins them in a multifaceted whole. The shifts in tone and register within individual poems and in the cycle as a whole reflect the complexity of Tsvetaeva's feelings for her addressee. Initially she stands apart—alongside Akhmatova's admirers—but then gradually enters Akhmatova's world and absorbs it into her own, incorporating identifying features of her addressee into her poems. Mythic, historical, folkloric, Tsvetaeva's Akhmatova is alternately threatening and reassuring. She is a muse, a folk heroine, a Madonna. Like Saint John Chrysostom, she is a "golden-lipped" (*zlatoustaia*) bearer of the sacred word, and like a sorceress, she commands language to cast spells. Akhmatova's breadth and scope, as Tsvetaeva's cycle announces, can be fully appreciated only by a poet whose reach encompasses hers.

As she addresses her sister poet, Tsvetaeva establishes her own poetic space and authority, claiming Moscow vis-à-vis Akhmatova's St. Petersburg and assuming the right to sanction the ties Akhmatova establishes with Push-kin in her cycle *In Tsarskoe Selo* (*V Tsarskom Sele*). Tsvetaeva's lyrics exhibit her grasp of Akhmatova's diverse personae and their corresponding voices but also the strength of her own creativity into which she incorporates them. The Akhmatova who emerges from this cycle is a complex myth of Tsve-taeva's making.[41] Kruglova notes that this mythologization is rooted in meta-poetic motifs,[42] but concrete ties also play a role. The maternity that figures in Tsvetaeva's letters to Akhmatova finds a place in the poems as well. The love that Tsvetaeva expresses is not that of a distant worshipper as it was in her poems to Blok. It is a love that derives from the creative exchange that Tsvetaeva accomplishes by first becoming absorbed in Akhmatova's lyrics and then absorbing them into her own world. With this exchange, Tsvetaeva models her concept of the ideal reader. Indeed, on the strength of her exceptional capacity for assimilation, the ideal reader and the poet are one.

What survives of the correspondence between Tsvetaeva and Akhma-tova shows mutual respect and affection, expressed in the distinct idioms characteristic of each.[43] The love, dreams, and desire for a meeting that fig-ure in Tsvetaeva's letters to Akhmatova appear in her correspondence with other poets as well.[44] In a notebook entry of 1920–21, Tsvetaeva observes, "I do not have a circle, I have [women] friends." Akhmatova appears—together with Karolina Pavlova and Evdokiia Rostopchina—in this list.[45] Tsvetaeva's letters express deep appreciation of Akhmatova's verse and convey loneli-ness and a sense of isolation. Some appear as drafts in her notebooks, as does a copy of her eight-year-old daughter Ariadna's letter to Akhmatova of March 17, 1921. Tsvetaeva's first surviving letter, dated April 26, 1921, is an exuberant reaction to Akhmatova's newly published *Plantain*. On July 1 of that year, Tsvetaeva wrote Akhmatova shortly after responding to a letter from her husband, Sergei Efron, who joined the White Army and had been missing since 1918.[46] She describes her joy to Akhmatova at hearing from her husband but also the guilt she experiences for taking time to write poetry. The letter that follows on August 31, 1921, is a reaction to the rumor that Akhmatova had committed suicide in the wake of Blok's death on the twenty-first and Gumilev's execution on the twenty-fifth of that month. Finally, in a letter from Bellevue, dated November 12, 1926, Tsvetaeva makes plans for Akhmatova's (falsely) rumored emigration to France.

As in her poems to Akhmatova, in the private space of her letters Tsvetaeva seeks to convey something about herself and to connect with her addressee. Tsvetaeva uses three facets of her own identity to establish ties with Akhmatova. To begin with, her exuberant praise of Akhmatova's poetry presents Tsvetaeva as an ideal reader for whom the poems are a life-changing experience. *Plantain*, as she writes, is "another joy in my life,"[47] the other joys being Akhmatova's collections *Rosary* and *White Flock* (*Belaia staia*, 1917). Second, Tsvetaeva's references to her daughter Ariadna Efron (Alia), her son, Georgii Efron, and Akhmatova's son, Lev Gumilev, mark the theme of maternity she uses to strengthen her ties with Akhmatova. Finally, Tsvetaeva presents herself as an active poet for whom Akhmatova, like other poets she admires, is a source of creative energy.

Alia is a constant in Tsvetaeva's self-presentations of that period, and her exceptionality figures as fundamental to Tsvetaeva's own identity: she is the poet-mother of a wunderkind. The eight-year-old's surviving letter to Akhmatova displays extraordinary perceptiveness, grasp of language, and sensitivity to poetry. At the same time, it conveys the poverty in which she and her mother live and situates their true existence in a realm beyond the discomforts of the here and now. Alia's letter expresses helpless naïveté but also wisdom and an extraordinary receptiveness to Akhmatova's poetry.

Akhmatova was not the prolific letter writer that Tsvetaeva was. Her letters are brief and infrequent. Tsvetaeva pleaded that she write more. Akhmatova apologized for her agraphia. Her two surviving letters to Tsvetaeva are brief but warm responses in which she expresses gratitude to Tsvetaeva for sending her two icons, for dedicating *On a Red Steed* to her, and for her thoughtfulness, which she finds "endlessly dear."[48] Akhmatova shows interest in Tsvetaeva's verse but responds with nothing like the accolades Tsvetaeva showers on her and, as yet, with no poetic dedications. Three volumes of Akhmatova's verse that Tsvetaeva treasured bear cordial inscriptions. In *Plantain* Akhmatova writes, "To Marina Tsvetaeva in hopes of a meeting, with love, Akhmatova. 1921." *Anno Domini MCMXXI* bears the inscription "To dear Marina Tsvetaeva, my enigmatic friend, with love, Akhmatova. 1921," and in *At the Very Edge of the Sea* she inscribes, "To Marina Tsvetaeva—Anna Akhmatova, in place of a letter."[49]

In 1921, Tsvetaeva dedicated *Mileposts* and *On a Red Steed* to Akhmatova and addressed two more poems to her. This was the year of Briusov's hostile review of Akhmatova's *At the Very Edge of the Sea, Plantain*, and *Anno Domini MCMXXI*, of Blok's death, and of Gumilev's arrest and execution. Rumors of Akhmatova's suicide moved Tsvetaeva to compose a poem that appears on August 30 in her notebook with the title "To Akhmatova"

("K Akhmatovoi") and the parenthetic explanation, "In response to the *persistent* rumor of her death."[50] Neither the title nor the explanatory note appear in the published version of the poem, which leaves Akhmatova and her falsely reported death for the reader to infer. In the poem, Tsvetaeva stresses that the living Akhmatova is vital to her own well-being as a poet. Rejecting notions of rivalry between them, she praises Akhmatova as an equal and presents their relationship as one of mutual appreciation.

The poem begins with a reaffirmation of a bond that leaves no room for competition and delineates the distinct cultural spaces they command:

> Соревнования короста
> В нас не осилила родства.
> И поделили мы так просто:
> Твой—Петербург, моя—Москва. (2:53)

> The scab of competition
> Did not overcome our kinship.
> And we divided so simply:
> Your—Petersburg, my—Moscow.

Tsvetaeva goes on to describe first how "blissfully" (*blazhenno*) and "disinterestedly" (*bezkorystno*—a play on *korosta* of the opening line) her own genius was uplifted by Akhmatova's, only to be brought down by her death. The description of the effect of Akhmatova's death shows Tsvetaeva at her best:

> Но вал моей гордыни польской—
> Как пал он!—С златозорных гор
> Мои стихи—как добровольцы
> К тебе стекались под шатер . . . (2:54)

> But the surge of my Polish pride—
> How it fell!—From the golden dawned mountains
> My poems, like volunteers,
> Flowed toward you beneath your tent . . .

The poem ends with Tsvetaeva questioning whether her verse can reach her departed addressee and expressing her desolation at losing a sister poet:

> Дойдет ли в пустоте эфира
> Моя лирическая лесть?
> И безутешна я, что женской лиры
> Одной, одной мне тягу несть. (2:54)

> In the emptiness of the ether
> Will my lyric flattery reach you?
> And I am inconsolable that I
> Alone, alone must bear the weight of the feminine lyre.

In a time flush with women poets, the despair at having to bear the feminine lyre alone attracts attention. Tsvetaeva, whose recognition was by then on a par with Akhmatova's, distinguishes herself and her addressee as the two leading women poets of the time. This, as she recognizes, can only intensify the tendency to see them as competitors. With her expression of bereavement, Tsvetaeva insists that she and Akhmatova are kindred spirits and not adversaries. Different but equal practitioners of their art, they are united by their shared dedication to poetry. In the course of mourning Akhmatova, Tsvetaeva honors her addressee, reaffirms her own status, and resists the estrangement of women poets from one another. She also indicates her need for a supportive relationship with a woman poet she genuinely admires. She does not desire Akhmatova's death. She desires only that they be read on their own terms and not against each other.

By the mid-1920s, the unremitting pairing of Tsvetaeva and Akhmatova became problematic. Critics and commentators increasingly judged the two poets on the basis of an entire host of contrasting criteria, framing their distinct creative personalities in terms of reductive binaries. The 1923 essay "Russian Poetesses: Marina Tsvetaeva and Anna Akhmatova" ("Russkie poetessy: Marina Tsvetaeva i Anna Akhmatova") by the émigré critic Konstantin Mochulsky is but one of a host of possible examples. Describing the two poets as representative of their time, Mochulsky inventories contrasts between them: "Tsvetaeva is a whirlwind, Akhmatova is silence. You cannot make out the face of the former because it is in motion, its mimicry is so varied. The latter has the pure line of an immobile profile. Tsvetaeva is all in movement—Akhmatova in contemplation. Where one barely smiles, the other rumbles with laughter."[51] He then juxtaposes Akhmatova's elegiac verse that treats of death, illness, and enervation with Tsvetaeva's poetry that "is a picture of health, filled with young blood, sunny, sensual."[52] Akhmatova read Mochulsky's essay in May of 1962 and passed it on to Chukovskaia, observing, "Yes, it's no good. Comparisons like this don't work for anyone, not even for Marina."[53]

Juxtapositions of the poets' temperaments, stylistics, appearance, and poetic voices, invocations of their distinct Moscow–St. Petersburg origins, and the painful, politics-laden divide of émigré-nonémigré projected discord onto them and positioned them as competitors. This intensified readers' propensity to choose one over the other, often on the basis of criteria extraneous to their verse, and upheld what Tricia Lootens describes as the "beauty pageant" bias that allows for the crowning of only one woman.[54] In 1926, Tsvetaeva sent Rainer Maria Rilke, with whom she began corresponding that year, a copy of her collection *Psyche* (*Psikheia*, 1921), which she annotated to assist his reading of the poems. Reprinted in that collection under the heading "Muse, for Anna Akhmatova" ("Muza, Anne Akhmatovoi") are poems from Tsvetaeva's 1916 cycle. The explanatory note Tsvetaeva supplies for Rilke identifies Akhmatova as "our greatest poet [fem.], from whom they (her readers and mine) always want to alienate me, as if 'hers' and 'mine' has any meaning here."[55]

Akhmatova's name crops up repeatedly in Tsvetaeva's prose essays that record her poetic becoming and explicate her thinking about poets and poetry. In these essays, Akhmatova figures among poets whom Tsvetaeva sees as gold standards of her art. She appears as an ally in Tsvetaeva's struggle against the antipoetical mundane and is part of her project to enable the woman poet. Among such essays are the 1922 "A Downpour of Light" ("Svetovoi liven'"), dedicated to Boris Pasternak, and "A Hero of Labor," the 1925 essay to Briusov discussed in the previous chapter. In "The Poet on Criticism/the Critic" ("Poet o kritike," 1926), Tsvetaeva scoffs at ignorant critics who trade in gossip and cites, by way of example, claims made in the press about Akhmatova's personal life. In "The History of a Dedication" ("Istoriia odnogo posviashcheniia") of 1931, Akhmatova appears side by side with Blok as exemplifying the genuine poet. In the 1932 essay "The Living about the Living" ("Zhivoe o zhivom"), Tsvetaeva clusters Cherubina de Gabriak, Akhmatova, and herself to create a composite portrait of the essential woman poet. In "Art in the Light of Conscience" ("Iskusstvo pri svete sovesti") of the same year, Tsvetaeva defends Akhmatova against Blok's harsh assessment of her early poems. In the 1933 "Poets with a History and Poets without a History" ("Poety s istoriei i poety bez istorii"), she writes, "Of my contemporaries, I will name three for the perfection of their lyrical uniqueness: Anna Akhmatova, Osip Mandel'shtam, and Boris Pasternak."[56] References to Akhmatova in Tsvetaeva's prose culminate with "An Otherworldly Evening" ("Nezdeshnii vecher").

"An Otherworldly Evening" is of particular interest here because in this essay, which she wrote in response to Kuzmin's death in 1936, Tsvetaeva enlarges on how she relates to Akhmatova. She does so in a way that counters the oppositional positions projected onto them and prompts other women poets to evade adversarial relations in favor of supportive ones. Motivating Akhmatova's inclusion in the essay is Tsvetaeva's mistaken notion—prompted apparently by Kuzmin's introduction to *Evening*—that she was commemorating "Akhmatova's last close friend," as she referred to him in a letter dated March 19 of that year.[57] As in her poems to Akhmatova, in "An

Otherworldly Evening" Tsvetaeva interweaves praise and self-affirmation. Her primary focus, however, remains on dispelling any notions of animosity between them. Addressed to her contemporary readers, "An Otherworldly Evening" also establishes Tsvetaeva's vision of her relationship with Akhmatova for posterity. I begin with a brief overview of the essay and then look at sections relevant to this study. The aim here again is not to test the essay's factual accuracy but to study how and to what purpose Tsvetaeva shapes her material.

"An Otherworldly Evening" describes Tsvetaeva's first meeting with Kuzmin in the winter of 1915/16, when she traveled to Petrograd with her lover Sophia Parnok.[58] The evening in question marks her poetic debut at a gathering of St. Petersburg poets that all the literary lights of the northern city attended[59]—all, that is, as Tsvetaeva apprises her reader, except Anna Akhmatova[60] and Nikolai Gumilev (4:288). The title of Tsvetaeva's essay invokes Kuzmin's 1921 collection *Otherworldly Evenings* (*Nezdeshnie vechera*), Akhmatova's *Evening*, for which he wrote the introduction, and Tsvetaeva's own debut collection *Evening Album*. Like all of Tsvetaeva's essays commemorating poets, the piece is a generic hybrid that is at once homage, memoir, commemoration, and oblique self-presentation. Characteristically, it champions the associative nature of poetic apprehension and documents how the intervening passage of time reshapes what past events come to signify in the future. Frankly subjective, "An Otherworldly Evening" shows Tsvetaeva filtering recollections of her St. Petersburg debut and configuring variously the synecdochal details and vignettes that embody them. These vividly convey the events she describes but—in a rich confluence of signifier and signified—also point beyond them. The recollected particulars appear in a kaleidoscopic array that draws details into ever-new configurations that continually expand their meaning. This gives rise to meaningful interactions among the various details and sections of the essay. My focus here remains on tracing the relationship with Akhmatova that emerges from these expansive dynamics.

Tsvetaeva's frequent protestations against seeing gender as constitutive of the poet reflect her cognizance of the negative effects of gender biases on readers' constructs of the woman poet and on the reception of her work. Throughout Tsvetaeva's writings affirmations of women as poetical in essence appear concomitantly with insistent erosions of the gender binary. In "An Otherworldly Evening" Tsvetaeva continues this dual project, focusing now on resisting the habitual casting of women poets in adversarial roles. Determined to dispel any notions of rivalry or disaffection between them, Tsvetaeva maps the present in which she writes her essay onto the early stages of her own poetic career and Akhmatova's. Her concurrent emphasis on her selfhood and her embrace of Akhmatova's differences demonstrate a constructive relationship that Tsvetaeva offers as a model for other women poets. Here it bears repeating that Tsvetaeva describes the evening in question not simply to re-create it but to revisit it from a new temporal vantage point and to convey ideas that are important to her. As she does so, she inculcates in her reader a new way to perceive events of the surrounding world and to relate to the essay that describes them. Emphasizing how misleading appearances are, Tsvetaeva raises her readers' conscious awareness of deeper strata beyond them. An undercurrent of homoeroticism that destabilizes the gender binary supports this project. Kuzmin, the homosexual dedicatee of Tsvetaeva's essay, the same-sex couples she mentions in it, and the description of the host's mistaking Esenin for Tsvetaeva herself participate in this destabilization. Here a biographical dimension also plays a part. Sophia Parnok, who harshly terminated her intense relationship with Tsvetaeva, accompanied her to Petrograd, though not to the poetry reading. In this context, Akhmatova "serves as a replacement (as emotional center) for Parnok" and thus "also a way of flouting Parnok's authority,"[61] adding another layer of import to Tsvetaeva's expressions of admiration for Akhmatova in this essay.

The evening Tsvetaeva describes marks her debut in St. Petersburg— then Petrograd—where Akhmatova was already an acclaimed poet. Akhmatova fit in easily with the beautiful woman aesthetic of the time. Tsvetaeva did not. Beneath the certainty that her poems would be compared with Akhmatova's is Tsvetaeva's unstated anxiety that her presence would also trigger comparisons of how they look. Mitigating this threat by emphasizing Akhmatova's absence, Tsvetaeva pursues an eager translation of flesh into words. Akhmatova remains a disembodied presence in a context that denies credence to physical appearances. There is more at stake here than Tsvetaeva's own reception. The fixation on the woman's body affects all women poets. Rather than focus directly on this gender-driven concern, Tsvetaeva absorbs it into the broader poetical imperative to privilege essences over outward forms. To make her point, she presents her argument through concrete, down-to-earth examples that prompt her readers to arrive at her conclusion together with her rather than receive it passively from her. In "An Otherworldly Evening," Tsvetaeva guides her readers to recognize the error of forming opinions based on how people look with accounts of her own erroneous assumptions. The disparity she highlights between seeming and being argues eloquently for looking beyond surface appearances.

Two examples from "An Otherworldly Evening" illustrate Tsvetaeva's method. The first involves the poet Leonid Kannegiser, whom Tsvetaeva meets for the first time that evening and whom she describes as effete. "Lënia is too fragile for me, tender . . . a flower . . . What can he do with such hands?"[62] His delicate appearance leads Tsvetaeva to surmise that he must certainly prefer Akhmatova to her. "Besides, Lënia obviously must dislike me—he constantly compares me, my simplicity and directness to the (then!) Akhmatovian bent—and nothing matches up" (4:283). This conjecture, in turn, prompts Tsvetaeva to assume that he, a quintessential St. Petersburgian, is irritated by her Muscovite manner of speech and to conclude that they are incompatible (4:283–84). It is only later that Tsvetaeva realizes how wrong she was. "After Lënia there remained a small book of verse—so simple that my heart contracted: how I understood nothing about this aesthete, how I believed this exterior" (4:285).

Significantly, it is Leonid Kannegiser's poetry that reveals the erroneousness of assumptions that Tsvetaeva based on his looks and shows that, contrary to appearances, they had much in common. That how Lënia looks and how he writes do not correspond and that his poetry is the corrective to her misapprehensions are essential to Tsvetaeva's argument. Meanwhile, the reader has already been prompted by the earlier question, "What can he do with such hands?" to recognize sooner than the authored self of the essay that her initial assessment of Lënia is wrong. In the winter of 1915/16, when the events she describes took place, Tsvetaeva did not yet know what Lënia was capable of doing with his delicate hands as she did in 1936, when she composed her essay. The answer to her question lies between her first encounter with Leonid Kannegiser at the "Otherworldly Evening" and her acquaintance with the posthumous volume of his verse that his father published in Paris in 1928. The point is that on August 30, 1918, Leonid Kannegiser, a member of an underground anti-Bolshevik organization, assassinated Moisei Uritsky, head of the Petrograd Cheka, and was executed by firing squad on October 21 of that year.[63] Tsvetaeva makes no mention of this in her essay, leaving it for her reader to summon up in affirmation of the deceptiveness of appearances. By allowing the reader to supply the missing information and to recognize her mistake before the authored self of her essay does, the authoring Tsvetaeva engages her reader in developing her argument, thus making her point the reader's own.

Between the account of her misapprehension of Leonid Kannegiser and the truth she learns from his verse, Tsvetaeva interjects what she describes as his close-knit friendship with Esenin, which, as readers know, was a homoerotic relationship. Against the background of this destabilization of the gender binary, Tsvetaeva lists diametrical features that their relationship conjoins: "Lënia. Esenin. Inseparable, indivisible friends. In their persons, in their so strikingly dissimilar faces came together, intertwined two races, two classes, two worlds. There came together—across all and sundry—poets" (4:285). She goes on to contrast Esenin's blond, curly hair and cornflower-blue eyes with Kannegiser's smooth black hair and brown, almond-shaped eyes and to sum up, "How pleasant, when something is antithetical and so close. Satisfaction as from a rare and full rhyme" (4:285). This replacement of mere binarism with a confluence of contraries lays the groundwork for Tsvetaeva's account of her relationship with Akhmatova and enhances the reader's receptivity to it.

Tsvetaeva bolsters her position with another example of how wrong it is to expect a correspondence between how a poet looks and writes. Gripped by Esenin's reading that evening, she marvels at how "this cherub, this baby face" (4:287) can write and feel so powerfully, adding parenthetically, "With Esenin I never ceased to marvel at this" (4:287). The false assumptions Tsvetaeva shows herself making prompt her readers to recognize and adjust similar tendencies in themselves. Significantly, these misguided assumptions based on how Kannegiser and Esenin look frame Tsvetaeva's account of her own reading that evening, which she now—at the time she writes her essay—uses to position herself vis-à-vis Akhmatova.

As she describes her St. Petersburg debut, Tsvetaeva counts on what she has taught her readers by negative example to persuade them to focus on her writing and not on how she looks. At the same time, she translates the differences between herself and Akhmatova into the capacious realm of poetry that obviates contention by easily accommodating their distinct creative personalities. Tsvetaeva's account of her recitation is consistent with this twofold design. As the narrator of the essay who looks out on the surrounding world, Tsvetaeva records what she sees and not how she is seen. Because Akhmatova is not present that evening, her physical appearance has no place in the essay either. The poems that, as Tsvetaeva describes, she directs exclusively to Akhmatova connect them in the disembodied realm of their art and situate them in a vast historical and cultural space. Their bodies bypassed, Tsvetaeva asserts her own creative identity. Giving Akhmatova high praise, she insists that her selfhood and her admiration of a dissimilar poet are mutually reinforcing.

Tsvetaeva's account of her reading underscores the uncompromising individuality that is a constant feature of her self presentations. In "A Hero of Labor," she shows herself reciting poems dedicated to the White Army to an audience of Reds. In "An Otherworldly Evening," she shows herself reciting the poem "To Germany" ("Germanii"), which she wrote at the start of World War I to express undying love for that country's natural beauty and culture. She follows this poem with her antiwar lyric "I know the truth" ("Ia znaiu pravdu"). Tsvetaeva turns to Akhmatova only after she has established both her rebellious creative identity and the success of the poems she recites to an admiring audience that clamors for more:

I read my entire poetic year 1915—but it's still not enough, and everyone wants still more. I clearly sense that I am reading on behalf of Moscow and that I am not disgracing myself, that I am rising to an Akhmatovian level. Akhmatova! The word has been uttered. With all my being, I sense the tense—inevitable—at every one of my lines—comparison (with some pitting us against each other): not only of Akhmatova and me but of St. Petersburg and Moscow poetry, of Petersburg and Moscow. But if some of Akhmatova's admirers are listening to me *against me*, I myself am reading not against Akhmatova but—to Akhmatova. I read as if Akhmatova were in the room—Akhmatova alone. I read for the absent Akhmatova. I need my success as a direct conduit to Akhmatova. (4:286–87; emphasis in the original)

Underscoring the presence of Akhmatova's absence, Tsvetaeva absorbs the patent differences between them into the broader cultural divide between their native cities. Tsvetaeva is the representative of poetic Moscow in the literary world of St. Petersburg, emblematized in the essay not by those gathered at the "otherworldly evening" but by the absent poet whom she designates as her sole addressee. By bestowing "her" Moscow on Akhmatova, Tsvetaeva both distinguishes herself from St. Petersburg poets and establishes herself among them. She engages Akhmatova in the company of other poets but also maintains the self-identifying heroic stance of one (Muscovite) against all (the poets of Petersburg) that she repeatedly invokes in her writings: "*All* of Petersburg read and *one* Moscow" (4:288; emphasis in the original). Tsvetaeva and the disembodied Akhmatova stand side by side, each presiding over her own cultural and geographical space. The obeisance to Akhmatova comes from a potentate with the power to bestow on her the gift of Moscow. "And if at this particular moment I want to represent Moscow as best as possible, it is not in order to defeat Petersburg but in order to make a gift of this Moscow to Petersburg, to make a gift to Akhmatova of this Moscow in me, in my love, to have it bow before Akhmatova" (4:287).

Explaining that her admiration of Akhmatova and desire to honor her gave rise to the cycles *Poems about Moscow* (*Stikhi o Moskve*) and *To Akhmatova*, which she composed in the spring and summer after her Petersburg visit, Tsvetaeva presents their differences as stimulating and transforms "rivalry" into a positive source of creative energy:

To say it all: for the poems about Moscow that followed my Petersburg trip I am indebted to Akhmatova, my love for her, my desire to give her something more eternal than love, to give her *that* which is more eternal than love. If I could simply have given her the Kremlin, I would probably not have written these poems. So there was competition, in some sense, with Akhmatova, but not to "do it better than she," rather—to do it so it could not be better, and to put this could not be better at her feet. Competition? Fervor. (4:287; emphasis in the original)[64]

Writing about Akhmatova and Tsvetaeva, Aiza Longo adduces passages from "An Otherworldly Evening" to support her assertion that "there was never any real competition or jealousy between them."[65] This is precisely the image of the relationship Tsvetaeva wished to project.

Tsvetaeva balances her admiration for Akhmatova with a passage showing how much Akhmatova valued the poems she wrote for her: "I know that later in 1916–17, Akhmatova did not part with my handwritten poems to her and carried them around in her purse so long that only folds and cracks remained. This story of Osip Mandel'shtam is one of the greatest joys of my life" (4:287). When in October of 1958 Chukovskaia read excerpts from "An Otherworldly Evening" (then circulating in typescript) to Akhmatova, she responded, "This never was. Neither her poems in my purse, nor the cracks and folds."[66] Akhmatova may have forgotten this detail, or preferred to deny it. Perhaps Mandel'shtam made it up it to please Tsvetaeva, and certainly Tsvetaeva, who also referred to it in a notebook entry of March 1925,[67] could have invented it.[68] In any event, on the pages of "An Otherworldly Evening" Akhmatova carrying Tsvetaeva's poems with her everywhere she goes and Tsvetaeva's joy upon learning this create an image that encapsulates vividly and economically the relationship between them that Tsvetaeva wishes to establish in her essay.

"An Otherworldly Evening" concludes with a shift from the past that Tsvetaeva recalls in the essay (the winter of 1915/16) to the present in which she composes it (1936).[69] From this temporal vantage point, the "otherworldliness" that describes the evening takes on additional meaning. Far from Symbolist metaphysics and no longer simply a signifier for a magical evening, it designates a culture that is now extinct. Tsvetaeva's commemoration of Kuzmin opens out into a commemoration of a bygone era that she captures on the eve of momentous historical events that transformed Russia and determined the fates of her poets.

Сидели и читали стихи. Последние стихи на последних шкурах у последних каминов. Никем за весь вечер не было произнесено слово фронт, не было произнесено—в таком физическом соседстве—имя Распутин.

Завтра же Сережа и Лёня кончали жизнь . . .

Завтра Ахматова теряла *всех*, Гумилев—жизнь . . .

Но сегодня вечер был наш! . . .

И—все заплатили. Сережа и Лёня—жизнью, Гумилев—жизнью, Есенин—жизнью, Кузмин, Ахматова, я—пожизненным заключением в самих себе, в этой крепости—вернее Петропавловской. (4:292; emphasis in the original, ellipses mine)[70]

We sat and read poems. The last poems on the last bearskins by the last fireplaces. The entire evening no one uttered the word front, no one uttered—in such close physical proximity—the name Rasputin.

Already the next day—Serezha and Lënia were ending their lives . . .
Tomorrow Akhmatova was losing *everyone*, Gumilev—his life . . .
But today the evening was ours! . . .
And everyone paid. Serezha and Lënia with their lives, Gumilev with his life, Esenin with his life, Kuzmin, Akhmatova, and I with a life sentence to confinement within ourselves, in this fortress that is more secure than Peter and Paul [Fortress].

As Tsvetaeva brings "An Otherworldly Evening" into this expanded temporality, she obviates the very need for her earlier strategic positioning vis-à-vis Akhmatova. The evening now emerges as a feast in time of the plague that supersedes the poet's physical self. "A feast in time of the Plague? *Yes*. But those feasted with wine and roses, we on the other hand— incorporeally, miraculously, like pure spirits—already shades of Hades— with words: *sounds* of words and the living blood of our senses" (4:292; emphasis in the original). It is here—in the loss and horror of their age—that Tsvetaeva establishes the closest ties with Akhmatova, ties that would be subsequently borne out in real life after Tsvetaeva's ill-starred repatriation.

Whatever Akhmatova's objections to specific details of "An Otherworldly Evening," the essay establishes a powerful bond among poets who staked their lives on their art and paid the high price exacted for its practice. Akhmatova later recognized this bond in three poems, none of which reached Tsvetaeva: "A Belated Reply" ("Pozdnii otvet"), "That's How I Am" ("Kakaia est'"), and "There Are Four of Us" ("Nas chetvero"). Akhmatova wrote her "Belated Reply" on March 16, 1940—some nine months after Tsvetaeva's return to Moscow in June of 1939, after seventeen years in emigration.[71] The title invokes the poems and letters Tsvetaeva wrote her decades earlier and to which Akhmatova now responds. The poem itself speaks of the horrific present as Akhmatova draws Tsvetaeva's early poems into the cruel context of Stalinist Russia. These temporalities inform two facets of her poem—one distant and the other deeply sympathetic.

Akhmatova's epigraph "My white-handed one, practitioner of black magic . . ." (*Beloruchen'ka moia, chernoknizhnitsa . . .*) comes from Tsvetaeva's 1921 folk-style lyric "For Akhmatova" (2:79), which references Blok's death and Gumilev's execution of that year and intimates the peril this double loss portends for Akhmatova and, by extension, all poets. In that lyric, Tsvetaeva takes on the voice, diction, and rhythm of a caster of spells to pose questions that highlight irredeemable loss and to forge ties with Akhmatova. (Gumilev famously attached the label "sorceress" [*koldun'ia*] to Akhmatova in his poem "From the Serpent's Lair" ["Iz logova zmieva," pub. 1911].) Tsvetaeva's designation of Akhmatova as a "practitioner of black magic" (*chernoknizhnitsa*) is one she applied to herself in the poem "Annunciation Eve" ("Kanun Blagoveshchen'ia," March 24–25, 1916), which she wrote shortly before beginning her cycle to Akhmatova in June of that year. This prompted E. A. Znosko-Borovskii to describe the poem "For Akhmatova" as Tsvetaeva's "challenge to a duel of sorceresses."[72] His reading appeared in the émigré publication *The Will of Russia* (*Volia Rossii*) in 1924, when recognition of Tsvetaeva and Akhmatova as the preeminent women poets of the time had already phased into debates on which poet was better.[73] How readers construe Akhmatova's and Tsvetaeva's relationship determines whether they read Tsvetaeva's "For Akhmatova" as a challenge she issues to establish primacy or as homage to a poet she values highly enough to absorb into her own creative world. It determines also whether readers see Akhmatova's "Belated Reply" as responding to Tsvetaeva's challenge to a duel or as joining with her in poetry.

The two lines from Tsvetaeva's poem that Akhmatova selects as the epigraph for her "Belated Reply" complete a quatrain that opens with the question, "Where are your helpers, / Those comrades in arms?" (*Gde spodruzhniki tvoi, / Te spodvizhnichki?* [2:79]). In the time Akhmatova composed her reply to Tsvetaeva, the fears sensed in 1921 had been realized. Akhmatova had witnessed the horrors of Stalinist repression and had suffered vilification, surveillance, imposed silence, repeated arrests of loved ones, and deaths of admired poets. She had just completed *Requiem*, which was to remain unpublished until 1963, and in the year of her reply to Tsvetaeva (1940) saw the collection *From Six Books*, which Stalin initially authorized, pulled from circulation. The new context in which she invokes Tsvetaeva's lines includes also the arrests of that poet's daughter and husband (August 27 and November 7, 1939) that left her a homeless pariah bereft of family, friends, and livelihood just months after her arrival in Stalinist Russia. The questions Tsvetaeva poses in her earlier poem to Akhmatova can now be asked of her as well.

"A Belated Reply" opens with nouns describing Tsvetaeva as an "invisible creature" (*nevidimka*), a "double" (*dvoinik*), and a "mockingbird" (*peresmeshnik*), all three of which deny the addressee a discrete identity. The incorporeality implicit in the first leaves her with no image of her own to inhabit. As a double she can only replicate someone else, and as a mockingbird she has no songs of her own and can only repeat those of others.[74] The appellation "mockingbird" harks back to Tsvetaeva's detractors, who saw her exceptional assimilative capacity as merely imitative.[75] What Shevelenko describes as the "interiorization of another's 'I'" (*interiorizatsiia chuzhogo "ia"*)[76] is in full evidence in the poems Tsvetaeva addressed to Akhmatova, who now responds. As Akhmatova understood, Tsvetaeva's emulation of her voice and stylistics is both homage and the assertion of a poetic self capable of engulfing her addressee. The images with which Akhmatova opens her "Belated Reply" appear to defuse Tsvetaeva's self-assertiveness.

Akhmatova continues "A Belated Reply" with expressions of loss articulated by her addressee. Echoing Tsvetaeva's frequently invoked onomastic association with her namesake Marina Mnishek, Akhmatova has her shout from the tower in which, as legend had it, Mnishek was held prisoner.[77]

> То кричишь из Маринкиной башни:
> «Я сегодня вернулась домой.
> Полюбуйтесь, родимые пашни,
> Что за это случилось со мной.
> Поглотила любимых пучина,
> И разграблен родительский дом». (1:469)

> Or you shout from Marinka's tower:
> "I returned home today.
> Feast your eyes, dear fields,
> On what happened to me for that.
> An abyss swallowed up my loved ones,
> And my parental home is pillaged."

Mnishek's triumphal entry into Moscow and high expectations of glory were dashed when her husband, the false Dimitri, was shot dead shortly after their coronation. Comparing Tsvetaeva to Mnishek recognizes the tragedy of her situation but suggests also the poet's false assumptions about the status she could claim in Moscow. In a notebook entry Akhmatova observes apropos Tsvetaeva's return, "Now, when she returned to her Moscow like such a queen and this time forever . . ."[78]

Alexandra Smith perceptively notes that the reference to Mnishek subtextually invokes Tsvetaeva's relations with Mandel'shtam and the verse they exchanged after her debut in Petrograd in the winter of 1915/16.[79] Between Tsvetaeva's return to Moscow from that trip and her composition of the cycle of poems to Akhmatova that it inspired, an intense relationship developed between Tsvetaeva and Mandel'shtam, whom she also presented with the gift of "her" Moscow and with whom she read and discussed Akhmatova's poetry.[80] Shortly before Tsvetaeva emigrated in May of 1922, Mandel'shtam wrote dismissively of women's poetry and delivered a deeply wounding misogynous attack on Tsvetaeva in an essay describing the literary scene in Moscow at the time.[81] Akhmatova, who developed a close friendship with Mandel'shtam, was privy to his disaffection with Tsvetaeva. The subtextual reference to Mandel'shtam folds yet another of Tsvetaeva's painful losses into her "Belated Reply."

At this juncture, a striking change occurs in Akhmatova's poem as it enters a "today" (*segodnia*) in which she and Tsvetaeva walk through the midnight streets of Moscow together and the addressee's isolation in the tower gives way to an image of shared suffering and poetic responsibility. Behind them are millions who follow in profound silence. The resonant glory of the city that Tsvetaeva bestowed on Petersburg poets in her early lyrics is radically transformed. The renowned Moscow bells now toll for the dead, and the only other sound is that of a blizzard that obliterates the poets' traces:

> А вокруг погребальные звоны,
> Да московские хриплые стоны
> Вьюги, наш заметающей след. (1:469)

> And all around is funereal ringing,
> And the hoarse Muscovite groans
> Of a blizzard sweeping away our traces.

If the first part of Akhmatova's poem (lines 1–10) can be seen as suggestive of rivalry or perhaps even a settling of scores, the second (lines 11–17) shows both poets, indeed everything around them, absorbed into a human tragedy of unspeakable proportions that dwarfs all else and swallows up individuating features. Territorial delineations of their spheres of influence are rendered moot as the distinction between Moscow and the city that now bears the name Leningrad is erased by the groaning blizzard. Any differences between Akhmatova and her addressee fall away in the face of the pain they endure and the annihilation that threatens them both.

This ending casts a new light on the opening of the poem, and what might initially be seen as haughty rejoinders to Tsvetaeva take on a warmer cast. In the context of the two poets walking side by side at the poem's end, its first section is more readily recognizable as pertinent not only to Tsvetaeva but to Akhmatova as well. The nouns that Akhmatova applies to her addressee in the first line of the poem are suggestive of her own mimicry in her later verse of defining characteristics of Tsvetaeva's. The concealment in secluded spots and the occasional sightings in places that mark loss apply also to Akhmatova, whose vilification and barring from publication followed on the celebrity that she enjoyed when Tsvetaeva first praised her. The fall of Tsvetaeva's prideful namesake Marina Mnishek is also that of

Akhmatova, who now comes to Moscow not as a luminary but as a supplicant to plead on behalf of her arrested son. Tsvetaeva's subtextually implied loss of Mandel'shtam is joined in the present by Akhmatova's own protracted loss of that poet—a close friend whose arrests, exile, deportation to a concentration camp, and death she witnessed. As she echoes Tsvetaeva, Akhmatova creates a shadow image of herself as well. This could be regarded as competition or dueling, but it can also be seen as an expression of solidarity—of Akhmatova joining in the creative interpenetration that Tsvetaeva practiced in her poetry and advocated in her prose. The ending of "A Belated Reply" and the echoes of Tsvetaeva's poetry that appear in Akhmatova's later verse argue for the latter reading.[82]

The closing lines of "A Belated Reply" suggest helplessness in the face of the elemental force that sweeps away all traces of the two poets and their mute followers. But the subtle ties with other poets suggest hope. Blok can be discerned in the blizzard. Tsvetaeva walks by her side, and the last two lines are linked by a characteristically Tsvetaevan enjambment.[83] In *Requiem*, which she spent five years composing just before beginning this poem to Tsvetaeva, Akhmatova vows to testify on behalf of silent fellow sufferers. In this poem, she has Tsvetaeva join her in the project. Shared suffering and the responsibility to give it voice unites them, but that they come together in their very differences is also the function of their shared appreciation of the effects of temporal passage on what and how things signify. The expanded temporality in which Tsvetaeva recontextualizes her relations with Akhmatova at the end of "An Otherworldly Evening" subsumes their differences. The belatedness of Akhmatova's reply to Tsvetaeva taps into a similar temporal expansion. In their chilling present, the differences between the two poets and the rivalry insistently projected onto them lose significance.

Chukovskaia records Akhmatova's regret that she did not share "A Belated Reply" with Tsvetaeva during their two-day meeting on the sixth and seventh of June in 1941: "I couldn't bring myself to read it to her. And now I am sorry. She dedicated so many poems to me. This would have been a reply, albeit decades later. But I couldn't because of the horrific line about her loved ones."[84] Tsvetaeva initiated the two meetings—the first via a friend and the second by direct request to Akhmatova. The encounters introduced correctives into how they envisioned each other and allowed them to exchange recent work. But they could not close the gap created by intervening time and unfamiliarity with each other's writings. Predispositions, fears, and uncertainties also had an effect. Tsvetaeva came to the meeting disappointed by Akhmatova's *From Six Books*: "Old, weak . . . But what did she do from 1917 to 1940? *Inside* herself. This book is an irreparably-blank page . . . Pity."[85] The excerpts Akhmatova shared with her from *A Poem without a Hero*, which she was working on at the time, seemed like a throwback to the

World of Art days. Akhmatova later quoted Tsvetaeva's retort, "One has to be possessed of great daring to write about harlequins and Pierrots in 1941."[86]

For her part, Akhmatova could not immediately appreciate *Poem of the Air* (*Poema vozdukha*), which Tsvetaeva copied out for her on the night between their two meetings and which struck Akhmatova as transsense (*zaum'*). Memoirists and commentators have much to say about these meetings—recording observations, speculating, repeating what they heard from others, and projecting their own notions about the poets onto what might have transpired between them. The poets themselves were reticent about their encounter. There is no mention of it in Tsvetaeva's notebooks, and considerable time passed before Akhmatova began describing it to friends, who variously recorded what she told them.[87] Her own plans to write an account of the meetings date to January 1963 but go no further than an excerpt titled "A This-Worldly Evening" ("Zdeshnii vecher").

Tsvetaeva's suicide a few months after their meetings deeply affected Akhmatova, and in December of 1941, Chukovskaia speaks anxiously of Akhmatova's "constant desire to draw a parallel between her fate and Tsvetaeva's."[88] The poem "That's How I Am," dated June 24, 1942, reveals Akhmatova's growing anxiety and survivor guilt in the face of the mounting casualties of the state. In it, Akhmatova speaks of her anguish and envisions her impending death. Comparing herself to Tsvetaeva, she frames suicide as submission to the inevitability of death.

> Но близится конец моей гордыне,
> Как той, другой—страдалице Марине,—
> Придется мне напиться пустотой. (4:279)

> But the end of my pride draws near,
> Like that other one—the sufferer Marina,—
> I will have to drink my fill of emptiness.

Yet if for Akhmatova their poetry and shared tragic fate drew them together, Tsvetaeva's prose was a source of dissent. Over the years, Akhmatova devoted considerable energy to refuting various fictions, images, and legends that grew up around her. Her retorts to Tsvetaeva's essays were part of an effort to set the record straight and to establish a creative identity of her own design.[89] As Akhmatova familiarized herself with essays Tsvetaeva had written in emigration, she objected to the mythologization that characterizes them. For Tsvetaeva, specific details and events were conduits to apprehending something larger that left behind the reductive world of facts to enter the generative realm of myth. Idiosyncratic readings of events and circumstances—whether actual or invented—were essential to her art and constitutive of her creative selfhood. Akhmatova directed her efforts toward different ends. Her project of self-invention was rooted in detachment and objectivity—or their semblance—and she did not often concur with Tsvetaeva's expansive treatment of her material.

Contrasting her own ostensible objectivity with Tsvetaeva's frank subjectivity, Akhmatova comments on essays that she read in April of 1959. She remarks that in "A Hero of Labor" Tsvetaeva was too easy on Briusov and praises "Mother and Music" ("Mat' i muzyka") as a work of genius ("eto genial'naia veshch'"). Three essays are dismissed out of hand: "My Pushkin" ("Moi Pushkin"); "A Captive Spirit" ("Plennyi dukh"), dedicated to Andrei Belyi; and the commemoration of Voloshin "Zhivoe o zhivom" ("The Living about the Living").[90] Akhmatova's reading of Tsvetaeva's essays is consistent with the relationship to the surrounding world that characterizes her own early writings. This relationship reveals itself not in the absence of subjectivity from her works but in a transparency that makes it unobtrusive. This combines with Akhmatova's need to push past the myths that enmeshed her and leads her to reinstate facts that Tsvetaeva used as points of departure for her creative explorations.

Akhmatova leaves the meaning with which Tsvetaeva invests these departures without notice. A case in point is her categorical statement on Tsvetaeva's "My Pushkin," which suggests competition for authority over the Golden Age poet. "Marina shouldn't be allowed to come within three versts of Pushkin, she does not understand a single sound in him" (2:351). In September of 1962, Akhmatova reiterates her categorical position: "Marina should not have written about Pushkin. She did not understand him and did not know him" (2:519). The reaction to Tsvetaeva's "The Living about the Living" is similarly harsh: "I didn't even begin reading about Voloshin. I know Marina worships him, but I cannot stand him: gossip always emanated from Koktebel'" (2:352).

Despite her claim that she ignored "The Living about the Living," Akhmatova read the essay and in her notebooks recorded objections to the Cherubina mystification and to Tsvetaeva's account of it. A Petersburg poet who had firsthand information about the episode and direct contact with some of its major players, Akhmatova registered her intense dislike of Dmitrieva, whom she branded an opportunist, and her disaffection with Voloshin for what she saw as his ill-treatment of Gumilev. Her remarks present the mystification and the conditions that fostered it in a different light:

Still, [Dmitrieva] miscalculated. She thought that a duel between two poets on her account would make her a fashionable Petersb<urg> lady and would secure her a place of honor in the literary circles of the capital, but for some reason she, too, had to leave almost forever . . . She wrote a hysterical letter to me and passionate poems to Nik<olai> Step<anovich> [Gumilev]. Nothing came of our meeting. No one knows all of this. In Kokt<ebel'> they babbled and [still] babble nonsense.[91]

Only hinting at Dmitrieva's relations with Gumilev as he courted Akhmatova and proposed marriage to them both, Akhmatova notes disagreements about which of Gumilev's poems were dedicated to her and which to Dmitrieva. Of primary interest to this study is that Akhmatova sees herself contending with Cherubina de Gabriak for the title of leading woman poet of the time:

> Apparently, at that time (1909–10) some kind of secret vacancy opened for a woman's place in Russian poetry. And Cherubina rushed for it. The duel or something in her verse prevented her from occupying that place. Destiny wanted it to become mine. It is remarkable that Marina Tsvetaeva somehow half understood this. (Find this passage in her *Prose*) pg. 152.[92]

Decades after her own literary debut when Cherubina de Gabriak was all but forgotten, Akhmatova still felt compelled to compete with Dmitrieva when she read about her in "The Living about the Living." On page 152, as Akhmatova notes, she found the passage she was looking for without specifying which passage this was. On that page Tsvetaeva comments apropos two lines of de Gabriak's verse, "—the image is Akhmatova's, the thrust—mine, verses written before both Akhmatova and me—that is how correct my assertion is that all poems that were, that are, and that will be are written by one, nameless woman."[93] This condensed, idiosyncratic expression of Tsvetaeva's expansive vision of unity among all women is followed on the same page by de Gabriak's burial: "This was the end of Cherubina. She wrote no more. Perhaps she wrote, but no one read her anymore, no one heard her voice anymore" (152). Given the tone of Akhmatova's reaction to Tsvetaeva's essay, she is likely referring to the latter of these two passages in her notebook entry.

Akhmatova further objects to disparities between fact and fiction that she discerns in "The Living about the Living." Into the twofold confabulation of the mystification itself and of Voloshin's fictionalized history of it on which Tsvetaeva relies in her presentation, Akhmatova interjects fact, but also her private notions:

> What nonsense, incidentally, that all of *Apollo* was in love with Cherubina. Who?—Kuzmin, Znosko-Borovsky?[94]—And where does that image of the modest schoolteacher come from? Dm<itrieva> had already been to Paris, shone in Koktebel', was friends with Margo [Voloshin's wife Margarita Sabash-

nikova], studied Provençal poetry, and then became a theosophic mother of god.

But Mak<ovsky> really did throw out Annensky's poems, from the first issue in order to publish her, which hastened the death of In<nokentii> Feod<orovich>. (See An<nensky> letter to Mak<ovsky> . . .). "Let us speak no more of this and try not to think about it." Tsvetaeva does not write about this but cultivates unimaginable, very shameful prattle around Voloshin.[95]

As Akhmatova must have understood, Tsvetaeva knew nothing about the displacement of Annensky's poems by de Gabriak's or about his letter to Makovsky of November 12, 1909, deploring it.

Akhmatova repeatedly distinguished her own way of relating events from Tsvetaeva's. Her dismissal of Tsvetaeva's purposeful subjectivity is encapsulated in a passage from the "Masquerade—New Year's Devilry" ("Maskarad—Novogodniaia chertovnia") section of her *Prose about a Poem* (*Proza o Poeme—Pro Domo Mea*), which speaks of "Marina Tsvetaeva, who arrived from Moscow to her 'Otherworldly Evening' and who muddled up everything in the world" (3:266). In her notes for a planned account of their meeting, which Akhmatova pointedly titles "A This-Worldly Evening, or Two Days (On Marina Tsvetaeva)" ("Zdeshnii vecher, ili Dva dnia [o Marine Tsvetaevoi]"), she observed, "It is frightening to think how Marina herself would have described these meetings if she remained alive and I died on Aug[ust] 31, '41. It would have been a 'perfumed legend,' as our grandfathers used to say. Maybe it would have been a lament for a 25-year love that turned out to be in vain, but in any event, it would have been magnificent."[96] Her own purpose, Akhmatova claims, is simple and straightforward: "I would like to remember these <u>Two days</u> simply, 'with no legend.'"[97] The project did not materialize.

Akhmatova's exasperation with Tsvetaeva's essays is balanced by her deep appreciation of Tsvetaeva's poetry and the tragic fate they shared with other poets in Stalinist Russia. The relaxation of repression and censorship ushered in by Khrushchev's Thaw enabled the tentative publication of poets who had been forced into silence or murdered in the Stalinist period and who now reappeared before readers. Among such publications were Tsvetaeva's *Selected Works* (*Izbrannoe*), which came out in Moscow in 1961. Four years in the making, the volume sparked interest in Tsvetaeva's work, which, together with Mandel'shtam's, was prominent in the samizdat at the time.[98] This allowed Akhmatova to familiarize herself with more of Tsvetaeva's poetry and to refer to her more openly. Beginning in 1961, Tsvetaeva's name recurs regularly in her works, notebooks, and sketches.[99] Akhmatova's name and works also edged their way back into the press, but a strong tendency to relegate her to a bygone era left her overshadowed by newly published poets, most of whom were no longer alive.[100] In the poem "There Are Four of Us" ("Nas chetvero"),[101] which she wrote in November of 1961, Akhmatova marks her strong ties with three such poets: Mandel'shtam, who perished in a transit camp in 1938; the vilified Pasternak, who died in 1960; and Tsvetaeva, who committed suicide in 1941. This marks the same four-some of poets that Tsvetaeva discusses in her 1933 essay "Poets with a History and Poets without a History."

"There Are Four of Us" references Tsvetaeva's poem "Elderberry" ("Buzina"). Dated September 11, 1931, Meudon–May 21, 1935, Vanves, the poem remained unpublished during Tsvetaeva's lifetime and first appeared in the truncated version that Akhmatova read in the 1961 *Selected Works*.[102] Recognizable even in the poem's incomplete state is the unfolding Russian Revolution that Tsvetaeva presents metaphorically through images of the el-derberry's transformations over the changing seasons of the year. It begins with the verdant foliage that bursts into the ominous flames of red berries, which, ripening, take on the color and taste of blood and fall from the "exe-cuted" (*kaznena*) elderberry bush to flood the garden "With the blood of the young and the blood of the pure" (*Krov'iu iunykh i krov'iu chistykh*). At the poem's end, only a solitary elderberry bush next to a moaning gate and an empty house remain. Akhmatova, who clearly grasped the underlying import of the elderberry's life cycle, responded to the poem with what Timenchik calls a lyric conversation with Tsvetaeva, initially titled "Komarov Sketches" ("Komarovskie nabroski") and augmented with Mandel'shtam's and Paster-nak's voices.[103]

More than an interlocutor, Akhmatova presents herself in this poem as the "spirit guardian" (*dukh-khranitel'*) of a richly symbolic locus—as a listener and a reader of signs. Having left worldly joys behind and only tenta-tively connected to the world of the living, the speaker of the poem perceives an ethereal exchange between two voices in the "aerial ways" (*vozdushnye puti*). The reference is to a 1924 story of that name in which Pasternak criti-cized for the first time the Revolution he initially supported. It alludes also to the almanac published in New York under the editorship of Roman Green-berg that took its name from Pasternak's story.[104] Among the contents of the almanac's five volumes, which came out between 1960 and 1967, are works of the four poets who appear in Akhmatova's poem, together with docu-ments and scholarly articles relating to them.[105] In 1961, when Akhmatova composed "There Are Four of Us," she, Pasternak, and Mandel'shtam had already been featured in *Aerial Ways*, while Tsvetaeva was to appear in later volumes. The "aerial ways" of Akhmatova's poem thus bring together Paster-nak's early criticism of the Revolution, the poets it attempted to stifle, and the almanac of that name in which their voices continue to be heard.

Akhmatova grants Tsvetaeva an entire stanza in the poem, featuring her as the author of a figurative letter—the "Dark, fresh branch of elderberry" (*Temnaia, svezhaia vetv' buziny*) that the speaker discerns in a thicket of raspberries. Recalling the poem "Elderberry" with the image of a living branch of that bush, which she describes as a message from Tsvetaeva, Akhmatova indicates the ties between them. Denying death dominion by recognizing signs from the deceased in the surrounding world is characteristic of Tsvetaeva herself—found in all her writings on the deaths of poets and loved ones. Such recognition is predicated on an interpenetration of subject and object that signals an interpenetration of life and death and removes the divide between them. With the reference to the branch of elderberry as a letter from Tsvetaeva, Akhmatova persists—even after Tsvetaeva's death—in the role of her addressee and responds to her metaphorical letter with a poem.

The three poets Akhmatova draws into "There Are Four of Us" are designated by epigraphs taken from poems that they addressed to her,[106] making her the center around which they come together. Contrasted with the ephemerality of lived life, which she describes as "but a habit" (*Zhit'— eto tol'ko privychka*),[107] are the abiding ties that hold—as the present tense of the title insists—among these poets even beyond their deaths. Tsvetaeva is represented with what now sounds like a prophetic apostrophe to Akhmatova, "O, Muse of Weeping." As Akhmatova composes "There Are Four of Us," it is clear that the "helpers" and "comrades in arms" after whom Tsvetaeva inquires in the poem "For Akhmatova" are other poets—past, present, and, as attested to by Akhmatova's mentorship of Brodsky, whom she met that year, future as well. In light of poetry's breach of the binary of life and death, the gender binary pales in significance.

Underlying Tsvetaeva's efforts to present her relationship with Akhmatova as one of mutually reinforcing differences that banished jealousy and enmity was a deep appreciation of her verse. References to Akhmatova and lines from her poems cited from memory appear throughout Tsvetaeva's notebooks, letters, and essays, whether by association or to illuminate points she wishes to make. Tsvetaeva responded to the seemingly inescapable comparisons between herself and Akhmatova and the rivalry they threatened to trigger by engaging Akhmatova in the space of her writings. Drawing Akhmatova into her own creative world, Tsvetaeva finds sustenance, affirms her selfhood, and enacts a productive relationship that embraces their differences. She also offers a model for other women poets. The relationship she promotes with Akhmatova precludes the sort of discord that worked to Pavlova's and Rostopchina's disadvantage. Forestalling contention, Tsvetaeva embraces her dissimilar sister poet to insist on the sustainability of their divergent selves in the vast realm of poetry they inhabit. Akhmatova upholds the verity of Tsvetaeva's thinking. Whatever her objections to Tsvetaeva's essays, her absorption of Tsvetaeva's poetry into her own in the latter years of her career is consistent with the poetic confluence that Tsvetaeva conceptualized in her prose, having first put it into practice when she assimilated Akhmatova's creative world into her own.

Conclusion

Yet our [critics'] words have real power. What
we say about a poet is what will be believed.
What we cite from a poem is what will be
remembered.
—Maximilian Voloshin, "Horoscope of Cherubina
de Gabriak"

THIS BOOK STUDIES how leading Russian women
poets of the nineteenth and early twentieth century worked to attain not
simply recognition, but creative self-realization, within a tradition that resisted their participation. As I explore inventions of women poets from both
sides of the divide between the authors and their readers, my focus is on
the woman poet as an active agent who folds available cultural vocabulary
into her negotiations between compliance with established norms and resistance to them. To this purpose, I attend to the specific sociopolitical and
cultural conditions in which these women wrote and in which their poems
were received. Using case studies as apertures into the cultures of the time, I
privilege what the women poets themselves write, calling attention to strategies they develop in response to changing constructs of the woman and the
unchanging biases underpinning them. Studying these women poets in dynamic interaction with their surrounding world, I show the sophisticated
encoding practices and largely overlooked subversive strategies that they
develop in response to their untenable circumstances. This leads me to foreground two categories of reading that alternately hold back and advance the
woman poet. On the one hand are superficial readings that leave women's
poems reaffirming the gender biases they subvert. On the other are women's
enabling rereadings that reposition them in the tradition.

Within conditions that bred "a tradition of self-restraint and evasive
tactics"[1] women poets had to develop means to sidestep not only the gov-
ernmental prohibitions that all poets confronted, but also the restrictions
imposed by prevailing gender norms. The vast encoding potential vested in
poetic language makes it particularly well suited for concealing proscribed
views, fostering a conspiratorial relationship between poets and readers who

could apprehend subversive meaning that remained opaque to the censor. This generic benefit entails a potential liability. The heightened interpretive responsibility that accrues to readers increases poets' dependency on how their poems are read and leaves them more vulnerable to misapprehension. The additional layer of gender-dictated restrictions that necessitated evasion intensified women poets' dependency on readers whose receptiveness to their poems, however, was compromised by prevailing notions of gender. Women poets veiled their resistance to constructs of the woman from the male establishment that determined them while readers brought these constructs to bear on their poems. In the absence of a readership that apprehends the deeper import of a poem, attaining publication loses value. Having gained recognition, women poets still contended with reductive readings.

Readers who penetrated the cultural vocabulary that men used to conceal subversive messages neglected to do the same for women who similarly invoked prevailing norms in order to undermine them. The deeper layers of meaning in Pavlova's "We are contemporaries, Countess" and Rostopchina's argument in "How Women Must Write" remained without notice because the feminine modesty and compliance with men's precepts delivered on the surface of these poems concurred with what was expected of women. Accordingly, Pavlova's poem is read as supporting inimical patriarchal norms rather than enacting the woman poet's capacity to write in restrictive conditions just as her male counterparts did. Rostopchina's strategic use of feminine masquerade and her injunction that women conceal their inner selves from men are similarly taken at face value. Her challenges to male authority and claims to ascendancy in poems addressed to Pushkin and Lermontov are seen, again in keeping with expectations, as unalloyed praise. Leaving Pavlova and Rostopchina celebrating a conformity with established norms that they in fact contravene, such reader-imposed censorship maintains the status quo they challenge.

Women poets' subordinate position and dependence on the male establishment for validation left them especially vulnerable to prejudicial assessments of influential critics. Changing constructs of the woman that combined with critics' gender biases exacerbated the situation. Belinsky's review of Rostopchina's *Poems* reflects his own shifting sociopolitical views but ultimately carries more weight than her writing. Untested against Rostopchina's oeuvre and insistently repeated over time, the critic's branding of Rostopchina as a frivolous society lady took on the semblance of truth. Failing to discern their critical edge, Belinsky drew disproportionate attention to poems in which Rostopchina describes social events. This selectivity joined shallow readings and citation of passages divorced from their contexts to perpetuate the image Belinsky forged, and this image further disinclined readers to give her writings closer attention.[2] His unjust assessment haunts Rostopchina to this day.

The growing number of women poets who emerged in the early twentieth century attracted increasing attention to the uncharted feminine domain. Women's creativity suggested new promise, stimulated curiosity, but also invited colonization and left the male establishment anxious to remain in control. As women grew in confidence and number, men's constructs of the woman strained harder against the women themselves. What was seen as the woman's threatening unknowability easily converted into the knowable of what men invented in their own writings and in their controlling mentorship of aspiring women poets. For all the differences between them, Cherubina de Gabriak and Nelli were both normative and aimed to contain rather than advance the woman poet. Cherubina accorded with the notion that women serve as material for men's projects, while Nelli was conceived as a disincentive to women poets' creative self-realization.

The expectation that the actual woman poet correspond to the image that men projected onto her continued to weigh on women, who, for all their progress, remained dependent on male authorization. The creative crisis that Dmitrieva—the alleged beneficiary of the Cherubina mystification—underwent emblematizes the tensions between the demands of the male establishment and the woman poet's selfhood. Curiously, even now when information about the episode has become available, publications of Dmitrieva's works make little distinction between the poems she wrote masquerading as Cherubina under Voloshin's direction and those she wrote on her own. The split in her creative identity precipitated by the mystification is similarly glossed over. The invented Cherubina de Gabriak and the actual poet who used "Cherubina de Gabriak" as a nom de plume in her subsequent work are scarcely differentiated—this despite the sharp distinction between them on which Dmitrieva herself insists. Along the same lines, Dmitrieva's "Autobiography" is not the poet's own account of herself, but a compendium of passages from her letters that Evgenii Arkhipov selected and arranged at will. Arkhipov was a close friend of Dmitrieva's, and the "Autobiogrpahy" prefaced a set of Dmitrieva's poems he preserved in typescript. I do not suggest malicious intent behind his compilation or, for that matter, behind Voloshin's invention of Cherubina but wish only to draw attention to the uncritical acceptance of men's routine management of women's words and images.

The beautiful woman aesthetic to which the invented Cherubina catered affected the reception of other women poets as well. Thus Akhmatova's title as one of the beauties of 1913 and the proliferating images of her at the outset of her career threatened to overwhelm her poetry.[3] The fact that decades later when de Gabriak was all but forgotten Akhmatova still saw herself in competition with her speaks volumes about the impact that this fiction born of male fantasies had on the living woman poet.

The creative vigor of Tsvetaeva's responses to the Nelli and the Cherubina de Gabriak mystifications is sparked by her cognizance of the challenge they pose to women's creative self-realization. In "A Hero of Labor," she asserts her poetic selfhood in terms of the adversarial stance she assumes toward Briusov, the powerful male poet and critic whom she quickly outgrows, while in "The Living about the Living," she supplants male mentorship with a mutually enriching friendship with Voloshin. The latter essay features a book that Tsvetaeva makes by binding together into a single volume the poems of Maximilian Voloshin and Adelaida Gertsyk. Encapsulated in this root metaphor is the equality of men and women poets.[4] The gender parity it epitomizes, Tsvetaeva insists, is within reach of all women who have only to reject male authority by refusing to act in accordance with men's expectations. Delivered obliquely in a wide variety of images and situations throughout her essays, the message is that all poets—regardless of their gender—must respond to the dictates of their art in accordance with their own creative needs.

The disadvantages of continued reliance on male endorsement from which Tsvetaeva urged women to free themselves were manifold. Bowing to men's demands, the woman poet opened herself to objectification and reinforced prevailing gender stereotypes that denied her selfhood. Intensified by a dearth of women role models, her efforts to win male approval heightened her self-consciousness and her preoccupation with how she would be received both as a woman and as a poet. This constrained her self-expression and fostered an intolerance to differences in how other women presented themselves. Discords bred in these circumstances closed down receptivity to what they could absorb from each other and intensified the propensity to position them as adversaries. Such pitting of women poets against one another that Barbara Johnson describes as the "divide and conquer" school of criticism[5] and that Tsvetaeva experienced at first hand motivates how Tsvetaeva writes about Akhmatova. Characteristically, the intensely personal, subjective dimension of her stance toward Akhmatova underpins a message with broader implications. Demonstratively eschewing discord like that between Pavlova and Rostopchina, Tsvetaeva shapes a relationship with her sister poet that does not simply neutralize their dissimilarities but presents them as mutually energizing. Using an argument analogous to the one she consistently advances against the gender binary, Tsvetaeva insists on the capacious poetic embrace of differences.

The oppositional pairing of the two poets persisted beyond Tsvetaeva's death when Akhmatova found herself in competition with her subsequently rehabilitated sister poet. It is in evidence even now, used to establish limiting typologies of women poets and fueling competition that calls on readers to choose a single winner. (I recently ran across a website that urged people to vote for one poet over the other.) The purportedly fair-minded solution that Kornilov offers in his essay "Antipodes (Tsvetaeva and Akhmatova)"

Conclusion

("Antipody [Tsvetaeva i Akhmatova]") highlights the enforced isolation of the lone woman on the peak of poetic success. "I hope that even a century from now Tsvetaeva and Akhmatova will replace one another in turn on the pinnacle of the Russian Olympus, and that readers' attention to one or the other will alternately pale and flare up again."[6] The enlargement of possibility for women poets that Tsvetaeva advocates with her strategically crafted image of how she relates to Akhmatova is a powerful counterargument to the "beauty pageant" bias that allows for the crowning of only one woman[7] and feeds into divide and conquer criticism.

Notably, the isolation of women poets from one another extends also over time as male critics and commentators repeatedly sever the developing line of women's poetry in the Russian tradition. Thus, for example, Khodasevich relegates Pavlova and Rostopchina to oblivion in a period that once again privileged poetry and reestablished ties with the Golden Age. In doing so, he undercuts not only their undisputed status in their time, but also their significance to women poets writing in his own day. Along similar lines, Pavel Gromov's introduction to a complete collection of Pavlova's poems, maintains (erroneously) that Pavlova had no successors.[8] Rostopchina, whom Tsvetaeva includes among the female friends who constituted her supportive virtual community, is still habitually read through the prism of Belinsky's sociopolitically motivated assessment of her verse. Beyond discounting her complex creative identity and poetic range, this denies her importance for subsequent women poets.

Opposite reader-imposed censorship that stems from and upholds entrenched gender biases and dismissive readings of women poets is the enabling rereading with which they respond. Lacking the power to change the actual circumstances in which they find themselves, women could newly frame them to their benefit. Pavlova derives advantage from connecting the marginalized woman with the marginalized poet. Rostopchina presents the modesty demanded of women as detrimental to the men who dictate it. Indicating the woman's inner world as a privileged space that is inaccessible to men, she turns the tables on the male establishment and attracts interest to women's creativity. Reading women's social comportment as a masquerade that conceals the real woman, she uses this feminine mask to smuggle subversive poems past government censors and male gatekeepers of the tradition alike. Tsvetaeva responds to the objectification that stalked women by framing concern with surface appearances as a sign of poetic insufficiency. She subverts the gender binary but also develops Rostopchina's argument for women's ascendancy over men. Women's dedication to interiority, the privileged space of Romantic lyricism, motivates Tsvetaeva's claim that all women—including even those who do not write—are poets in essence. In her argument, powerlessness in the material world legitimizes women

181

in the privileged domain of the male Romantics. Such enabling rereading counters reader-imposed censorship and weakens the hold of gender-driven preconceptions that readers bring to women's poems. Women's rereading of the existing order and their situation in it allows them to redraw prescribed boundaries, gaining them space in which to work and to claim parity with men.

Tsvetaeva augments enabling rereading by teaching her readers new ways to approach her writing and guiding them into a new relationship with her works. Her prose essays provide instructive examples of a poetic apprehension of meaning-bearing details both in literary texts and in the actual world and draw her reader into a cocreative venture that dissolves the divide between poet and reader. Ultimately, the kind of reading that Tsvetaeva advocates and herself demonstrates in her essays is optimal for all writers and readers regardless of their gender.

As they enlarge the tradition, women poets challenge notions about gender that hold them back with powerful counterarguments that are still relevant today. The close attention I give to the poems in this book and to the specific contexts in which they arose and signified challenges belittling pronouncements of authoritative male critics and offsets unconsciously received biases that continue to affect reception of women's writing. Such attention, which men's poems routinely command, mitigates reader-imposed censorship of women's poems that persists into our own time to affect even serious scholarly work devoted to women's writing. Thus, for example, it counters reductive conclusions like the one Patrick Vincent draws in his important study where he maintains that "the entire 'feud' between Rostopchina and Pavlova, itself a footnote in the debate between Slavophiles and Westernizers, was fought for nothing."[9] This assertion unintentionally upholds precisely those prejudices that blinded Pavlova's and Rostopchina's contemporaneous readers to the underlying import of their disaffection.

The case studies assembled here are unique but illustrative episodes in Russian cultural history. Each shows women poets actively responding to the cultures of their time, deriving possibility from straitened conditions, and working purposefully not to overthrow the tradition, but to gain a rightful place in it. Taken together, these case studies reveal a variously expressed but consistent set of strategies that women poets develop to resist a consistent set of disincentives. These include subversive strategies that push against male authority and enabling strategies that raise women poets' consciousness and self-esteem. Individually and in concert, the case studies in this book enhance mindfulness of the biases and ideological partialities that all readers bring to texts and urge supplanting reader-imposed censorship with enabling rereadings that are informed but not constrained by new approaches.

Notes

PREFACE

1. This title is in keeping with the translation of the poem that appears in Pamela Perkins and Albert Cook, *The Burden of Sufferance: Women Poets of Russia* (New York: Garland Publishing, 1993), 48. The poem has also been translated as "How Women Should Write."

2. Readers seeking broader coverage of Russian women poets can benefit, as I have, from a wide array of studies and anthologies, including Viktoriia Uchenova, ed., *Tsaritsy muz: Russkie poetessy XIX-nachala XX vv* (Moscow: Sovremennik, 1989); Barbara Heldt, *Terrible Perfection: Women and Russian Literature* (Bloomington: Indiana University Press, 1992); Frank Göpfert, *Dichterinnen und Schriftstellerinnen in Russland von der Mitte des 18. bis zum Beginn des 20. Jahrhunderts: Eine Problemskizze* (Munich: Verlag Otto Sagner, 1992); Toby W. Clyman and Diana Green, eds., *Women Writers in Russian Literature* (London: Praeger, 1994); Catriona Kelly, *A History of Russian Women's Writing, 1820–1992* (Oxford: Clarendon Press, 1994); Marina Ledkovsky, Charlotte Rosenthal, Mary Zirin, eds., *A Dictionary of Russian Women Writers* (Westport, Conn.: Greenwood Press, 1994); M. Sh. Fainshtein, ed., *Russkie pisatel'nitsy i literaturnyi protsess* (Wilhelmshorst, Ger.: F. K. Göpfert Verlag, 1995); Rosalind Marsh, trans. and ed., *Gender and Russian Literature: New Perspectives* (Cambridge: Cambridge University Press, 1996); Wendy Rosslyn, *Anna Bunina (1774–1829) and the Origins of Women's Poetry in Russia* (Lewiston, N.Y.: Mellen Press, 1997); Christine Tomei, ed., *Russian Women Writers*, vols. 1 and 2 (New York: Garland Publishing, 1999); Adele Marie Barker and Jehanne M. Gheith, eds., *A History of Women's Writing in Russia* (Cambridge: Cambridge University Press, 2002); Arja Rosenholm and Frank Göpfert, eds., *Vieldeutiges Nicht-zu-Ende-Sprechen: Thesen und Momentaufnahmen aus der Geschichte russischer Dichterinnen* (Fichtenwalde, Ger.: Frank Göpfert Verlag, 2002); Diana Greene, *Reinventing Romantic Poetry: Russian Women Poets of the Mid-Nineteenth Century* (Madison: University of Wisconsin Press, 2004); Wendy

Rosslyn and Alessandra Tosi, eds., *Women in Nineteenth-Century Russia: Lives and Culture* (Cambridge: Open Book Publishers, 2012).

3. Sandra Gilbert and Susan Gubar, *The Madwoman in the Attic: The Woman Writer and the Nineteenth-Century Literary Imagination* (New Haven, Conn.: Yale University Press, 1984), 65.

4. A comprehensive list of scholars who have made major contributions to our appreciation of Russian women's writing requires far more space than is available here. A perforce partial list includes Joe Andrew, Kirsti Ekonen, Sibelan Forrester, Susanne Fusso, Jehanne Gheith, Frank Göpfert, Diana Greene, Barbara Heldt, Catriona Kelly, Marianna Landa, Marina Ledkovsky, Arja Rosenholm, Charlotte Rosenthal, Stephanie Sandler, Irina Savkina, Ursula Stohler, Christine Tomei, Judith Vowles, and Mary Zirin.

5. Leo Strauss, "Persecution and the Art of Writing," in *Persecution and the Art of Writing* (Chicago: University of Chicago Press, 1988), 22–37; Annabel Patterson, *Censorship and Interpretation: The Conditions of Writing and Reading in Early Modern England* (Madison: University of Wisconsin Press, 1984); and Lev Loseff, *On the Beneficence of Censorship: Aesopian Language in Modern Russian Literature* (Munich: Verlag Otto Sagner, 1984).

6. Wolfgang Iser, "The Reading Process: A Phenomenological Approach," in *The Implied Reader: Patterns in Communication in Prose Fiction from Bunyan to Beckett* (Baltimore: Johns Hopkins University Press, 1974), 274–94; Wolfgang Iser, "Interaction between Text and Reader," in *The Reader and the Text: Essays on Audience and Interpretation*, ed. Susan R. Suleiman and Inge Crosman (Princeton, N.J.: Princeton University Press, 1980), 106–19.

7. Erika Greber, *Textile Texte: Poetologische Metaphorik und Literaturtheorie; Studien zur Tradition des Wortflechtens und der Kombinatorik* (Cologne: Böhlau, 2002), 313–72; Schamma Schahadat, "Die Geburt des Autors aus der Mystifikation: Valerij Brjusov, die Signatur und der Stil," in *Mystifikation—Autorschaft—Original*, ed. Susi Frank, Renate Lachmann, et al. (Tübingen: Gunter Narr Verlag, 2001), 183–208.

8. Luce Irigaray, *Speculum of the Other Woman*, trans. Gillian C. Gill (Ithaca, N.Y.: Cornell University Press, 1985); Joan Riviere, "Womanliness as a Masquerade," in *Formations of Fantasy*, ed. Victor Burgin, James Donald, and Cora Kaplan (London: Routledge, 1989), 35–44; Liliane Weissberg, ed., *Weiblichkeit als Maskerade* (Frankfurt: Fischer Taschenbuch, 1994); Stephen Heath, "Joan Riviere and the Masquerade," in *Formations of Fantasy*, ed. Victor Burgin, James Donald, and Cora Kaplan (London: Methuen, 1986), 45–61; Kathleen Woodward, "Youthfulness as a Masquerade," *Discourse* 11, no. 1 (1988–89): 119–42.

9. Used widely in the social and life sciences, case-study methodology is gaining increasing recognition for its value to other fields as well. See the magis-

terial *Case Studies*, ed. Malcolm Tight (London: Sage Publications, 2015), especially vol. 4, *The Use of Case Studies in Other Disciplines*.

10. Suzan van Dijk and Ursula Stohler, "NEWW: New Approaches to European Women's Writing (before 1900)," *Aspasia* 2, no. 1 (2008): 267.

11. Van Dijk and Stohler, "NEWW," 266.

INTRODUCTION

1. Informing my approach are Leo Strauss, "Persecution and the Art of Writing," in *Persecution and the Art of Writing* (Chicago: University of Chicago Press, 1988), 22–37; Annabel Patterson, *Censorship and Interpretation: The Conditions of Writing and Reading in Early Modern England* (Madison: University of Wisconsin Press, 1984); and Lev Loseff, *On the Beneficence of Censorship: Aesopian Language in Modern Russian Literature* (Munich: Verlag Otto Sagner, 1984).

2. This term comes from Wayne Koestenbaum, *The Queen's Throat: Opera, Homosexuality, and the Mystery of Desire* (New York: Poseidon Press, 1993), 11.

3. Barbara Johnson, "Gender and Poetry: Charles Baudelaire and Marceline Desbordes-Valmore," in *Displacements: Women, Traditions, Literatures in French*, ed. Joan DeJean and Nancy K. Miller (Baltimore: Johns Hopkins University Press, 1991), 164.

4. Tricia Lootens, *Lost Saints: Silence, Gender, and Victorian Literary Canonization* (Charlottesville: University Press of Virginia, 1996), 161.

CHAPTER ONE

1. Other women poets of this period include Zinaida Volkonskaia, Anna Gotovtseva, Ekaterina Timasheva, Elizaveta Shakhova, Iulia Zhadovskaia, Nadezhda Khvoshchinskaia, Praskov'ia Bakunina, and Anna Barykova.

2. Arja Rosenholm and Irina Savkina note that Pavlova's poem "Three Souls" ("Tri dushi," 1845) "displays the very type of woman author as Rostopchina," without referring to her directly ("'How Women Should Write': Russian Women's Writing in the Nineteenth Century," in *Women in Nineteenth-Century Russia: Lives and Culture*, ed. Wendy Rosslyn and Alessandra Tosi [Cambridge: Open Book Publishers, 2012], 169).

3. Judith Vowles, "The 'Feminization' of Russian Literature: Women, Language, and Literature in Eighteenth-Century Russia," in *Women Writers in Russian Literature*, ed. Toby W. Clyman and Diana Greene (Westport, Conn.: Praeger, 1994), 35–60.

4. Judith Vowles, "The Inexperienced Muse: Russian Women and Poetry in the First Half of the Nineteenth Century," in *A History of Women's Writing in*

Russia, ed. Adele Marie Barker and Jehanne M. Gheith (Cambridge: Cambridge University Press, 2002), 72.

5. Gary Kelly, "Feminine Romanticism, Masculine History, and the Founding of the Modern Liberal State," *Essays and Studies* 51 (1998): 3.

6. Marlon B. Ross writes, "The categories of gender, both in their lives and in their work, help the Romantics establish rites of passage toward poetic identity and toward masculine empowerment. Even when the women themselves are writers, they become anchors for the male poets' own pursuit for masculine self-possession" ("Romantic Quest and Conquest: Troping Masculine Power in the Crisis of Poetic Identity," in *Romanticism and Feminism*, ed. Anne K. Mellor [Bloomington: Indiana University Press, 1988], 29). See also Margaret Homans, *Women Writers and Poetic Identity: Dorothy Wordsworth, Emily Brontë, and Emily Dickinson* (Princeton, N.J.: Princeton University Press, 1980), especially the introduction and chapter 1, "The Masculine Tradition." For a comprehensive list of critics who describe Romanticism as inimical to women, see Diana Greene, *Reinventing Romantic Poetry: Russian Women Poets of the Mid-Nineteenth Century* (Madison: University of Wisconsin Press, 2004), 219n3.

7. Greene, *Reinventing Romantic Poetry*, 23–27; Diana Greene, "Mid-Nineteenth-Century Domestic Ideology in Russia," in *Women and Russian Culture: Projections and Self-Perceptions*, ed. Rosalind Marsh (New York: Berghahn Books, 1998), 78–97.

8. Ol'ga Demidova, "Russian Women Writers of the Nineteenth Century," in *Gender and Russian Literature: New Perspectives*, trans. and ed. Rosalind Marsh (Cambridge: Cambridge University Press, 1996), 96.

9. Volume 9 of Pushkin's collected works appeared in 1841. The years 1842–44 saw the publication of Lermontov's collected poems.

10. E. M. Shneiderman, ed., *Poety 1840–1850 godov* (Leningrad: Sovetskii pisatel', 1972), 9–10.

11. Diana Greene, "Nineteenth-Century Women Poets: Critical Reception vs. Self-Definition," in Clyman and Greene, *Women Writers in Russian Literature*, 95–97. See also Diana Greene, "Praskov'ia Bakunina and the Poetess's Dilemma," in *Russkie pisatel'nitsy i literaturnyi protsess v kontse XVII-pervoi treti XX vekov*, ed. M. Sh. Fainshtein (Wilhelmshorst, Ger.: F. K. Göpfert, 1995), 43–45.

12. Susanne Fusso, "Pavlova's *Quadrille*: The Feminine Variant of (the End of) Romanticism," in *Essays on Karolina Pavlova*, ed. Susanne Fusso and Alexander Lehrman (Evanston, Ill.: Northwestern University Press, 2001), 118.

13. Diana Greene, "The Menagerie or the Visitor's Pass? Aleksandra Zrazhevskaia and Praskov'ia Bakunina on Russian Women Writers," *Carl Beck Papers in Russian and East European Studies*, no. 1803 (2007): 10.

14. Marlon Ross, *The Contours of Masculine Desire: Romanticism and the Rise of Women's Poetry* (Oxford: Oxford University Press, 1989), 301.

15. In his novel in verse, *Eugene Onegin*, Pushkin characterizes Tatiana Larina in terms of what and how she reads.

16. Stephanie Sandler and Judith Vowles, "Beginning to Be a Poet: Baratynsky and Pavlova," in *Russian Subjects: Empire, Nation, and the Culture of the Golden Age*, ed. Monika Greenleaf and Stephen Moeller-Sally (Evanston, Ill.: Northwestern University Press, 1998), 152.

17. Olga Lee Briker, "The Poetic Personae of Karolina Pavlova (1807–1893)" (Ph.D. diss., Columbia University, 1996), 3. On this characteristic of Pavlova's love poetry, see also Briker's chapter 4, "The Poet-Lover," 151–77.

18. Catriona Kelly, *A History of Russian Women's Writing, 1820–1992* (Oxford: Oxford University Press, 1994), 102.

19. Greene, "Nineteenth-Century Women Poets," 105.

20. In the lyric where children appear—"Temptation" ("Iskushenie")—a mother watches over her sleeping children, wishing she were at a ball.

21. In his commentary to Pavlova's poem E. N. Lebedev writes that in it "the poetess polemicizes with E. P. Rostopchina, who in her poems spoke of her departure from the customs and manners of old Moscow" (Karolina Pavlova, *Stikhotvoreniia* [Moscow: Sovetskaia Rossiia, 1985], 223). N. M. Gaidenkov's commentary echoes this explanation in Karolina Pavlova, *Polnoe sobranie stikhotvorenii* (Moscow: Sovetskii pisatel', 1964), 553. Frank Göpfert similarly writes, "Rostopchina hatte 1840 in ihren Gedichten 'V Moskvu' und 'Vid Moskvy' ihre Entfremdung von Moskau beschrieben" (*Dichterinnen und Schriftstellerinnen in Russland von der Mitte des 18. bis zum Beginn des 20. Jahrhunderts: Eine Problemskizze* [Munich: Verlag Otto Sagner, 1992], 214n19).

22. Vissarion Belinskii, "Russkaia literatura v 1840 godu," in *Polnoe sobranie sochinenii*, 13 vols. (Moscow: Akademiia nauk, 1953–59), 4:441.

23. Beginning in 1834, most of Rostopchina's poems appeared in Moscow; see M. Sh. Fainstein, *Pisatel'nitsy pushkinskoi pory: Istoriko-literaturnye ocherki* (Leningrad: Nauka, 1989), 89.

24. Thus, for example, in a review article that appeared in 1839, the authoritative critic Vissarion Belinsky, who had high praise for the "manly energy" of Pavlova's translation of Pushkin into French, observes that "the amazing talent of Mme. Pavlova (née Jaenisch) to translate poems from and into all the languages she knows is finally gaining widespread recognition," but he makes no mention of her original poems (Belinskii, *Polnoe sobranie sochinenii*, 3:191).

25. Sandler and Vowles, "Beginning to Be a Poet," 152.

26. Paula R. Feldman and Theresa M. Kelley, eds., *Romantic Women Writers: Voices and Countervoices* (Hanover, N.H.: University Press of New England, 1995), 9.

27. Kelly, *History of Russian Women's Writing*, 94.

28. Boris Rapgof, *Karolina Pavlova: Materialy dlia izucheniia zhizni i tvorchestva* (Petrograd: Izdatel'stvo Trirema, 1916), 20.

29. Munir Sendich, "Moscow Literary Salons: Thursdays at Karolina Pavlova's," *Die Welt der Slaven* 17 (1972): 341.

30. Vissarion Belinskii, "Stikhotvoreniia grafini E. Rostopchinoi," in *Polnoe sobranie sochinenii*, 5:456–61.

31. Belinskii, "Stikhotvoreniia grafini E. Rostopchinoi," 5:458.

32. Briusov's two-volume collection of Pavlova's works erroneously gives the date of this poem as 1841; Karolina Pavlova, *Sobranie sochinenii*, 2 vols. (Moscow: Knigoizdatel'stvo K. F. Nekrasova, 1915), 1:30.

33. Boris Rapgof maintains that together with "The Poet" ("Poet"), "We are contemporaries, Countess" best expresses Pavlova's views on poetry; Rapgof, *Karolina Pavlova*, 23.

34. Pavlova, *Polnoe sobranie stikhotvorenii*, 135. Unless otherwise noted, subsequent citations of Pavlova's poetry are to this edition, with page numbers provided parenthetically. For a penetrating discussion of the intertextuality of the "stern judgment" Pavlova notes, see Romy Taylor, "Autobiographical Poetry or Poetic Autobiography? K. Pavlova's 1847 Invective Epistle 'We are contemporaries, Countess,'" in *Models of Self: Russian Women's Autobiographical Texts*, ed. Marianne Liljeström, Arja Rosenholm, and Irina Savkina (Helsinki: Kikimora Publications, 2000), 40.

35. Patrick H. Vincent, *The Romantic Poetess: European Culture, Politics, and Gender, 1820–1840* (Durham: University of New Hampshire Press, 2004), 80, 81.

36. M. Aronson describes the growth of domesticity "at the expense of the suppressed public sphere" ("Kruzhki i salony," in *Literaturnye kruzhki i salony*, by M. Aronson and S. Reiser [Leningrad: Priboi, 1929], 18).

37. The point is that here, too, it remains a question of how domesticity is read. Thus, to consider a prominent historical example, the demonstrative marital fidelity of the Decembrists' wives who followed their husbands into Siberian exile was a strategic way to register contempt for the autocrat who had sent them there. Yet because this defiant gesture was consistent with patriarchal norms that dictated women's self-sacrifice to their husbands' needs, reading it as conforming to established norms could defuse its rebelliousness. To focus exclusively on the spousal loyalty under whose cover the women defied the state is to read them back into the norms they defy. An enabling rereading of their actions would frame the Decembrist wives' move to Siberia as courageous, well-considered rebellion.

38. The most comprehensive study of George Sand's impact in Russia to date is Lesley Singer Herrmann, "George Sand and the Nineteenth Century Russian Novel: The Quest for a Heroine" (Ph.D. diss., Columbia University, 1979). My account of Sand's influence in Russia draws on the background material that Herrmann provides. Dawn D. Eidelman's *George Sand and the Nineteenth-Century Russian Love-Triangle Novels* (Lewisburg, Pa.: Bucknell

University Press, 1994) relies heavily on the work of Herrmann, whose name she misspells. General discussions of Sand's importance in Russia appear, inter alia, in Richard Stites, *The Women's Liberation Movement in Russia: Feminism, Nihilism, and Bolshevism, 1860–1930* (Princeton, N.J.: Princeton University Press, 1990), 19–24; Ol'ga Demidova, "Russian Women Writers of the Nineteenth Century," in *Gender and Russian Literature: New Perspectives*, ed. Rosalind Marsh (Cambridge: Cambridge University Press, 1996), 92–111; Helena Goscilo, introduction to *Russian and Polish Women's Fiction*, ed. and trans. Helena Goscilo (Knoxville: University of Tennessee Press, 1985), 10–11; Barbara Alpern Engel, *Mothers and Daughters: Women of the Russian Intelligentsia in Nineteenth-Century Russia* (Evanston, Ill.: Northwestern University Press, 1983), 36–37.

39. Herrmann, "George Sand," 16. Viardot's letter is also cited in Belinda Jack, *George Sand: A Woman's Life Writ Large* (New York: Knopf, 2000), 275.

40. Herrmann, "George Sand,"177–78.

41. Stites, *Women's Liberation*, 23.

42. These included *Indiana*, 1832; *Valentine*, 1833; *Lélia*, 1833; and *Jacques*, 1834. See Demidova, "Russian Women Writers," 98, 109n46.

43. I argue that this view of Tatiana does not do justice to the complexity and creative energy with which Pushkin invests his beloved heroine; see Olga P. Hasty, *Pushkin's Tatiana* (Madison: University of Wisconsin Press, 1999).

44. For an extended comparison of Indiana and Tatiana, see Herrmann, "George Sand," 77–79; Herrmann notes that "Indiana and Tatyana in Russian fiction of the 1840s complement and compete with each other" (78).

45. The trajectory of Belinsky's attitude to Sand parallels her reception among the Russian intelligentsia of the time. Initially the critic was hostile toward the French "libertine," but by the early 1840s he had become an enthusiastic admirer. He pestered his friends to translate her works, having tried earnestly, but in vain, to learn French to read the originals rather than the versions altered by censors who oversaw Sand's publication in Russian. See V. I. Kondorskaia, "V. G. Belinskii o Zh. Sand," *Uchenye zapiski*, no. 28 (1958): 141–65.

46. Sand's active role in the Revolutions of 1848 showed that Nicholas I's fears were justified; see Herrmann, "George Sand," 9.

47. Herrmann, "George Sand," 34–35.

48. Herrmann, "George Sand," 23.

49. Stites, *Women's Liberation*, 22–23.

50. A. V. Druzhinin, "Pol'inka Saks: Povest'," in *Povesti: Dnevnik* (Moscow: Nauka, 1986), 8.

51. Engel, *Mothers and Daughters*, 37.

52. Goscilo, *Russian and Polish Women's Fiction*, 10–11.

53. Leo Strauss, "Persecution and the Art of Writing," in *Persecution and the Art of Writing* (Chicago: University of Chicago Press, 1988), 36.

54. For a sketch of Nikolai Pavlov's life, see Rapgof, *Karolina Pavlova*, 14–16.

55. In a letter to the poet Nikolai Iazykov, cited in Rapgof, *Karolina Pavlova*, 31.

56. Rapgof, *Karolina Pavlova*, 25–26.

57. See Louis Pedrotti, "The Scandal of Countess Rostopchina's Polish-Russian Allegory," *Slavic and East European Journal* 30, no. 2 (1986): 196–214.

58. In his reminiscences, the writer and translator Nikolai Vasil'evich Berg, who claims he heard the story from Rostopchina, maintains that she sent "A Forced Marriage" to the *Northern Bee* at the prompting of Nikolai Gogol, who persuaded her that the censors would be too dense to catch the allegorical meaning of the poem; "Grafinia Rostopchina v Moskve (Otryvok iz vospominanii)," in *Schastlivaia zhenshchina: Literaturnye sochineniia*, by E. P. Rostopchina (Moscow: Pravda, 1991), 392–93. This account is contested. E. S. Nekrasova insists that Gogol, knowing how damaging this escapade could be for Rostopchina, with whom he was on excellent terms, would not have done her such a bad turn; "Grafinia E. P. Rostopchina," *Vestnik Evropy*, March 1885, 55–57. Diana Greene sees the claim that Rostopchina sent "A Forced Marriage" to Bulgarin at Gogol's suggestion as an attempt "to give credit to Gogol and depict him as a liberal, while decreasing Rostopchina's responsibility for her own political act" (*Reinventing Romantic Poetry*, 90). Given the consequences of the ballad's appearance, it is also possible that Rostopchina invoked Gogol in an attempt to diminish her responsibility for the publication. We do not know what really transpired, but the various constructions of the events are themselves instructive.

59. Pedrotti includes excerpts from this letter in "The Scandal of Countess Rostopchina's Polish-Russian Allegory." I offer a brief taste, drawing on his translation: "With all assurances of my esteem, I ask you to accept the expression of my wishes that success ever and everywhere reward your estimable efforts on behalf of our literature, as well as the services of your long-standing and inexhaustible talent, which every Russian recognizes" (199).

60. Bulgarin heeded Rostopchina's request that the first three poems she sent him appear in the order she presented them. "A Forced Marriage" came out framed by the poems "The Lover and the Sailor" ("Liubovnik i moriak") and "The Pine at Cornish" ("Sosna na Kornishe").

61. Unbeknownst to himself, Bulgarin was not off the mark when he invoked "the inscrutable heart of a woman." As Vladimir Kiselev-Sergenin documents, the poems Rostopchina sent Bulgarin together with "A Forced Marriage" encoded private messages to Andrei Karamzin (the eldest son of the author and historian), with whom she had been amorously involved. Her relations and private correspondence with Karamzin cut off by his recent marriage, she resorted to communicating with him in a public forum whose very openness promised the best form of concealment. Details with which she invested the

poems carried personal significance that only Karamzin would understand even as—at another level—the poems engaged a wider, uninitiated readership. Because the *Northern Bee* came out daily, Kiselev-Sergenin plausibly suggests that the urgency of her need to convey her feelings to Karamzin may have motivated Rostopchina's startling choice of venue. In the wake of the "Forced Marriage" scandal, the second installment of the poems she sent Bulgarin remained unpublished. See Vladimir Kiselev-Sergenin, "Taina grafini E. P. Rostopchinoi," *Neva* 9 (1994): 281.

62. Cited in Pedrotti, "Scandal," 199.

63. Berg claims that Russian readers remained unaware of the allegorical dimension of Rostopchina's ballad until alerted to it by an article in a French newspaper that came out some weeks after "A Forced Marriage" had appeared in the *Northern Bee*; Berg, "Grafinia Rostopchina v Moskve," 393. This account sounds improbable, though possible in light of the unthinkability of the publication and the fact that Russian readers who recognized the import of the poem would be unlikely to broadcast it.

64. For Grech's letter to Count Orlov, see V. Kiselev, "Poetessa i tsar'" (Stranitsy istorii Russkoi poezii 40-kh godov)," *Russkaia literatura*, no. 1 (1965): 148–49.

65. For Bulgarin's letter to Orlov, see Kiselev, "Poetessa i tsar'," 149–50.

66. For fuller coverage of this episode, see Pedrotti, "Scandal," 203; Kiselev, "Poetessa i tsar'," 147–51; Kiselev-Sergenin, "Taina grafini E. P. Rostopchinoi," 281; and Taylor, "Autobiographical Poetry," 33–48.

67. Kiselev, "Poetessa i tsar'," 148. First, the individual poems had to be passed by the government censor for publication. Next, the entire issue of the *Northern Bee* had to be submitted to the censor for approval.

68. In 1856, Rostopchina's ballad appeared in print in London in Aleksandr Herzen's liberal journal *The Polar Star* (*Poliarnaia zvezda*). The note Herzen appended to the poem had this to say: "This poem was published; the censorship did not guess at first that 'A Forced Marriage' is an outstanding depiction of Nicholas and Poland; then they realized it and the 'old baron' sent its famous author out of Petersburg." Cited in Evdokiia Rostopchina, *Stikhotvoreniia, proza, pis'ma* (Moscow: Sovetskaia Rossiia, 1986), 420.

69. Pedrotti, "Scandal," 203.

70. Kiselev, "Poetessa i tsar'," 151.

71. For examples of such responses, see Fainshtein, *Pisatel'nitsy pushkinskoi pory*, 95, and Taylor, "Autobiographical Poetry," 46n17.

72. Fainshtein, *Pisatel'nitsy pushkinskoi pory*, 95.

73. Lidiia Rostopchina, "Semeinaia khronika, fragmenty," in Rostopchina, *Schastlivaia zhenshchina*, 408.

74. Rostopchina, "Semeinaia khronika," 408–9.

75. Greene, *Reinventing Romantic Poetry*, 95.

76. Pedrotti, "Scandal," 203–4. In the wake of the failed Revolutions of 1848, censorship became even more stringent.

77. Dmitrii M. Pogodin, "Grafinia E. P. Rostopchina i ee vechera," in Rostopchina, *Schastlivaia zhenshchina*, 401.

78. Romy Taylor describes the poem as "an answer, of sorts, to Rostopchina's allegory" ("Autobiographical Poetry," 33–48). My discussion builds on this important observation.

79. "Autobiographical Poetry," 39. For an extended discussion of the intertextual references in Pavlova's poem, see Taylor, "Autobiographical Poetry," 41–43.

80. For a discussion of how Pavlova "borrows Rostopchina's language in 'A Forced Marriage' to invert certain images as well as the overall message," see Briker, "Poetic Personae," 55.

81. Pavlova, *Polnoe sobranie stikhotvorenii*, 231.

82. Sarah M. Zimmerman, "Dost thou not know my voice? Charlotte Smith and the Lyric's Audience," in *Romanticism and Women Poets: Opening the Doors of Reception*, ed. Harriet Kramer Lenkin and Stephen C. Behrendt (Lexington: University Press of Kentucky, 1999), 105.

83. Judith Pascoe, *Romantic Theatricality: Gender, Poetry, and Spectatorship* (Ithaca, N.Y.: Cornell University Press, 1997), 116, citing Dorinda Outram, *The Body and the French Revolution: Sex, Class, and Political Culture* (New Haven, Conn.: Yale University Press, 1989), 84.

84. Pavlova, "Moi vospominaniia," in *Sobranie sochinenii*, 2:302–3.

85. Tomas Venclova, "Almost a Hundred Years Later: Toward a Comparison of Karolina Pavlova and Marina Cvêtaeva," in *Essays on Karolina Pavlova*, ed. Susanne Fusso and Alexander Lehrman (Evanston, Ill.: Northwestern University Press), 201–3.

86. Jaenisch had purchased this house from Rostopchin; see Sendich, "Moscow Literary Salons," 344.

87. Pavlov's authorship of the offending piece was brought to light by Rostopchina, who in the aftermath of the "Forced Marriage" scandal was under suspicion of having written it and was eager to prove her innocence; see Taylor, "Autobiographical Poetry," 47–48n25.

88. Rapgof, *Karolina Pavlova*, 32.

89. Munir Sendich, "The Life and Works of Karolina Pavlova" (Ph.D. diss., New York University, 1968), 62–65.

90. Cited in Sendich, "Life and Works of Karolina Pavlova," 63.

91. For the text of Aksakov's letter, see Sendich, "Life and Works of Karolina Pavlova," 75.

92. For a discussion of the poem see Sendich, "Life and Works of Karolina Pavlova," 207–10.

93. Rapgof, *Karolina Pavlova*, 33–34.

94. These include the *Northern Bee*, where the poem first appeared, *Notes of the Fatherland*, *The Contemporary*, *The Muscovite*, *Pantheon*, and *The St. Petersburg Gazette*. See O. V. Grishanova, "Zhanr 'Razgovora' v lirike K. K. Pavlovoi," in *Naukovi zapiski Kharkivs'kogo natsional'nogo pedagogicheskogo universiteta im. G. S. Skovorodi* (Kharkiv: Literaturoznavstvo, 2011), 40.

95. Positive responses came primarily from Slavophiles, who (erroneously) saw Pavlova as one of their own; see Sendich, "Life and Works of Karolina Pavlova," 207.

96. "Bibliografiia," *Sovremennik* 47, no. 1 (1854): 34–38.

97. Pavlova, *Sobranie sochinenii*, 2:323.

98. Pavlova, *Sobranie sochinenii*, 2:333–34.

99. For the text of this letter, see Pavlova, *Sobranie sochinenii*, 2:416–18.

100. For the text of the parody, see Pavlova, *Polnoe sobranie stikhotvorenii*, 566–67. Rostopchina's opening line echoes Panaev's parody "As If from Heine" ("Budto iz Geine"), in which he lampoons German Romanticism.

101. Pavlova, *Polnoe sobranie stikhotvorenii*, 567.

102. The description of Pavlova by A. Ia. Panaeva, the wife of the "learned man" in question, provides a characteristic example: "At the Granovskys' I met Karolina Karlovna Pavlova and heard her read poems she had just composed and recited from memory over the course of her visit. In her conversation she constantly inserted stanzas from Goethe's poems in German, from Byron's in English, from Dante's in Italian, and as for Spanish, she cited some sort of saying . . . Pavlova, no longer young, was unattractive, very thin, but with a grand manner" (A. Ia. Panaeva [Golovacheva], *Vospominaniia* [Moscow: Khudozhestvennaia literatura, 1972], 148–49). Panaeva's memoir covers the years 1824 to 1870, described through the prism of ideas developed in the early 1860s. It was first published in 1889 in *Istoricheskii vestnik*.

103. For a comprehensive account of hostilities Pavlova endured from her contemporaries, see Venclova, "Almost a Hundred Years Later," 187–214.

104. The dearth of models available to self-reliant and creative women led to their indiscriminate alignment with exceptional women (often heavily fictionalized or entirely authored by men). Accolades to women from critics frequently came in the form of comparison with famous women on little more ground than their shared gender. Figuring most prominently in such accolades were "Sapphos," "Joans of Arc," and "Corinnes." Thus, for example, Belinsky designated George Sand as a Joan of Arc and Rostopchina as a Muscovite Sappho. At the height of de Staël's popularity in Russia, Rostopchina herself numbered among the Russian "Corinnes" of her time. On April 10, 1846, when she visited Tivoli, a group of her admiring compatriots presented her with a laurel wreath in a gesture taken directly from the pages of de Staël's novel. In her poem "To My Two Friends [fem.]" ("Moim dvum priiatel'nitsam," 1851), Rostopchina invokes Corinne to describe the painful split between her public identity and her private

world. See Sergei Ernst, "Karolina Pavlova i gr. Evdokiia Rastopchina [*sic*]," *Russkii bibliofil'*, no. 6 (1916): 34.

105. Vincent, *The Romantic Poetess*, 77; for a discussion of *Corinne*'s reception and influence in Europe, see 18–25.

106. The pronouncement of Lady Edgermond, a character in the novel, summarizes the view held in England against which Corinne struggles: "I esteem not those talents which divert a woman from her real duties. There must be actresses, musicians, and artists in order to amuse the world; but women of our rank have nothing to do but obey their husbands, and attend to the bringing up of their children" (Germaine de Staël, *Corinne, or Italy*, 2 vols., trans. George Saintsbury [Philadelphia: Lippincott, 1894], 2:172).

107. Vincent, *The Romantic Poetess*, 20. This applies directly to Rostopchina. In "To My Two Friends [fem.]," Rostopchina insists that beyond the public accolades she has won is a private world of pain and suffering. Describing herself not as a Corinne crowned in glory but as someone who knows suffering—a woman with "a heart full of tears," Rostopchina draws attention to the private pain that underlies celebrity. Vincent reads this poem not as confirming his observation about women's focus on the tragic guise of de Staël's heroine but as Rostopchina's rejection of the image of Corinne (105–6). I would argue instead that it is in keeping with Rostopchina's efforts to draw attention to the woman's hidden inner world. See Rostopchina, *Stikhotvoreniia, proza, pis'ma*, 221.

108. Vladislav Khodasevich, *Sobranie sochinenii*, ed. John E. Malmstad and Robert P. Hughes, 2 vols. (Ann Arbor, Mich.: Ardis, 1990), 2:218.

CHAPTER TWO

1. Evdokiia Rostopchina, *Stikhotvoreniia, proza, pis'ma* (Moscow: Sovetskaia Rossiia, 1986), 377. De Staël writes, "Nature and society make women quite accustomed to suffering, and I think it is clear that most women today are better than men. In an age when the universal malady is egoism, men are necessarily less generous and sensitive than women" (*Major Writings of Germaine de Staël*, trans. Vivian Folkenflik [New York: Columbia University Press, 1987], 294).

2. Rostopchina, *Stikhotvoreniia, proza, pis'ma*, 378.

3. Iurii Lotman, "Zhenskoe obrazovanie v XVIII—nachale XIX veka," in *Besedy o russkoi kul'ture: Byt i traditsii russkogo dvorianstva (XVIII—nachalo XIX veka)* (St. Petersburg: Iskusstvo, 1994), 75.

4. Diana Greene, "Nineteenth-Century Women Poets: Critical Reception vs. Self-Definition," in *Women Writers in Russian Literature*, ed. Toby W. Clyman and Diana Greene (Westport, Conn.: Praeger, 1994), 104.

5. See, inter alia, Luce Irigaray, *Speculum of the Other Woman*, trans. Gillian C. Gill (Ithaca, N.Y.: Cornell University Press, 1985); Joan Riviere, "Womanliness as a Masquerade," in *Formations of Fantasy*, ed. Victor Burgin, James

Donald, and Cora Kaplan (London: Routledge, 1989), 35–44; Liliane Weissberg, ed., *Weiblichkeit als Maskerade* (Frankfurt: Fischer Taschenbuch, 1994).

6. Leo Strauss, "Persecution and the Art of Writing," in *Persecution and the Art of Writing* (Chicago: University of Chicago Press, 1988), 22–37.

7. Laura Jo McCullough, "Evdokiia Rostopchina," in *Russian Women Writers*, ed. Christine D. Tomei, 2 vols. (New York: Garland Publishing, 1999), 1:96.

8. M. Sh. Fainshtein, *Pisatel'nitsy pushkinskoi pory: Istoriko-literaturnye ocherki* (Leningrad: Nauka, 1989), 93. The passage is from a letter of 1857 to the historian and journalist Mikhail Pogodin.

9. V. G. Belinskii, *Polnoe sobranie sochinenii*, 13 vols. (Moscow: Akademiia nauk, 1953–59), 5:457–58. George Sand abhorred being called by her married name, as Belinsky refers to her here. My translation conveys the awkwardness of Belinsky's prose.

10. Belinskii, *Polnoe sobranie sochinenii*, 5:458.

11. There was a clear separation between frivolous social events and literary salons, as Rostopchina emphasized in the 1838 poem "Where I Feel Good" ("Gde mne khorosho"), which appeared in the collection Belinsky reviewed. In it, Rostopchina distinguishes sharply between the vacuous pastimes that she abhors and the refuge she finds in E. A. Karamzina's salon, where poetry reigns and where the poet finds a welcome opportunity to be herself; see E. P. Rostopchina, *Talisman* (Moscow: Moskovskii rabochii, 1987), 49–50. On Rostopchina's salons, see M. Aronson and S. Reiser, *Literaturnye kruzhki i salony* (Leningrad: Priboi, 1929), 199–203, 287–89.

12. Belinskii, *Polnoe sobranie sochinenii*, 5:458.

13. Belinskii, *Polnoe sobranie sochinenii*, 5:458.

14. Viktor Afanasiev adduces this fact in defense of Rostopchina's subject matter; "Da, zhenskaia dusha dolzhna v teni svetit'sia," in Rostopchina, *Talisman*, 10.

15. For an account of the woman's circumscribed sphere of activity at the time, see Diana Greene, *Reinventing Romantic Poetry: Russian Women Poets of the Mid-Nineteenth Century* (Madison: University of Wisconsin Press, 2004), 21–37; on Rostopchina's situation in particular, see 88–111.

16. Judith Vowles, "The Inexperienced Muse: Russian Women and Poetry in the First Half of the Nineteenth Century," in *A History of Women's Writing in Russia*, ed. Adele Marie Barker and Jehanne M. Gheith (Cambridge: Cambridge University Press, 2002), 76–77.

17. Vowles, "The Inexperienced Muse," 77.

18. Belinskii, *Polnoe sobranie sochinenii*, 5:457 (emphasis in the original).

19. Vowles, "The Inexperienced Muse," 75.

20. Rostopchina, *Stikhotvoreniia, proza, pis'ma*, 229.

21. Arja Rosenholm and Irina Savkina, "'How Women Should Write': Russian Women's Writing in the Nineteenth Century," in *Women in Nineteenth-*

Century Russia: Lives and Culture, ed. Wendy Rosslyn and Alessandra Tosi (Cambridge: Open Book Publishers, 2012), 167.

22. Rostopchina described society as a false masquerade in private conversations as well. Complaining to Pletnev about the social life she was compelled to lead, she repeatedly quoted the lines from Pushkin's *Eugene Onegin* in which Tatiana speaks of her social role as a burdensome masquerade: "I would be happy to give up / All these tatters of masquerade" (*Otdat' by rada / Vsiu etu vetosh' maskerada*) (*Talisman*, 286).

23. Judith Pascoe, *Romantic Theatricality: Gender, Poetry, and Spectatorship* (Ithaca, N.Y.: Cornell University Press, 1997), 43.

24. Lotman, "Zhenskoe obrazovanie," 105.

25. In Rostopchina, *Talisman*, 276.

26. See, for example, Belinskii, *Polnoe sobranie sochinenii*, 2:409, 496. In a letter to A. I. Turgenev, Viazemsky ranked Rostopchina's lyric "Poslednii tsvetok" ("The Last Flower") with the best of Zhukovsky's, Pushkin's, and Baratynsky's poems; cited in Rostopchina, *Talisman*, 6.

27. This, too, had its risks. Thus, for example, Iazykov found Pavlova's poetry more original than Rostopchina's, which, as he held, was imitative of Pushkin's; Rostopchina, *Talisman*, 284.

28. V. Brio, "Pushkin o vozmozhnostiakh zhenskoi literatury," *Pushkinskii sbornik* 1, no. 1 (1997): 192–93; see also B. V. Tomashevskii, *Pushkin i Frantsiia* (Leningrad: Sovetskii pisatel', 1960).

29. Tomashevskii, *Pushkin i Frantsiia*, 52, cited in Brio, "Pushkin o vozmozhnostiakh zhenskoi literatury," 192. Among de Staël's influential works that devote attention to women are *De la littérature considérée dans ses rapports avec les institutions sociales* (1800) with its chapter on women writers and *De l'Allemagne* (1810) with its chapter on women in society.

30. Brio, "Pushkin o vozmozhnostiakh zhenskoi literatury," 187–200.

31. Marina Tsvetaeva, *Sobranie sochinenii v semi tomakh*, 7 vols. (Moscow: Ellis Lak, 1994), 4:602.

32. Fainshtein, *Pisatel'nitsy pushkinskoi pory*, 87.

33. Vladimir Kiselev-Sergenin, "Taina grafini E. P. Rostopchinoi," *Neva* 9 (1994): 273–74.

34. Zhukovsky had given Pushkin this notebook, which was returned to him after the poet's death; see Kiselev-Sergenin, "Taina grafini Rostopchinoi," 278.

35. Rostopchina, *Stikhotvoreniia, proza, pis'ma*, 412–13. Here Zhukovsky refers to Rostopchina's pregnancy.

36. Rostopchina, *Stikhotvoreniia, proza, pis'ma*, 92.

37. Greene, *Reinventing Romantic Poetry*, 109.

38. Rostopchina, *Stikhotvoreniia, proza, pis'ma*, 93.

39. David Bethea, "A Protean Look at the Russian Proteus: Pushkin Studies in Its Maturity," *Russian Review* 64, no. 1 (January 2005): 104.

40. Strauss, "Persecution and the Art of Writing," 36.

41. These appear in Zhukovsky's collected works under the heading "From the Album Presented to Countess Rostopchina" ("Iz al'boma podarennogo gr. Rostopchinoi"); V. A. Zhukovskii, *Sobranie sochinenii v chetyrekh tomakh*, 4 vols. (Moscow: Gosudarstvennoe izdatel'stvo khudozhestvennoi literatury, 1959), 1:392–93; commentary, 1:467.

42. The Russian *nemoi* (mute) that characterizes the "behest" is a homonym for "not mine" (*ne moi*) and emphasizes acoustically that it is not for Zhukovsky to fill the notebook.

43. Greene, *Reinventing Romantic Poetry*, 109.

44. These include Pushkin's epigrams on Arakcheev, Bulgarin, and A. Golitsyn. See Fainshtein, *Pisatel'nitsy pushkinskoi pory*, 92.

45. V. Kiselev, "Poetessa i tsar'" (Stranitsy istorii russkoi poezii 40-kh godov)," *Russkaia literatura*, no. 1 (1965): 154. The notebook itself is now in *Pushkinskii Dom*.

46. Rostopchina, *Stikhotvoreniia, proza, pis'ma*, 152. "I was one of the last to press his hand," Rostopchina wrote in a letter of 1858 (391). In its published version, Lermontov's poem opens with the lines: "I believe: you and I / Were born under the same star" ("Ia veriu: pod odnoi zvezdoiu / My s vami byli rozhdeny"); M. Iu. Lermontov, *Polnoe sobranie sochinenii v dvukh tomakh*, 2 vols. (Leningrad: Sovetskii pisatel', 1989), 2:72.

47. Ol'ga Demidova, "Russian Women Writers of the Nineteenth Century," in *Gender and Russian Literature: New Perspectives*, trans. and ed. Rosalind Marsh (Cambridge: Cambridge University Press, 1996), 108n39.

48. Cited in Rostopchina, *Stikhotvoreniia, proza, pis'ma*, 413.

49. Rostopchina, *Stikhotvoreniia, proza, pis'ma*, 94. All cited passages from *Two Meetings* are taken from this edition, pp. 94–98.

50. Consider, for example, the following excerpt from the first poem of the cycle:

> Пестро и пышно убрана,
> В одежде праздничной, она
> Слила, смешала без вниманья
> Сословья все, все сочетанья.
> На день один, на краткий час
> Сошлись друг дургу на показ,
> Хмельной разгул простолюдина
> С степенным хладом знати чинной,
> Мир черни с миром богачей
> И старость с резвостью детей.

51. Stephanie Sandler, *Commemorating Pushkin: Russia's Myth of a National Poet* (Stanford, Calif.: Stanford University Press, 2004), 40.

52. Pushkin, who remained unaware of the first "meeting," was apparently taken by Mlle. Sushkova at the second, which took place in December of 1827 at the home of Prince D. V. Golitsyn, the governor-general of Moscow.

53. Rostopchina, *Talisman*, 265. Cited also in Fainshtein, *Pisatel'nitsy pushkinskoi pory*, 87.

54. Here I part company with Stephanie Sandler, who describes Rostopchina's accounts of these two meetings as "being eroticized"; Sandler, *Commemorating Pushkin*, 39.

55. A syntactic ambiguity allows "artless" to pertain to her poetry and to her whispered recitation.

56. Belinskii, *Polnoe sobranie sochinenii*, 5:458.

57. Rostopchina, *Stikhotvoreniia, proza, pis'ma*, 133–34.

58. Viktor Afanasiev cites it as Rostopchina's "L'art poétique"; Rostopchina, *Talisman*, 9. Frank Göpfert calls it "ein kunstprogrammatisches Gedicht" (*Dichterinnen und Schriftstellerinnen in Russland von der Mitte des 18. bis zum Beginn des 20. Jahrhunderts: Eine Problemskizze* [Munich: Verlag Otto Sagner, 1992], 86). Kiselev-Sergenin suggests that the poem describes how women should write about love; "Taina grafini Rostopchinoi," 268.

59. Belinskii, *Polnoe sobranie sochinenii*, 5:457.

60. Review cited in Rostopchina, *Talisman*, 280. To contemporary readers, the terms in which Shevyrev couched his praise of Rostopchina and his emphasis on the feminine in his review sound decidedly sexist. The point is that he judges her a worthy recipient of Pushkin's notebook.

61. Rostopchina, *Talisman*, 278–79.

62. Rostopchina, *Talisman*, 279.

63. Rostopchina, *Talisman*, 280.

64. For a comprehensive account of how Rostopchina was referred to at this time, see Greene, *Reinventing Romantic Poetry*, 259n44.

65. McCullough, "Evdokiia Rostopchina," 1:99.

66. Strauss, "Persecution and the Art of Writing," 36.

67. Strauss, "Persecution and the Art of Writing," 36.

68. Greene summarizes the dissimilarity in different terms: "While Rostopchina appeared to revel in the feminine role, Pavlova directly protested against the strictures that made it almost impossible for a woman to be strong and creative" ("Nineteenth-Century Women Poets," 105).

69. For the subsequent intensification of this trend, see Arja Rosenholm, who describes progressive social critics' "deprecating attitude to women writers who failed to meet the criteria of the rationalist canon, such as Evdokiia Rostopchina, whose work both Chernyshevsky and Dobroliubov criticized with censorial irony. Her incontestable 'learning' was no guarantee of being the ideal 'enlightened woman' for in addition to representing the 'old' aristocratic power

and romantic individualism, Rostopchina's female consciousness and her repudiation of asexual experience posit a 'second sex' alongside abstract gender" ("The 'Woman Question' of the 1860s and the Ambiguity of the 'Learned Woman,'" in Marsh, *Gender and Russian Literature*, 117).

70. Dargomyzhsky, Glinka, Tchaikovsky, and Rubenstein are among the many composers who set Rostopchina's lyrics to music.

71. Vladislav Khodasevich, *Sobranie sochinenii*, ed. John E. Malmstad and Robert P. Hughes, 2 vols. (Ann Arbor, Mich.: Ardis, 1990), 2:56.

72. Khodasevich, *Sobranie sochinenii*, 2:46–65.

73. Khodasevich, *Sobranie sochinenii*, 2:58–59.

CHAPTER THREE

1. Ol'ga Kushlina and Tat'iana Nikol'skaia, who call their anthology of women poets of this period *101 Poetesses of the Silver Age*, explain in the introduction that the difficulty they encountered in putting the volume together was not in finding enough women poets for it but in establishing criteria for selecting from the vast number available to them; *Sto odna poetessa Serebriannogo veka* (St. Petersburg: Dean, 2000), 3. While not all the "poetesses" among the 101 represented are well-known, the volume includes an impressive number of recognized women poets who are representative of the era, including (in Russian alphabetical order, as they appear in the collection) Adalis, Akhmatova, Barkova, Berberova, Vasil'eva, Vil'kina, Gertsyk, Gippius, Guro, Zviagintseva, Zinov'eva-Annibal, Il'ina, Inber, Kuz'mina-Karavaeva, Lokhvitskaia, L'vova, Merkur'eva, Moravskaia, Nagrodskaia, Odoevtseva, Parnok, Petrovskaia, Polonskaia, Sabashnikova, Solov'eva, Stolitsa, Teffi, Figner, Tsvetaeva, Shaginian, and Shkapskaia.

2. See Charlotte Rosenthal, "The Silver Age: Highpoint for Women?," in *Women and Society in Russia and the Soviet Union*, ed. Linda Edmondson (Cambridge: Cambridge University Press, 1992), 32–47.

3. Kirsti Ekonen, *Tvorets, sub"ekt, zhenshchina: Strategii zhenskogo pis'ma v russkom simvolizme* (Moscow: Novoe literaturnoe obozrenie, 2011), 55 (emphasis in the original).

4. Ekonen, *Tvorets, sub"ekt, zhenshchina*, 8–9.

5. Catriona Kelly, *A History of Russian Women's Writing, 1820–1992* (Oxford: Oxford University Press, 1994), 133.

6. Examples include *Women's World, Women's Treasure, Women's Messenger, Women's Lyre* (*Zhenskii mir, Zhenskoe bogatstvo, Zhenskii vestnik, Zhenskaia lira*).

7. On Russian women poets as critics, see Catriona Kelly, "Missing Links: Russian Women Writers as Critics of Women Writers," in *Russian Writers on Russian Writers*, ed. Faith Wigzell (Oxford: Berg Publishers, 1994), 67–79;

Diana Greene, "The Menagerie or the Visitor's Pass? Aleksandra Zrazhevskaia and Praskov'ia Bakunina on Russian Women Writers," *Carl Beck Papers in Russian and East European Studies*, no. 1803 (2007): 12–17.

8. Rosenthal, "The Silver Age," 33.

9. Sergei Makovskii, *Portrety sovremennikov* (New York: Izdatel'stvo imeni Chekhova, 1955), 336.

10. These included Viacheslav Ivanov, Maximilian Voloshin, Elizaveta Dmitrieva, Nikolai Gumilev, Innokentii Annensky, Aleksei Tolstoi, Johannes von Guenther, Sergei Auslender, and Mikhail Kuzmin; see Makovskii, *Portrety*, 337, and Marianna Landa, "Mif i sud'ba," in *Ispoved'*, by Cherubina de Gabriak, ed. Vladimir Kupchenko, Marianna Landa, and Irina Repina (Moscow: Agraf, 1998), 11.

11. Makovsky mistakenly writes that Lansere's graphics ornamented both installments of de Gabriak's poems. Some accounts of the mystification perpetuate this error.

12. Maksimilian Voloshin, "Zhenskaia poeziia," in *Sobranie sochinenii*, 13 vols. (Moscow: Ellis Lak 2003–2015), vol. 6, bk. 1, 319–22. For an extended account of de Gabriak's progress, see Landa, "Mif i sud'ba," 5–44, and Vladimir Kupchenko's timeline "Khronika zhizni i tvorchestva E. I. Dmitrievoi" in the same volume, 318–36. See also Larisa Ageeva, *Nerazgadannaia Cherubina: Dokumental'noe povestvovanie* (Moscow: Dom-muzei Mariny Tsvetaevoi, 2006), and the section "Khronologicheskaia kanva zhizni i tvorchestva E. I. Dmitrievoi-Vasil'evoi (Cherubiny de Gabriak)," 291–314. My brief outline of the mystification draws on these two chronologies.

13. Landa, "Mif i sud'ba," 10. On Dmitrieva's connections with anthroposophy, see Kristi A. Groberg, "Behind the Veil of 'Cherubina de Gabriak,'" *Theosophical History* 6, no. 8 (October 1997): 285–97.

14. Estranged from his wife, Margarita Sabashnikova, at the time, Voloshin was considering divorce in order to marry Dmitrieva.

15. For Dmitrieva's life, see Ageeva, *Nerazgadannaia Cherubina*, 292–95.

16. Irina Shevelenko, *Literaturnyi put' Tsvetaevoi: Ideologiia—poetika—identichnost' avtora v kontekste epokhi* (Moscow: Novoe literaturnoe obozrenie, 2002), 71 (emphasis in the original).

17. Studies that provide historical background and published documents include Z. D. Davydov and V. P. Kupchenko, "Maksimilian Voloshin: Rasskaz o Cherubine de Gabriak," in *Pamiatniki kul'tury: Novye otkrytiia; Ezhegodnik 1988* (Moscow: Nauka, 1989), 41–61, and Cherubina de Gabriak, *Iz mira uiti nerazgadannoi*, ed. Vladimir Kupchenko and Roza Khruleva (Moscow: Izdatel'skii dom Koktebel', 2009). Landa, "Mif i sud'ba," 20, provides historical background and discusses creative play and the personal and ethical dimensions of this "experiment in myth-creation." Erika Greber describes it as a "metamys-

tification" in "Mystifikation und Epochenschwelle (Cherubina de Gabriak und die Krise des Symbolismus)," *Wiener Slawistischer Almanach* 32 (1993): 175–206. Elsewhere Greber considers de Gabriak in the context of word weaving and mystification theory: *Textile Texte: Poetologische Metaphorik und Literaturtheorie; Studien zur Tradition des Wortflechtens und der Kombinatorik* (Cologne: Böhlau, 2002), 313–72.

18. On Voloshin's mentoring of women poets and complications attendant on the mix of the poetical and the amorous, see Barbara Walker, "Voloshin and the Modernist Problem of the Ugly Poetess," in *Maximilian Voloshin and the Russian Literary Circle: Culture and Survival in Revolutionary Times* (Bloomington: Indiana University Press, 2005), 66–83. Walker bases her account of the mystification on Voloshin's fictionalized version.

19. Writing of the mystification, Svetlana Boym summarizes, "Woman-as-subject-of-writing was appropriated by a more culturally accepted image, woman-as-object-of-courtly love" (*Death in Quotation Marks: Cultural Myths of the Modern Poet* [Cambridge, Mass.: Harvard University Press, 1991], 45). This is an important point, to which the mystification adds yet another dimension: inventing the woman who becomes the object.

20. Accounts of a hoax played out in the imaginative sphere of a targeted readership and sustained by rumors and flights of fancy cannot remain strictly accurate. Accounts of the episode are subjective narratives that interweave facts and confabulation. Different people were privy to different pieces of information at different times, giving rise to inconsistencies. Details that were variously assembled and interpreted or that remained out of the picture skewed accounts of the events, generating inaccuracies perpetuated in retellings of the story and scholarly treatments of the mystification. Thickly mediated, recounted often decades later in accordance with its tellers' biases, the story of the phantom poet remained elusive and illusory. Recent scholars have provided a more factual underpinning for what transpired, rectifying numerous inexactitudes and unsound assertions. Prominent among publications that help set the record straight are de Gabriak, *Ispoved'*; Ageeva, *Nerazgadannaia Cherubina*; Davydov and Kupchenko, "Maksimilian Voloshin"; Groberg, "Behind the Veil"; V. Palacheva, "Rodoslovnaia Cheruviny de Gabriak," *Russkaia literatura v XX veke: Imena, problemy, kul'turnyi dialog*, no. 9 (September 2008): 4; de Gabriak, *Iz mira uiti nerazgadannoi*; Marianna Landa, "The Poetic Voice of Cherubina de Gabriak in Russian Symbolism," *Slavic and East European Journal* 30, no. 1 (2013): 49–66.

21. Makovskii, *Portrety*, 333–58.

22. Makovskii, *Portrety*, 339. The peculiar punctuation is in the original.

23. Makovskii, *Portrety*, 349.

24. Makovskii, *Portrety*, 349.

25. Johannes von Guenther, *Ein Leben im Ostwind: Zwischen Petersburg*

und München, Erinnerungen (Munich: Biederstein Verlag, 1969), 284. "We were collectively in love with the poetess Cherubina de Gabriak."

26. Makovskii, *Portrety*, 346.

27. Makovskii, *Portrety*, 331.

28. Aleksei Tolstoi, who was among Voloshin's guests at Koktebel' in the summer of 1909, later said he recognized verses Dmitrieva recited there in some of de Gabriak's poems but chose to keep this to himself. Gofman and Kuzmin were among those who doubted Cherubina. Viacheslav Ivanov spoke highly of the poems, adding that if this was a mystification it was genius; Voloshin, *Sobranie sochinenii*, vol. 6, bk. 1, 701.

29. Events came thick and fast for Dmitrieva. A few days before November 11, 1909, Dmitrieva revealed in strict confidence to von Guenther that she was the author of de Gabriak's poems. On November 11, von Guenther divulged her secret to Kuzmin. On November 14, Gumilev proposed to Dmitrieva and, angered by her refusal, spoke ill of her in public. On November 15 the first installment of de Gabriak's poems appeared on the pages of *Apollo*, which also featured Voloshin's "Horoscope of Cherubina de Gabriak." On the following day, Dmitrieva confessed the truth to Makovsky. On the November 19 Voloshin slapped Gumilev for the way he spoke of Dmitrieva, precipitating a challenge. On the November 22 the duel took place, and Dmitrieva praised Voloshin's chivalrous act.

30. Accounts of von Guenther's behavior vary. In his memoirs, *Ein Leben im Ostwind*, von Guenther writes that Dmitrieva needed to confide in someone and excuses his betrayal of her secret as a youthful indiscretion (284–300). Voloshin claims that von Guenther won Dmitrieva's trust in order to elicit this information from her; "Vospominaniia o Cherubine de Gabriak," in *Sobranie sochinenii*, vol. 7, bk. 2, 470. Landa describes the part von Guenther played as self-serving and deceitful; "Mif i sud'ba," 33. Kushlina and Nikol'skaia maintain that von Guenther resorted to hypnosis to elicit the information from Dmitrieva; *Sto odna poetessa*, 219.

31. Makovskii, *Portrety*, 351.

32. Palacheva, "Rodoslovnaia Cherubiny de Gabriak," 4. Scholars differ in their assessments of the authorship of the de Gabriak poems, with Landa giving Dmitrieva full credit for their composition while Kushlina and Nikol'skaia describe them as a joint effort on Voloshin's and Dmitrieva's part. As noted in chapter 5, Tsvetaeva designates Dmitrieva as the sole author of the poems.

33. Makovskii, *Portrety*, 352.

34. For an example, see "Ispanskii znak," in de Gabriak, *Ispoved'*, 65–66.

35. Makovskii, *Portrety*, 351; ellipsis in original.

36. See the chronologies in de Gabriak, *Ispoved'*, 322–23, and Ageeva, *Nerazgadannaia Cherubina*, 296–99, which inform my brief summary.

37. De Gabriak, *Ispoved'*, 323.

38. Landa, "Mif i sud'ba," 38.

39. Ageeva, *Nerazgadannaia Cherubina*, 136.

40. De Gabriak, *Ispoved'*, 306.

41. T. N. Zhukovskaia and E. A. Kallo, eds., *Sub rosa* (Moscow: Ellis Lak, 1999), 69.

42. Zhukovskaia and Kallo, *Sub rosa*, 65. The projected volume did not materialize.

43. De Gabriak, *Ispoved'*, 271.

44. Rusina Volkova, "Vnuki Cherubiny," *Neva*, no. 5 (May 2009): 74–120.

45. Landa, "Mif i sud'ba," 22–27.

46. Groberg, "Behind the Veil," 293.

47. Landa, "Mif i sud'ba," 35.

48. Voloshin, "Goroskop Cherubiny de Gabriak," in *Sobranie sochnenii*, vol. 6, bk.2, 60–66.

49. Voloshin, "Vospominaniia o Cherubine de Gabriak," in *Sobranie sochnenii*, vol. 7, bk. 2, 451–71. The same piece was published as "Istoriia Cherubiny de Gabriak" ("History of Cherubina de Gabriak") by Davydov and Kupchenko, who argue persuasively for the appropriateness of this particular title, which I adopt here; "Maksimilian Voloshin," 41–52.

50. Accounts that rely on Anna Akhmatova's response to the mystification as set down by Lydia Chukovskaia perpetuate that poet's erroneous assertion that the de Gabriak poems appeared in the first issue of the journal; see Lidiia K. Chukovskaia, *Zapiski ob Anne Akhmatovoi v trekh tomakh*, 3 vols. (Moscow: Soglasie, 1977), 1:176.

51. Voloshin, "Goroskop Cherubiny de Gabriak," 260.

52. Ageeva, *Nerazgadannaia Cherubina*, 100. Voloshin's essays devoted to Villiers de L'Isle-Adam and Barbey d'Aurevilly are similar in tone and style to the "Horoscope" and to other essays he published in *Apollo*.

53. See Landa, "Mif i sud'ba," 353, on Voloshin's notebook in which he recorded detailed interpretations of the signs of the zodiac—both astrological and chiromantic.

54. This came in response to a question on the "Turgenev Survey," which a French journalist had sent to the Russian novelist in the preceding century and which Voloshin copied and distributed to his friends; see Voloshin, *Sobranie sochinenii*, vol. 7, bk. 2, 281 and the commentary on p. 585.

55. Voloshin, *Sobranie sochinenii*, vol. 6, bk. 1, 263.

56. De Gabriak, *Ispoved'*, 291–92.

57. In speaking of the de Gabriak poems, Kristi Groberg and Catriona Kelly write, "These verses achieve a clever fusion of the Decadent female persona, as it had earlier been developed by Mariia Bashkirtseva in her diary, Mirra Lokhvitskaia in poetry, and Lidiia Zinov'eva-Annibal in prose, with a Catholic religiosity drawing partly on French Symbolism and partly on Dmitrieva's reading of the

Counter-Reformational mystics St. Teresa and St. Ignatius Loyola" ("De Gabriak, Cherubina," in *Dictionary of Russian Women Writers*, ed. Marina Ledkovsky, Charlotte Rosenthal, and Mary Zirin [Westport, Conn.: Greenwood Press, 1994], 145). Landa also compares de Gabriak with Maria Bashkirtseva; "Mif i sud'ba," 29–32. Ageeva also invokes Lokhvitskaia; *Nerazgadannaia Cherubina*, 34.

58. De Gabriak, *Ispoved'*, 290.

59. Maksimilian Voloshin, "Vil'e de Lil'-Adan [*sic*]," in *Sobranie sochinenii*, vol. 6, bk. 1, 149.

60. "Villiers de L'Isle-Adam" (1908) and "The Apotheosis of Dream and Death (Villiers de L'Isle-Adam's Tragedy *Axel* and the Tragedy of His Own Life)" ("Apofeoz mechty i smerti [Tragediia Vil'e de Lil'-Adana [*sic*] i tragediia ego sobstvennoi zhizni]") (pub.1912), Voloshin, *Sobranie sochinenii*, vol. 6, bk. 1, 138–49 and 3:462, respectively.

61. Marilyn Gaddis Rose, translator's foreword to *Axel*, by Villiers de L'Isle-Adam (Dublin: Dolmen Press, 1970), ix.

62. Announced in the December 1909 issue of *Apollo*, Voloshin's translation of *Axel* remained unpublished during his lifetime.

63. Rose, translator's foreword, xi.

64. My English rendering of Voloshin's Russian translation; Voloshin, *Sobranie sochinenii*, vol. 6, bk. 1, 261. Voloshin takes this passage from his own translation of the original.

65. Voloshin was responding to a "Turgenev Survey." In earlier questionnaires of this kind, he privileged Sonia Marmeladova from *Crime and Punishment*, Hannele from Gerhardt Hauptmann's *Hanneles Himmelfahrt*, and Gretchen from Goethe's *Faust*; Voloshin, *Sobranie sochinenii*, vol. 7, bk. 2, 285.

66. Rose, translator's foreword, x.

67. In a climactic speech, Axel has to persuade Sara to relinquish the untold wealth and love that life promises them in order to transcend the material world. The speech concludes with the famous line "Live? The servants will do that for us" (*Vivre? Les serviteurs feront cela pour nous*).

68. These are "The Life of Jules Barbey d'Aurevilly" ("Zhizn' Zhulia Barbe d'Orevil'i") and "The Personality and Works of Barbey d'Aurevilly" ("Lichnost' i tvorchestvo Barbe d'Orevil'i"), his compendium "Opinions on Jules Barbey d'Aurevilly by His Contemporaries" ("Mneniia soveremennikov o Zhule Barbe d'Orevil'i"), and the bibliography "Books by Barbey d'Aurevilly" ("Knigi Barbe d'Orevil'i"); Voloshin, *Sobranie sochinenii*, 3:41–70 and the commentary on page 472.

69. Voloshin, *Sobranie sochinenii*, vol. 7, bk. 1, 261.

70. Voloshin, *Sobranie sochinenii*, vol. 7, bk. 2, 644.

71. Tat'iana Borisovna Shan'ko recorded Voloshin's tale. For an account of its textological history, see Davydov and Kupchenko, "Maksimilian Voloshin,"

41–43, 55–61. In Voloshin's collected works, the piece appears under the title "Vospominaniia o Cherubine de Gabriak"; vol. 7, bk. 2, 451–71.

72. In the West, the major source was initially Tsvetaeva's version of the mystification, which she knew only through Voloshin's retelling and discussed in her essay "The Living about the Living" ("Zhivoe o zhivom").

73. See Voloshin's "Response to Valerii Briusov" ("Otvet Valeriiu Briusovu"), in *Sobranie sochinenii*, vol. 6, bk. 1, 650.

74. Davydov and Kupchenko, "Maksimilian Voloshin"; de Gabriak, *Ispoved'*; and Ageeva, *Nerazgadannaia Cherubina*.

75. The injustice of Voloshin's characterization of Makovsky is noted in Davydov and Kupchenko, "Maksimilian Voloshin," 56n36.

76. Voloshin, *Sobranie sochinenii*, vol. 7, bk. 2, 451. Dmitrieva's limp resulted from a childhood illness.

77. See Voloshin's "Istoriia moei dushi," diary entries documenting his interest in childhood and the importance he ascribed to the formative years of an individual, in *Sobranie sochinenii*, vol. 7, bk.1, 304–8.

78. Landa, "Mif i sud'ba," 17–18.

79. "Today one would probably identify the aura that emanated from her as 'sexy'" (*das Fluidum, das von ihr ausging würde man heute vermutlich als "sexy" bezeichnen*); von Guenther, *Ein Leben im Ostwind*, 287–88.

80. Anna Akhmatova, *Zapisnye knizhki Anny Akhmatovoi 1958–1966*, ed. K. N. Suvorova (Moscow: Rossiiskii gosudarstvennyi arkhiv literatury i iskusstva na russkom iazyke, 1996), 268.

81. Voloshin, *Sobranie sochinenii*, vol. 7, bk. 2, 455.

82. Voloshin, "Istoriia moei dushi," vol. 7, bk. 1, 45.

83. See, inter alia, M. V. Mikhailova, who as late as 2000 writes of the "beautiful mysterious Spanish woman Cherubina de Gabriak, who replaced the unattractive, limping Elizaveta Dmitrieva, whose poems no one wanted to notice and hear—in contrast to the poems of her double" ("Dialog muzhskoi i zhenskoi kul'tur v russkoi literature Serebrianogo veka: 'Cogito ergo sum'—'Amo ergo sum,'" *Russian Literature* 48 [2000]: 55).

84. Landa, "Mif i sud'ba," 12–20.

85. Landa, "Mif i sud'ba," 12–13.

86. Landa, "Mif i sud'ba," 13.

87. See Voloshin, *Sobranie sochinenii*, vol. 7, bk. 2, 650.

88. Ageeva, *Nerazgadannaia Cherubina*, 295.

89. Makovskii, *Portrety*, 341.

90. Voloshin, *Sobranie sochinenii*, vol. 7, bk. 2, 456, 458.

91. Voloshin, *Sobranie sochinenii*, vol. 7, bk. 2, 467.

92. Voloshin emphasizes the split by describing Dmitrieva and de Gabriak in poetic dialogue with each other. Von Guenther's memoirs echo the notion of

the double: "It was a split in her personality. Could this really be possible? As unbelievable as that sounded, circumstances seemed to prove that housed in Dmitrieva were two completely different poets" (*Ein Leben im Ostwind*, 293).

93. Otto Weininger, *Sex and Character* (New York: Fertig, 2003), 210.

94. Otto Rank, *The Double: A Psychoanalytic Study*, trans. Harry Tucker Jr. (Chapel Hill: University of North Carolina Press, 1971), xxi n9.

95. Published in 1878, the novel popularized the term "android." Its Russian title is *Griadushchaia Eva*.

96. Voloshin's article appeared in the October 12, 1911, issue of the *Moscow Gazette* (*Moskovskaia gazeta*); *Sobranie sochinenii*, vol. 6, bk. 1, 431–33.

97. Auguste Villiers de L'Isle-Adam, *Tomorrow's Eve*, trans. Robert Martin Adams (Urbana: University of Illinois Press, 1982).

98. Marie Lathers, *The Aesthetics of Artifice: Villiers's L'Eve future* (Chapel Hill: University of North Carolina Press, 1996), 137 (emphasis in the original).

99. Villiers, *Tomorrow's Eve*, 31.

100. Asti Hustvedt, "Science Fictions: The Future Eves of Villiers de L'Isle-Adam and Jean-Martin Charcot," in *The Decadent Reader: Fiction, Fantasy, and Perversion from Fin-de-Siècle France* (New York: Zone Books, 1998), 500.

101. Many modernists embraced Weininger's postulate of feminine, passive material contrasted with the active male artist who shaped it; see Ekonen, *Tvorets, sub"ekt, zhenshchina*, 97.

102. Makovskii, *Portrety*, 346.

103. Landa, "Mif i sud'ba," 43.

104. Groberg and Kelly, "De Gabriak, Cherubina," 145. In a fuller treatment of the de Gabriak poems Groberg describes them as "a Symbolist *tour de force*" and lauds their form and multifaceted imagery; "Behind the Veil," 285–97.

105. Cited in Ageeva, *Nerazgadannaia Cherubina*, 136, 361n292.

106. Landa, "Mif i sud'ba," 44.

107. Palacheva, "Rodoslovnaia Cherubiny de Gabriak," 8–9.

CHAPTER FOUR

1. Irina Shevelenko, *Literaturnyi put' Tsvetaevoi: Ideologiia—poetika—identichnost' avtora v kontekste epokhi* (Moscow: Novoe literaturnoe obozrenie, 2002), 72.

2. A. V. Lavrov, "'Novye stikhi Nelli'—literaturnaia mistifikatsiia Valeriia Briusova," in *Pamiatniki kul'tury: Novye otkrytiia; Ezhegodnik 1985* (Moscow: Nauka, 1987 [*sic*]), 75.

3. D. E. Maksimov, *Poeziia Valeriia Briusova* (Leningrad: Khudozhestvennaia literatura, 1940), 258.

4. Lavrov, "'Novye stikhi Nelli.'"

5. Schamma Schahadat, "Die Geburt des Autors aus der Mystifikation: Valerij Brjusov, die Signatur und der Stil," in *Mystifikation—Autorschaft—Original*, ed. Susi Frank, Renate Lachmann, et al. (Tübingen: Gunter Narr Verlag, 2001), 183–208.

6. Lavrov, "'Novye stikhi Nelli,'" 70. Noting that Briusov's adoption of a feminine mask was a means to expand his poetic horizons, Lavrov cites other examples from literary history of the effective use of this strategy by male writers (71).

7. Lavrov, "'Novye stikhi Nelli,'" 71.

8. Lavrov, "'Novye stikhi Nelli,'" 77.

9. Lavrov, "'Novye stikhi Nelli,'" 76.

10. Vladislav Khodasevich, *Nekropol': Vospominaniia; Literatura i vlast'; Pis'ma B.A. Sadovskomu* (Moscow: SS, 1996), 42.

11. Pavel Antokol'skii, introduction to *Sobranie sochinenii v semi tomakh*, by Valerii Briusov, 7 vols. (Moscow: Khudozhestvennaia literatura, 1973–75), 8. "Briusov loved to 'discover' young [poets] the way sailors love to discover islands, chemists—new elements in Mendeleev's table. For Briusov there was in this pursuit the passion of a great game."

12. N. A. Bogomolov, *Russkaia literatura pervoi treti XX veka: Portrety, problemy, razyskaniia* (Tomsk: Vodolei, 1998), 228.

13. Kirsti Ekonen, *Tvorets, sub"ekt, zhenshchina: Strategii zhenskogo pis'ma v russkom simvolizme* (Moscow: Novoe literaturnoe obozrenie, 2011), 73.

14. Vladislav Khodasevich, *Sobranie sochinenii*, ed. John E. Malmstad and Robert P. Hughes, 2 vols. (Ann Arbor, Mich.: Ardis, 1990), 2:129.

15. Vladislav Khodasevich, *Sobranie sochinenii v chetyrekh tomakh*, 4 vols. (Moscow: Soglasie, 1997), 4:32. See also Joan Delaney Grossman, ed. and trans., *The Diary of Valery Bryusov (1893–1905)* (Berkeley: University of California Press, 1980), 17–20.

16. Sofiia Parnok, *Sobranie stikhotvorenii* (Ann Arbor, Mich.: Ardis, 1979), 166. The reference here is to Pushkin's "Little Tragedy" *Mozart and Salieri*.

17. Olga P. Hasty, "Tsvetaeva's Briusov, Mozart, and Salieri," in *Word, Music, History: A Festschrift for Caryl Emerson*, ed. Lazar Fleishman, Gabriella Safran, and Michael Wachtel (Stanford, Calif.: Department of Slavic Languages and Literatures, Stanford University, 2005), 693–706.

18. Cherubina de Gabriak, "Avtobiografiia," in *Ispoved'*, ed. Vladimir Kupchenko, Marianna Landa, and Irina Repina (Moscow: Agraf, 1998), 268.

19. Khodasevich, *Nekropol'*, 37.

20. Valerii Briusov, *Nochi i dni* (Moscow: Skorpion, 1913), page unnumbered.

21. N. S. Ashukin, comp., *Valerii Briusov v avtobiograficheskikh zapiskakh, pis'makh, vospominaniiakh sovremennikov i otzyvakh kritiki* (Moscow: Federatsiia, 1929), 301.

22. We see a similar project in Briusov's 1913 "Sharà: The Diary of a Young

Woman" ("Sharà: Dnevnik devushki"), which was published posthumously; see Valerii Briusov, *Neizdannoe i nesobrannoe* (Moscow: Kliuch, 1998), 150–74.

23. M. V. Mikhailova, "V. Ia. Briusov o zhenshchine (analiz gendernoi problematiki tvorchestva)," *Gendernye issledovaniia* 9 (2003): 147.

24. Briusov, *Neizdannoe i nesobrannoe*, 118–37.

25. Mikhailova notes the racism of the story, in which the African women have an easier time dealing with abuse than the white woman narrator; "V. Ia. Briusov o zhenshchine," 150.

26. The matrophobia in these stories had found powerful manifestation already in Briusov's poem "The Woman" ("Zhenshchina"), from the cycle *Sonnets and Terza Rima* (*Sonety i tertsiny*) of 1901–3.

27. Two examples, one fictional and one real, come readily to mind: de Staël's Corinne and Anna Gorenko, whose father's opprobrium prompted her to write as Anna Akhmatova.

28. Lavrov, "'Novye stikhi Nelli,'" 72–73. That Lavrov sees the courtesan as an emancipated woman shows the degree to which the sexualization has been normalized.

29. Lavrov notes Briusov's plans for poetry collections by a Mariia Raiskaia and an Ira Ialtinskaia; "'Novye stikhi Nelli,'" 71.

30. Subsequent citations of Nelli's verse are to the original 1913 Skorpion edition, with page numbers provided parenthetically.

31. The pet name "Nelli" was not reserved for L'vova alone. Elena Aleksandrovna Syreishchikova, another of Briusov's woman poet paramours, signed her letters to him "Tvoia Nelli" (Your Nelli). Lavrov plausibly links the name to Igor' Severianin's 1911 poem "Nelli"; Lavrov, "'Novye stikhi Nelli,'" 78.

32. Lavrov, "'Novye stikhi Nelli,'" 80–81.

33. Lavrov, "'Novye stikhi Nelli,'" 79.

34. N. Gumilev, *Sobranie sochinenii v chetyrekh tomakh*, 4 vols. (Washington, D.C.: Kamkin, 1968), 4:319–21.

35. In a letter of September 5, 1913, Khodasevich wrote to a friend, "I published a most amusing little piece on Nelli. The ladies laughed a lot" (*Nekropol'*, 341).

36. Khodasevich, *Sobranie sochinenii*, 2:133; first published August 29, 1913, in *Voice of Moscow* (*Golos Moskvy*).

37. Lavrov, "'Novye stikhi Nelli,'" 79.

38. For the text of this draft, see "'Novye stikhi Nelli,'" 81.

39. "Kholod utra, Otryvki," in *Marina Tsvetaeva v kritike sovremennikov, 1910–1941 gody: Rodstvo i chuzhdost'*, comp. and ed. L. A. Mnukhin, (Moscow: Agraf, 2003), 63–64.

40. Cited in Lavrov, "'Novye stikhi Nelli,'" 80.

41. Ekonen, *Tvorets, sub"ekt, zhenshchina*, 77.

42. Khodasevich relates an anecdote that illustrates Briusov's condescension: "Once the late poetess Nadezhda L'vova told him that she did not like some of his poems. Briusov bared his teeth . . . and replied: But they will be learned by heart in high schools, while girls like you will be punished if they learn them badly" (*Nekropol'*, 38).

43. Mikhailova, "V. Ia. Briusov o zhenshchine," 152.

44. In chapter 15 of Briusov's *The Fiery Angel* (*Ognennyi angel*) (St. Petersburg: Azbuka, 2001), octopus tentacles similarly invoke despair ("kak shchupal'tsy morskogo spruta" [347]).

45. Lavrov, "'Novye stikhi Nelli,'" 73.

46. Lavrov is citing a review of *Nelli's Poems* by V. Shmidt, which appeared in *Russkaia mysl'* shortly after the publication of the volume; "'Novye stikhi Nelli,'" 92n32.

47. "'Novye stikhi Nelli,'" 73.

48. "'Novye stikhi Nelli,'" 75.

49. Valerii Briusov, *Polnoe sobranie sochinenii i perevodov*, vols. 1–4, 12, 13, 15, 21 (St. Petersburg: Sirin, 1913–14), 21:253.

50. Charles Baudelaire, *The Painter of Modern Life and Other Essays*, trans. J. Mayne (New York: Garland Publishing, 1978), 12.

51. Milica Banjanin, "The Female 'Flâneur': Elena Guro in Petersburg," *Australian Slavonic and East European Studies*, 11, nos. 1–2 (1997): 54.

52. Keith Tester, ed., *The Flâneur* (London: Routledge, 1994), 7.

53. Baudelaire, *Painter of Modern Life*, 13.

54. Priscilla Parkhurst Ferguson, "The *Flâneur* on and off the Streets of Paris," in Tester, *The Flâneur*, 22–23.

55. Ferguson, "*Flâneur*," 31.

56. Deborah Epstein Nord, "The Urban Peripatetic: Spectator, Streetwalker, Woman Writer," *Nineteenth-Century Literature* 46, no. 3 (December 1991): 365.

57. Nord, "The Urban Peripatetic," 365–66.

58. Ferguson, "*Flâneur*," 35.

59. See, inter alia, Griselda Pollock, *Vision and Difference: Femininity, Feminism and Histories of Art* (London: Routledge, 1988).

60. Baudelaire, *Painter of Modern Life*, 9 (emphasis in the original).

61. Tester, *The Flâneur*, 2.

62. Tester, *The Flâneur*, 2.

63. Janet Wolff, "The Invisible *Flâneuse*," in *Feminine Sentences: Essays on Women and Culture* (Oxford: Polity Press, 1990), 42.

64. Laura Engelstein, *The Keys to Happiness: Sex and the Search for Modernity in Fin-de-Siècle Russia* (Ithaca, N.Y.: Cornell University Press, 1992), 398.

65. Engelstein, *The Keys to Happiness*, 399.

66. Anna Akhmatova, *Zapisnye knizhki Anny Akhmatovoi 1958–1966*, ed. K. N. Suvorova (Moscow: Rossiiskii gosudarstvennyi arkhiv literatury i iskusstva na russkom iazyke, 1996), 612.

CHAPTER FIVE

1. See Olga Peters Hasty, "On Women Poets: Gender in Cvetaeva's Commemorations of Brjusov and Vološin," *Russian Literature* 73, no. 4 (2013): 497–512, which informs this chapter.

2. See Antonina Filonov Gove, "The Feminine Stereotype and Beyond: Role Conflict and Resolution in the Poetics of Marina Tsvetaeva," *Slavic Review* 36, no. 2 (June 1977): 231–55.

3. Irina Shevelenko, *Literaturnyi put' Tsvetaevoi: Ideologiia—poetika—identichnost' avtora v kontekste epokhi* (Moscow: Novoe literaturnoe obozrenie, 2002), 15–18.

4. Anastasia Tsvetaeva notes that her sister avoided the prominent publishing houses Musaget and Skorpion because she "did not want anyone monitoring or controlling her" (*Vospominaniia* [Moscow: Sovetskii pisatel', 1983], 355n1).

5. Marina Tsvetaeva, "Zhivoe o zhivom," in *Sobranie sochinenii v semi tomakh*, 7 vols. (Moscow: Ellis Lak, 1994), 4:172. All subsequent references to Tsvetaeva's writings are to this edition, with volume and page numbers provided parenthetically in the main text.

6. Shevelenko, *Literaturnyi put' Tsvetaevoi*, 71 (emphasis in the original).

7. Olga P. Hasty, "Marina Cvetaeva on Influence and Other Russian Poets," in *A Companion to Marina Cvetaeva: Approaches to a Major Russian Poet*, ed. Sibelan Forrester (Leiden: Brill, 2017), 37–65.

8. For a comprehensive discussion of the critical reception of *Evening Album*, see Shevelenko, *Literaturnyi put' Tsvetaevoi*, 27–34.

9. Shaginian, still in the early stages of her own poetic career, had published her first volume of verse, *Pervye vstrechi* (*First Meetings*), at her own expense the previous year. Symbolist in tenor, its poems reflect the mentorship of a woman poet—Zinaida Gippius, to whose verse Shaginian devoted a critical study in 1912. Shaginian's own rise to celebrity came in 1912 with the publication of her second volume of poetry, *Orientalia*, which went through seven editions and placed her as a leading woman poet of the time. Tsvetaeva may have modeled her own debut on that of Shaginian, who was also establishing a precedent by writing criticism under her own name rather than a male pseudonym.

10. *Marina Tsvetaeva v kritike sovremennikov, 1910–1941 gody: Rodstvo i chuzhdost'*, comp. and ed. L. A. Mnukhin (Moscow: Agraf, 2003), 29.

11. Mnukhin, *Marina Tsvetaeva v kritike sovremennikov*, 29.

12. Briusov included only sixteen poets in his survey "New Collections of Poetry" ("Novye sborniki stikhov," 1911), republished in 1912 as "Poems of the

Year 1911" ("Stikhi 1911 goda") in *Dalekie i blizkie* (Moscow: Skorpion, 1912), 188–202.

13. Vladimir Kupchenko, *Trudy i dni Maksimiliana Voloshina: Letopis' zhizni i tvorchestva*, vol. 1, *1877–1916* (St. Petersburg: Aleteia, 2002), 259.

14. Shevelenko, *Literaturnyi put' Tsvetaevoi*, 67.

15. Voloshin, *Sobranie sochinenii*, vol. 6, bk. 1, *Proza, 1906–1916: Ocherki, stat'i, retsenzii* (Moscow: Ellis Lak, 2007), 319. Subsequent references to his review are to this edition, volume, and book. Page numbers are provided parenthetically.

16. For Anastasia Tsvetaeva's summary of Voloshin's story, see her *Vospominaniia*, 359.

17. Cited here as it appears in Voloshin's review without line breaks.

18. S. Iu. Kornienko, "Anri de Ren'e v kruge chteniia Mariny Tsvetaevoi," *Vestnik VGU: Seriia filologiia, zhurnalistika*, no. 1 (2014): 56.

19. Kornienko, "Anri de Ren'e v kruge chteniia Mariny Tsvetaevoi," 56.

20. Valerii Briusov, "Novye sborniki stikhov," in Mnukhin, *Marina Tsvetaeva v kritike sovremennikov*, 28.

21. Briusov, "Novye sborniki stikhov," 1:28.

22. Briusov, "Novye sborniki stikhov," 1:28.

23. Briusov, "Novye sborniki stikhov," 1:28.

24. Briusov, "Novye sborniki stikhov," 1:28–29.

25. Vladislav Khodasevich, *Nekropol': Vospominaniia; Literatura i vlast'; Pis'ma B.A. Sadovskomu* (Moscow: SS, 1996), 34.

26. See Olga Hasty, "Valerii Briusov as Marina Tsvetaeva's Anti-Muse," in *Vieldeutiges Nicht-zu-Ende-Sprechen: Thesen und Momentaufnahmen aus der Geschichte russischer Dichterinnen*, ed. Arja Rosenholm and Frank Göpfert (Fichtenwalde, Ger.: F. K. Göpfert Verlag, 2002), 196–97. Tsvetaeva, who owned a copy of the 1863 *Poems of K. Pavlova* (*Stikhotvoreniia K. Pavlovoi*), was familiar with the poet before Briusov's 1915 publication of her writings. Indeed, as Tomas Venclova shows, Tsvetaeva already knew Pavlova when she wrote the poems of *Evening Album*; "Almost a Hundred Years Later: Toward a Comparison of Karolina Pavlova and Marina Cvêtaeva," in *Essays on Karolina Pavlova*, ed. Susanne Fusso and Alexander Lehrman (Evanston, Ill.: Northwestern University Press, 2001), 187–214.

27. Venclova, "Almost a Hundred Years Later," 190.

28. Venclova, "Almost a Hundred Years Later," 190.

29. Karolina Pavlova, *Polnoe sobranie stikhotvorenii* (Moscow: Sovetskii pisatel', 1964), 154. Briusov invokes Pavlova's lines in his collection *A Mirror of Shadows* (*Zerkalo tenei*, 1912) in a section titled "Sacred Craft" ("Sviatoe remeslo") with its epigraph "My misfortune! my treasure! / My sacred craft!" The exclamation "My sacred craft!" appears again as an epigraph to a lecture Briusov delivered in April of 1918 that described his views on poetry and was later published in the collection *Experiments: Poems, 1912–1918* (*Opyty: Stikhi, 1912–1918*).

30. Briusov, "Novye sborniki stikhov," 50.

31. Briusov, "Novye sborniki stikhov," 51.

32. Valerii Briusov, "Ob otnoshenii k molodym poetam," *Literaturnoe nasledstvo* 85 (1976): 205.

33. Nadezhda L'vova, "Kholod utra," in Mnukhin, *Marina Tsvetaeva v kritike sovremennikov*, 65.

34. L'vova, "Kholod utra," 65.

35. The question of authorship came up again in connection with the essay "On the Poems of N. L'vova" ("O stikhakh N. L'vovoi"), which appeared in *Russian Thought (Russkaia mysl')* in 1914, under Anna Akhmatova's name. On the strength of textual evidence and the fact that this is the only critical essay in Akhmatova's oeuvre, V. A. Chernykh argues persuasively that this essay was written by Gumilev as a response to Briusov, whom he held to be the author of "The Chill of Morning"; "Akhmatova ili Gumilev? Kto avtor retsenzii 'O stikhakh N. L'vovoi'?," *Novoe literaturnoe obozrenie*, no. 14 (1985): 80–84.

36. N. Bogomolov, "Vazhnaia stupen'," review of *Marina Tsvetaeva: Stranitsy zhizni i tvorchestva, 1910–1922*, by Anna Saakiants, *Voprosy literatury*, no. 9 (1987): 251.

37. R. S. Voitekhovich, "Tri zametki na temu 'Tsvetaeva i Voloshin,'" in *Marina Tsvetaeva: Lichnye i tvorcheskie vstrechi, perevody ee sochinenii; Vos'maia tsvetaevskaia mezhdunarodnaia nauchno-tematicheskaia konferentsiia* (Moscow: Dom-muzei Mariny Tsvetaevoi, 2001), 144–57. See also his "'Exegi monumentum . . . ,' ili poedinok Tsvetaevoi s Briusovym," in *A. S. Pushkin–M. I. Tsvetaeva: Sed'maia tsvetaevskaia mezhdunarodnaia nauchno-tematicheskaia konferentsiia* (Moscow: Dom-muzei Mariny Tsvetaevoi, 2000), 263–67, which traces the Roman theme in Tsvetaeva's confrontation with Briusov.

38. Shevelenko, *Literaturnyi put' Tsvetaevoi*, 289–90; see also 312.

39. Bogomolov, "Vazhnaia stupen'," 251.

40. Briusov, "Novye sborniki stikhov," 28.

41. Nadezhda L'vova's suicide prepared fertile ground for the arguments Tsvetaeva presents in "A Hero of Labor." The resistance that Tsvetaeva continually offered Briusov in her writings is a sign that he was important to her as a gadfly. Beyond the early "Enchantment in Briusov's Poems," the two poems titled "To V. Ia. Briusov," and the essay "A Hero of Labor" is Tsvetaeva's distinct treatment of thematic material that she shares with her stern critic. Prominent examples of such material include the Pied Piper, Orpheus and Eurydice, Theseus and Ariadne, Pushkin, and the juxtaposition of Mayakovsky and Pasternak.

42. In a letter of September 9, 1925, to her Czech friend Anna Tesková, Tsvetaeva writes in connection with her work on "A Hero of Labor," "I wrote, alas, without sources, quoting from memory" (*Pis'ma k Anne Teskovoi* [Prague: Academia, 1969], 32).

43. In 1921, Zinaida Gippius commented that although Briusov had not died physically, he died as a poet in the course of securing power in Bolshevik Russia; "Oderzhimyi," in *Zhivye litsa* (Tbilisi: Merani, 1991), 38. The same essay speaks of "that intense thirst for grandeur and power by which Briusov was possessed," 40. Briusov's readiness to change direction was another characteristic that supported his comparisons with Pushkin's Salieri.

44. As Simon Karlinsky describes, Briusov "systematically opposed, from 1918 to 1922, the acceptance of any Tsvetaeva manuscripts by the state publishers" (*Marina Tsvetaeva: The Woman, Her World, and Her Poetry* [Cambridge: Cambridge University Press, 1985], 96).

45. Alexandra Smith, "Sverzhenie s Olimpa: Briusov v otsenke Zinaidy Gippius i Mariny Tsvetaevoi," in *Perom i prelest'iu: Zhenshchiny v panteone russkoi literatury*, ed. Wanda Laszczak and Daria Ambroziak (Opole, Pl.: Opole University Press, 1999), 124.

46. This is the pen name of poet and translator Adelina Efimovna Efron (1900–1969).

47. Although different in tone, Briusov's insistence on the essential similarity of all women poets accords with Voloshin's description of women poets as types rather than individuals in his review "Women's Poetry" ("Zhenskaia poeziia"), Voloshin, *Sobranie sochinenii*, vol. 6, bk. 1, 322.

48. Veronika Losskaia maintains that in "The Evening of Poetesses" Tsvetaeva was expressing loyalty to the White Army and not commenting on the woman poet; *Pesni zhenshchin: Anna Akhmatova i Marina Tsvetaeva v zerkale russkoi poezii XX veka* (Moscow: Redaktsiia zhurnala *Moskovskii zhurnal*, 1999), 199.

49. Quoting from memory, Tsvetaeva mistakenly gives the title of Briusov's poem as "To Young Ladies" ("Devushkam" [4:53]).

50. "A Hero of Labor" mentions L'vova in passing (4:42).

51. For a more extensive treatment of the Pushkinian theme in "A Hero of Labor," see Olga P. Hasty, "Tsvetaeva's Briusov, Mozart, and Salieri," in *Word, Music, History: A Festschrift for Caryl Emerson*, ed. Lazar Fleishman, Gabriella Safran, Michael Wachtel (Stanford, Calif.: Department of Slavic Languages and Literatures, Stanford University, 2005), 693–706.

52. Sibelan Forrester, "The Poet as Pretender: Poetic Legitimacy in Tsvetaeva," *Slavic and East European Journal* 52, no. 1 (2008): 43.

53. On the image of the pretender in Tsvetaeva's poetry, see Forrester, "The Poet as Pretender," 37–53.

54. Hasty, "On Women Poets," 509.

55. Tsvetaeva's claim that the visual holds no interest for her is not strictly factual. See the insightful study by Molly Thomas Blasing, "Marina Cvetaeva and the Visual Arts," in Forrester, *Companion to Marina Cvetaeva*, 191–238.

56. See Anya M. Kroth, "Androgyny as an Exemplary Feature of Marina Tsvetaeva's Dichotomous Poetic Vision," *Slavic Review* 38, no. 4 (December 1979): 563–82. Kroth's account of "the androgynous make-up of Tsvetaeva's characters" is insightful, but her assertion that Tsvetaeva was unaffected by her cultural milieu is not persuasive. Tsvetaeva was clearly aware of the challenges to the gender binary during the Symbolist period, when homoeroticism, androgyny, and cross-dressing were part of the cultural scene.

57. Tsvetaeva praises Rainer Maria Rilke along similar lines in a letter to him: "Ich glaub nur an Muttersöhne. Sie sind auch ein Muttersohn. Ein *Mann* nach der *weiblichen* Linie darum so *reich*. (Zweifaltigkeit)" (I believe only in mother-sons. You, too, are a mother-son. A *man* along the *feminine* line—hence so *rich*. [Duality]); see Konstantin M. Asadowskij, ed., *Rainer Maria Rilke und Marina Zwetajewa: Ein Gespräch in Briefen* (Frankfurt am Main: Insel, 1992), 48–49 (emphasis in the original).

CHAPTER SIX

1. Tricia Lootens describes such treatment of women writers as a beauty pageant that allows for the crowning of a single woman and dismisses the rest; *Lost Saints: Silence, Gender, and Victorian Literary Canonization* (Charlottesville: University Press of Virginia, 1996), 161.

2. Tsvetaeva initially dedicated *On a Red Steed* to the poet Evgenii Lann, then to Akhmatova, and finally removed the dedication altogether.

3. Simon Karlinsky writes of these attacks, "The hostility was prompted less by the fact of Tsvetaeva's emigration (poets who remained in Russia, such as Akhmatova, were often treated even worse in the Soviet press) than by undisguised misogyny" (*Marina Tsvetaeva: The Woman, Her World, and Her Poetry* [Cambridge: Cambridge University Press, 1985], 128).

4. Vladislav Khodasevich, *Sobranie sochinenii*, ed. John E. Malmstad and Robert P. Hughes, 2 vols. (Ann Arbor, Mich.: Ardis, 1990), 2:364–68.

5. Lidiia K. Chukovskaia, *Zapiski ob Anne Akhmatovoi v trekh tomakh*, 3 vols. (Moscow: Soglasie, 1977), 2:458. Nabokov's satirization of this fashion in *Pnin* offended Akhmatova, who saw it as directed against her. Chukovskaia counters that Nabokov was aiming not at Akhmatova herself but at the epigones that the fashion spawned. See also Anna Akhmatova, *Zapisnye knizhki Anny Akhmatovoi 1958–1966*, ed. K. N. Suvorova (Moscow: Rossiiskii gosudarstvennyi arkhiv literatury i iskusstva na russkom iazyke, 1996), 116.

6. Vladimir Kornilov, "Antipody (Tsvetaeva i Akhmatova)," in A Centennial Symposium Dedicated to *Marina Tsvetaeva, 1892–1992*, ed. Svetlana Elnitsky and Efim Etkind, 2 vols. (Northfield, Vt.: Russian School of Norwich University, 1992), 2:189. As Kornilov documents, Tsvetaeva was certain to have seen the

poem, which, as he states, appeared in *Anno Domini—2*, Berlin, 1923, together with Annenkov's sketch of Akhmatova.

7. See Anatolii Naiman, "O sviazi mezhdu 'Poemoi bez geroia' Akhmatovoi i 'Poemoi vozdukha' Tsvetaevoi," in *Marina Tsvetaeva, 1892–1992*, 196–205; and Inna Lisnianskaia, "Zametki o 'Poeme bez geroia,'" *Literaturnoe obozrenie*, no. 5 (1989): 34–36.

8. Alexandra Smith, "The Tsvetaeva Theme in Akhmatova's Late Poetry," *Australian Slavonic and East European Studies*, no. 2 (November 1996): 139–56. Smith states that Tsvetaeva "appears to be an invisible co-author of *Poema bez geroia*" (149).

9. Chukovskaia, *Zapiski*, 1:411.

10. Roberta Reeder translates this title as "I am what I am." I avoid the reference to Shakespeare's *Othello*.

11. Kornilov, "Antipody," 190–91.

12. See also the sketch of the relationship that Ariadna Efron provided to Veronika Losskaia, in *Marina Tsvetaeva v zhizni* (Tenafly, N.J.: Hermitage, 1989), 238–40.

13. Anna Akhmatova, *Sobranie sochinenii v shesti tomakh*, ed. N. V. Koroleva, 6 vols. (Moscow: Ellis Lak, 1998–2005), 1:708. Unless otherwise noted, subsequent citations of Akhmatova's works are to this edition, with volume and page numbers provided parenthetically. Like Rostopchina's relatives in the previous century, Akhmatova's father objected to the poet's disgracing her family name by appearing in print. Rostopchina postponed publishing until after her marriage. Akhmatova settled on a defiant choice of pseudonym.

14. Valerii Briusov, *Sobranie sochinenii v semi tomakh*, 7 vols. (Moscow: Khudozhestvennaia literatura, 1973–75), 6:373.

15. Cited in Akhmatova, *Sobranie sochinenii*, 1:572.

16. Cited in Akhmatova, *Sobranie sochinenii*, 1:583.

17. Briusov, *Sobranie sochinenii*, 6:508.

18. Briusov, *Sobranie sochinenii*, 6:508.

19. Akhmatova, *Zapisnye knizhki*, 254.

20. Akhmatova, *Zapisnye knizhki*, 612.

21. Chukovskaia, *Zapiski*, 2:352.

22. No. 4 of *Apollo* for that year carried Akhmatova's poems "The Gray-Eyed King" ("Seroglazyi korol'"), "In the Forest" ("V lesu"), "Above the Water" ("Nad vodoi"), and "I No Longer Need My Legs" ("Mne bol'she nog moikh ne nado").

23. Some of Akhmatova's best-known poems appeared in *Apollo* in 1913–17.

24. These included Somov, Lancere, Golovin, Kustodiev, Trubetskoi, Ul'ianov, and Leonid Pasternak; Natal'ia Dzutseva, "'Krasavitsa trinadtsatogo goda . . .' (Zhenskii portret v zerkale kul'tury predvoennoi epokhi)," in *Russkaia kul'tura*

v tekstakh, obrazakh, znakakh 1913 goda, ed. G. Iu. Sternin, N. O. Osipova, and N. I. Pospelova (Viatsk: Viatskii gosudarstvennyi gumanitarnyi universitet, 2003), 55.

25. This category included also Ol'ga Glebova Sudeikina, Pallada Bogdanova-Bel'skaia, and Salomeia Andronikova. See Dzutseva, "'Krasavitsa trinadtsatogo goda . . . ,'" 56.

26. Veronika Losskaia, "Akhmatova i Tsvetaeva: 1913 god," in Sternin, Osipova, and Pospelova, *Russkaia kul'tura,* 97–98.

27. Chukovskaia, *Zapiski,* 2:235 and 2:329, respectively.

28. Evgenii Tager, "K nei tianulis', znakomstva s nei dobivalis'," in *Marina Tsvetaeva v vospominaniiakh sovremennikov,* ed. and comp. L. Mnukhin and L. Turchinskii, 3 vols. (Moscow: Agraf, 2002), 3:62.

29. Akhmatova, *Sobranie sochinenii,* 1:567–69. The reference to Tsvetaeva is on page 568.

30. Noted in Marina Tsvetaeva, *Neizdannoe: Sem'ia, istoriia v pis'makh,* ed. E. B. Korkina (Moscow: Ellis Lak, 1999), 469.

31. Irina Shevelenko, *Literaturnyi put' Tsvetaevoi: Ideologiia—poetika—identichnost' avtora v kontekste epokhi* (Moscow: Novoe literaturnoe obozrenie, 2002), 53, 57.

32. Khodasevich, *Sobranie sochinenii,* 2:144 and 2:155–56, respectively.

33. Shevelenko, *Literaturnyi put' Tsvetaevoi,* 57.

34. Shevelenko, *Literaturnyi put' Tsvetaevoi,* 109. Poets continued to consider and call themselves St. Petersburg poets even after the official renaming of the city. In speaking of these poets and their cultural orientation, I do the same, otherwise using the offical name of the city.

35. Alyssa Dinega notes insightfully that Tsvetaeva's Blok and Akhmatova cycles are not tributes but means to find "a solution to her own inspirational impasse." These two purposes are not mutually exclusive. See Alyssa Dinega, *A Russian Psyche: The Poetic Mind of Marina Tsvetaeva* (Madison: University of Wisconsin Press, 2001), 37.

36. Adamovich is correct.

37. G. Adamovich, "Vecher Mariny Tsvetaevoi," in *Marina Tsvetaeva v kritike sovremennikov, 1910–1941 gody: Rodstvo i chuzhdost',* comp. and ed. L. A. Mnukhin (Moscow: Agraf, 2003), 383.

38. The cycle to Akhmatova has attracted considerable scholarly attention, most frequently in conjunction with the cycle *Poems to Blok (Stikhi k Bloku).* See, inter alia, Shevelenko, *Literaturnyi put' Tsvetaevoi,* 116–31; Dinega, *A Russian Psyche,* 56–71; L. V. Zubova, "Traditsii stilia 'pleteniia sloves' u Mariny Tsvetaevoi," *Vestnik LGU,* no. 9 (1985): 47–52; Olga Peters Hasty, "Tsvetaeva's Onomastic Verse," *Slavic Review* 45, no. 2 (1986): 245–56.

39. Olga P. Hasty, "Marina Cvetaeva on Influence and Other Russian Poets,"

in *A Companion to Marina Cvetaeva: Approaches to a Major Russian Poet*, ed. Sibelan Forrester (Leiden: Brill, 2017), 37–65.

40. Shevelenko, *Literaturnyi put' Tsvetaevoi*, 130.

41. Alyssa Dinega notes the discrepancy between Tsvetaeva's image of Akhmatova and that poet's self-image; *A Russian Psyche*, 59. Anna Saakiants sees Tsvetaeva's Akhmatova as a lyric heroine; *Marina Tsvetaeva: Stranitsy zhizni i tvorchestva, 1910–1922* (Moscow: Sovetskii pisatel', 1986), 102.

42. T. S. Kruglova, "Liricheskii dialog M. Tsvetaevoi i A. Akhmatovoi v zhanrovom aspekte," *Vestnik novgorodskogo gosudarstvennogo universiteta*, no. 56 (2010): 38.

43. The epistolary exchange appears in Tsvetaeva, *Sobranie sochinenii*, 6:200–207.

44. For a study of the poetics of Tsvetaeva's letters, see Natal'ia Kapoche, *Poetika pisem Mariny Tsvetaevoi* (Vilnius: EHU, 2014).

45. Marina Tsvetaeva, *Neizdannoe: Zapisnye knizhki*, ed. E. B. Korkina and M. G. Krutikova, 2 vols. (Moscow: Ellis Lak, 2001), 2:138.

46. Ariadna Efron, "Stranitsy vospominanii," in *Marina Tsvetaeva v vospominaniiakh sovremennikov*, 1:256.

47. Tsvetaeva, *Sobranie sochinenii*, 6:200.

48. Tsvetaeva, *Sobranie sochinenii*, 6:206.

49. *Marina Tsvetaeva: Poet i vremia; Vystavka k 100-letiiu so dnia rozhdeniia 1892–1992* (Moscow: GALART, 1992), 100.

50. Marina Tsvetaeva, *Neizdannoe: Svodnye tetradi*, ed. E. B. Korkina and I. D. Shevelenko (Moscow: Ellis Lak, 1997), 55 (emphasis in the original).

51. K. Mochulskii, "Russkie poetessy: Marina Tsvetaeva i Anna Akhmatova," in *Marina Tsvetaeva v kritike sovremennikov*, 1:129. The essay first appeared in the Parisian paper *Link* (*Zveno*) on March 5, 1923.

52. Mochulskii, "Russkie poetessy," 129.

53. Chukovskaia, *Zapiski*, 2:489. Akhmatova is referring to Tsvetaeva's comparison of Mayakovsky and Pasternak in the essay "The Epic and the Lyric in Contemporary Russia" ("Epos i lirika sovremennoi Rossii").

54. Lootens, *Lost Saints*, 262.

55. The copy Tsvetaeva annotated for Rilke is in the archives of the Bibliothèque Nationale, Bern, Switzerland. Tsvetaeva's notes in it appear in F. Ph. Ingold, "M. I. Cvetaevas Lese- und Verständnishilfen für R. M. Rilke," *Die Welt der Slawen* 2 (1979): 352–68.

56. Tsvetaeva, *Sobranie sochinenii*, 5:404.

57. Tsvetaeva, *Sobranie sochinenii*, 6:435.

58. For Tsvetaeva's relations with Parnok, see S. Poliakova, *Zakatnye ony dni: Tsvetaeva i Parnok* (Ann Arbor, Mich.: Ardis, 1983).

59. The event took place at the home of naval engineer Ioakim Kannegiser

and his two sons, Leonid and Sergei. Among those present were Kuzmin, Mandel'shtam, Esenin, Georgii Ivanov, Adamovich, Landau, and Otsup. For an account of the evening and its place in Tsvetaeva's poetic development, see Shevelenko, *Literaturnyi put' Tsvetaevoi*, 108–10.

60. Akhmatova was in the Crimea undergoing treatment for tuberculosis.

61. I gratefully acknowledge the insightful anonymous reader of my manuscript who shared this observation with me.

62. Tsvetaeva, *Sobranie sochinenii*, 4:283. Subsequent citations of Tsvetaeva's "An Otherworldly Evening" are to this edition, with volume and page numbers provided parenthetically.

63. Coinciding with the attempt on Lenin's life that was planned for the same day, the assassination contributed to unleashing the Red Terror.

64. A paronomastic chain strengthens the developing argument: *sravnivanie-stravlivanie-sorevnovania-rvenie* (comparison-pitting-competitions-fervor).

65. Aiza Pessina Longo, "Dva poeta: Anna Akhmatova i Marina Tsvetaeva," in *La Pietroburgo di Anna Achmatova*, ed. Elio Ballardini and Tatiana V. Tsivian (Bologna: Grafis, 1996), 94.

66. Chukovskaia, *Zapiski*, 2:329.

67. Tsvetaeva, *Neizdannoe: Svodnye tetradi*, 349.

68. Amanda Haight speaks of Tsvetaeva's poems in Akhmatova's purse as fact; *Anna Akhmatova: A Poetic Pilgrimage* (New York: Oxford University Press, 1976), 110.

69. An intermediate temporality obtains between these in the form of a letter that Tsvetaeva wrote to Kuzmin in 1921 in response to his collection *Otherworldly Evenings*, a draft of which serves as the basis of this essay; Tsvetaeva, *Sobranie sochinenii*, 6:207–10.

70. Tsvetaeva's use of tenses in this passage (which I attempt to convey in my translation) is indicative of the complex temporal framework she creates and the multiple perspectives it affords her.

71. After making revisions to the poem, Akhmatova dated it 1961. For variants, the cycles and collections in which Akhmatova included or planned to include it, and its publication history, see Akhmatova, *Sobranie sochinenii*, 1:927–30. For a discussion of variants of the poem, see Elena Aisenshtein, *Obrazy i mify Tsvetaevoi* (Moscow: Izdatel'skie resheniia po litsenzii Ridero, 2017), 134–37.

72. Cited in Roman Timenchik, *Anna Akhmatova v 1960-e gody* (Moscow: Volodei; Toronto: University of Toronto Press, 2005), 201.

73. Timenchik, *Anna Akhmatova*, 616n194.

74. Timenchik suggests that Akhmatova takes the image of the double from Tsvetaeva's cycle *Poems about Moscow*, which Akhmatova first read on February 19, 1917; Timenchik, *Anna Akhmatova*, 618n200. The suggestion is plausible. In the fourth poem of the Moscow cycle, "The Day Will Come, a Sad One,

As They Say" ("Nastanet den', pechal'nyi, govoriat," April 11, 1916), Tsvetaeva envisions her death and describes the moment of transition from corporeality to disembodiment as a meeting of doubles.

75. Khodasevich notes that Briusov "once called her an eternal imitator" and insists that Tsvetaeva's own voice is always heard through the poets that she assimilates; V. Khodasevich, "Rets.: Marina Tsvetaeva; Posle Rossii; Stikhi 1922–1925," in Mnukhin, *Marina Tsvetaeva v kritike sovremennikov*, 1:346.

76. Shevelenko, *Literaturnyi put' Tsvetaevoi*, 117.

77. In 1936, Akhmatova visited the tower purported to be the one in which Mnishek was imprisoned; Timenchik, *Anna Akhmatova*, 616n193.

78. Akhmatova, *Zapisnye knizhki*, 278.

79. Smith, "Tsvetaeva Theme," 143–44.

80. On Tsvetaeva's relations with Mandel'shtam, see, inter alia, Viktoria Shveitser, *Byt i bytie Mariny Tsvetaevoi* (Fontenay-aux-Roses, Fr.: Syntaxis, 1988), 152–74. Shveitser describes Tsvetaeva's poems to Mandel'shtam as important precursors to her cycles to Blok and Akhmatova (174).

81. Karlinsky, *Marina Tsvetaeva*, 128–29.

82. For more on Tsvetaeva in Akhmatova's later verse, see, inter alia, Veronika Losskaia, *Pesni zhenshchin: Anna Akhmatova i Marina Tsvetaeva v zerkale russkoi poezii XX veka* (Moscow: Redaktsiia zhurnala *Moskovskii zhurnal*, 1999), 280–83; Naiman, "O sviazi mezhdu," 196–205; Lisnianskaia, "Zametki," 34–36; and Smith, "Tsvetaeva Theme," 139–56.

83. Timenchik, *Anna Akhmatova*, 201.

84. Chukovskaia, *Zapiski*, 2:199.

85. Tsvetaeva, *Sobranie sochinenii*, 4:611; emphasis in the original. For a discussion of Tsvetaeva's comments on Akhmatova's collection, see Aisenshtein, *Obrazy i mify Tsvetaevoi*, 114–15.

86. This remark appears twice in Akhmatova's *Prose about A Poem* [*without a Hero*] (*Proza o poeme*); Akhmatova, *Sobranie sochinenii*, 3:241, 254.

87. See, inter alia, Chukovskaia, *Zapiski*, 2:488, and the accounts by E. G. Gershtein and N. I. Khardzhiev cited in Akhmatova, *Sobranie sochinenii*, 5:683 and 5:684, respectively.

88. Chukovskaia, *Zapiski*, 1:349.

89. On the complexity of this process, Akhmatova's "ambiguous attitude to her own reputation," and her "ghosting her own biography," see Catriona Kelly, *A History of Women's Writing, 1820–1992* (Oxford: Oxford University Press, 1994), 217–21. Recently Akhmatova's efforts to shape and retain control over her own image have met with resistance. The most prominent example is the attack by Alexander Zholkovsky, "The Obverse of Stalinism: Akhmatova's Self-Serving Charisma of Selflessness," in *Self and Story in Russian History*, ed. Laura Engelstein and Stephanie Sandler (Ithaca, N.Y.: Cornell University Press, 2000), 46–68; see also the selected recollections—those of Akhmatova's friends

and relations and her own—compiled by D. Vorob'iev, *Akhmatova bez gliantsa* (St. Petersburg: Amfora, 2007), which purports, as the title indicates, to show Akhmatova as she really was in life.

90. Chukovskaia, *Zapiski*, 2:352–53. Akhmatova's comments on Tsvetaeva's essays, as recorded by Chukovskaia, are from this edition, with volume and page numbers provided parenthetically. As Chukovskaia notes (2:720), these essays first appeared in the émigré press and made their way into Soviet publications only sporadically in the 1960s. Chukovskaia does not give Akhmatova's source, but the list of essays makes it clear that she read them in Marina Tsvetaeva, *Proza* (New York: Chekhov Publishing House, 1953).

91. Akhmatova, *Zapisnye knizhki*, 268.

92. Akhmatova, *Zapisnye knizhki*, 268. The note to find the passage is Akhmatova's.

93. Tsvetaeva, *Proza*, 152–53. References hereafter to Akhmatova's reactions to Tsvetaeva's prose are to this edition.

94. Both poets were homosexual.

95. Akhmatova, *Zapisnye knizhki*, 268. Akhmatova attributed the heart attack Annensky suffered on November 30, 1909, to the fact that Makovsky used the space allotted for his poems in *Apollo* to publish de Gabriak's verse instead. Akhmatova is mistaken when she states that Annensky's poems were to have appeared in the first issue of *Apollo* (October 1909). While both he and de Gabriak were listed as contributors in that issue, de Gabriak's poems replaced Annensky's in the second issue, which came out the following month. References to what Akhmatova called Annensky's last tragedy come up a number of times in her notes.

96. The "twenty-five year love" is a reference to Tsvetaeva's inscription in the copy of *Poema vozdukha* (*Poem of the Air*) that she copied out by hand overnight and presented to Akhmatova on the second day of their meeting.

97. Akhmatova, *Zapisnye knizhki*, 278.

98. Timenchik, *Anna Akhmatova*, 144.

99. Akhmatova, *Sobranie sochinenii*, 5:683.

100. As Timenchik describes in *Anna Akhmatova*, "The majority of readers relegated her to archives" (19); see also 337nn111, 112.

101. After the poem's first appearance in *Literary Gazette* (*Literaturnaia gazeta*) in 1962 under the heading "Komarovskie kroki," Akhmatova included it in various cycles and collections, with and without the epigraphs and with various emendations. Here I discuss the version that appears in vol. 2, bk. 2, 119 of her collected works. For a history of the publications and variants of the poem, see Akhmatova, *Sobranie sochinenii*, vol. 2, bk. 2, 401–2.

102. Marina Tsvetaeva, *Izbrannoe* (Moscow: Gosudarstvennoe izdatel'stvo khudozhestvennoi literatury, 1961), 212. This version omits Meudon and Vanves, the indicated places of composition, differs in punctuation, and leaves out stan-

zas 6 and 8 of the more complete version of the poem that appears in the 1994 edition of Marina Tsvetaeva's collected works (2:296–97). Here I use the version of "Elderberry" that Akhmatova read and responded to in her poem. The two poems of Tsvetaeva's 1934 cycle *Bush* (*Kust*), with its perceptible links to "Elderberry," had to wait until the 1965 Moscow edition of Tsvetaeva's selected works for publication. The 1961 edition carried only one poem from Tsvetaeva's cycle to Akhmatova—the 1916 "You Cannot Fall Behind." ("Ne otstat' tebe"), which appears with no reference to its addressee. The 1965 edition carries four of Tsvetaeva's poems under the heading "From the Cycle *To Akhmatova*" ("Iz tsikla *Akhmatovoi*").

103. Timenchik, *Anna Akhmatova*, 144–45. The poem first appeared in *Literary Gazette* on January 16, 1961, as "Komarov Sketches" ("Komarovskie kroki") without the epigraphs and the second quatrain; see Chukovskaia, *Zapiski*, 2:485. For a detailed analysis of this poem and its genesis, see Roman Timenchik, "Rozhdenie stikha iz dukha prozy, 'Komarovskie kroki' Anny Akhmatovoi," in *Analysieren als Deuten: Wolf Schmid zum 60. Geburtstag*, ed. Lazar Fleishman, Christine Gölz, and Aage A. Hansen-Löve (Hamburg: Hamburg University Press, 2004), 541–61. For a different reading of "Nas chetvero," see Smith, "Tsvetaeva Theme," 155–56.

104. This reference prevented Akhmatova from seeking to publish the poem. In November 1963, its full text appeared under the title "There Are Four of Us" as the first poem in the third number of the almanac *Aerial Ways* (*Vozdushnye puti*).

105. Among the primary texts published in the almanac are Akhmatova's *Poem without a Hero* in vols. 1 and 2 (1960 and 1961, respectively) and her recollections of Modigliani and Mandel'shtam in vol. 4 (1965); poems by Mandel'shtam in vol. 2; Pasternak's "Sketches for the Fantasy 'Poem about the Nearest'" ("Nabroski k fantazii 'Poema o blizhnem'") in vol. 4 (1965); and Tsvetaeva's *Perekop* and "Posmertnyi podarok" ("Posthumous Gift") in vol. 5 (1967). The issues also carried articles devoted to these poets by Struve, Veidle, Adamovich, Filippov, and Margolin, as well as portraits of Pasternak, Akhmatova, and Tsvetaeva.

106. The epigraphs are lines from Pasternak's "To Anna Akhmatova" ("Anne Akhmatovoi"), Mandel'shtam's "The Facial Features Are Distorted . . ." ("Cherty litsa iskazheny . . ."), and Tsvetaeva's "O, Muse of Weeping" ("O, muza placha").

107. Akhmatova, *Sobranie sochinenii*, 4:440.

CONCLUSION

1. I borrow this felicitous formulation from Annabel Patterson, *Censorship and Interpretation: The Conditions of Writing and Reading in Early Modern England* (Madison: University of Wisconsin Press, 1984), 243.

2. Diana Greene issues inspiring challenges to the unjust treatment to which Rostopchina continues to be subjected, which prompt the poet's reassessment; "Evdokiia Rostopchina," in *Reinventing Romantic Poetry: Russian Women Poets of the Mid-Nineteenth Century* (Madison: University of Wisconsin Press, 2004), 88–111.

3. In his 1918 essay, pointedly titled "Inglorious Glory" ("Besslavnaia slava"), Khodasevich warns that her fame looks too much like fashion and notes that he loves Akhmatova, but not her admirers; Vladislav Khodasevich *Sobranie sochinenii*, ed. John E. Malmstad and Robert P. Hughes, 2 vols. (Ann Arbor, Mich.: Ardis, 1990), 2:288.

4. Marina Tsvetaeva, *Sobranie sochinenii v semi tomakh*, 7 vols. (Moscow: Ellis Lak, 1994), 4:177, 178, 181.

5. Barbara Johnson, "Gender and Poetry: Charles Baudelaire and Marceline Desbordes-Valmore," in *Displacements: Women, Traditions, Literatures in French*, ed. Joan DeJean and Nancy K. Miller (Baltimore: Johns Hopkins University Press, 1991), 164.

6. Vladimir Kornilov, "Antipody (Tsvetaeva i Akhmatova)," in A Centennial Symposium Dedicated to *Marina Tsvetaeva, 1892–1992*, 2 vols., ed. Svetlana Elnitsky and Efim Etkind (Northfield, Vt.: Russian School of Norwich University, 1992), 2:193.

7. Tricia Lootens, *Lost Saints: Silence, Gender, and Victorian Literary Canonization* (Charlottesville: University Press of Virginia, 1996), 161.

8. Pavel Gromov, "Karolina Pavlova," in *Polnoe sobranie stikhotvorenii*, by Karolina Pavlova (Moscow: Sovetskii pisatel', 1964), 72.

9. Patrick H. Vincent, *The Romantic Poetess: European Culture, Politics, and Gender, 1820–1840* (Durham: University of New Hampshire Press, 2004), 88.

Index

Index

("Odna iz zabytykh"), 65; reviews by, 41, 95, 98–99, 123, 151, 181, 222n3; "There or Here?" ("Tam ili zdes'?"), 147
Khomiakov, Aleksei, 30
Kiselev-Sergenin, Vladimir, 190n61
Kollontai, Aleksandra, 112
Kornienko, S. Iu., 121
Kornilov, Vladimir, 148, 149, 180–81, 214n6
Kuzmin, Mikhail, 12, 75, 151, 158, 202n28; *Otherworldly Evenings* (*Nezdeshnie vechera*), 159

Lathers, Marie, 87
Lavrov, A. V., 94, 98, 107, 207n6, 208nn28–29
Lebedev, E. N., 187n21
Lermontov, Mikhail, 19, 54–55, 81, 178, 197n46
Lokhvitskaia, Mirra, 70–71, 204n57
Longo, Aiza, 164
Lootens, Tricia, 157–58
Losskaia, Veronika, 151
Lotman, Iurii, 44, 49
L'vova, Nadezhda, 149–50; "The Chill of Morning" ("Kholod utra"), 100–101, 125–26; *An Old Fairytale* (*Staraia skazka*), 95, 98

Makovsky, Sergei, 71, 73–77, 78, 83, 84–85, 200n11; "Cherubina de Gabriak," 74
male projections and definitions of women, 69–70, 186n6
Mandel'shtam, Osip, 158, 164, 167–68, 169, 173–74
masquerade. *See* feminine masquerade
maternity and motherhood, poets on, 23, 29, 38–39, 110, 135–36, 143, 155, 187n20
Mickiewicz, Adam, 22, 32
Mnishek, Marina, 167
Mochulsky, Konstantin: "The Russian Poetesses: Marina Tsvetaeva and Anna Akhmatova" ("Russkie poetessy: Marina Tsvetaeva i Anna Akhmatova"), 157
Moravskaia, Mariia, 78
Moscow, 23, 24, 147, 187n21
mystification theory, x, 8

Nabokov, Vladimir, 214n5
Nelli: creation of, 91, 93–94, 98; as model of "new woman," 111–12
WORKS: "At Dawn" ("Na rassvete"), 106; "At the Skating Rink" ("Na sketinge"), 104; *Nelli's Poems* (*Stikhi Nelli*), 8–9, 92, 98–107; "The Ninth Wave" ("Deviatyi val"), 107; "Nocturnal Murmur" ("Nochnoi ropot"), 104–5
Nicholas I, 28, 30, 33–34, 37
Nikitenko, Aleksandr Vasil'evich, 63
Northern Bee (*Severnaia pchela*, newspaper), 31, 32, 33, 37, 190n58, 191n67
Northern Flowers (*Severnye tsvety*, journal), 57

Orlov, Aleksei, 33

Panaev, Ivan Ivanovich, 37, 39, 40, 63, 193n102
Parnok, Sophia, 9, 36, 70, 95, 96
Pascoe, Judith, 49
Pasternak, Boris, 149, 158, 174
Pavlov, Nikolai Filippovich, 30–31, 37–38
Pavlova, Karolina, 4–7; Briusov on, 94–95; description of, 193n102; husband of, 30–31, 37–38; self-presentation of, 21–25, 36–37, 42, 64; Tsvetaeva on, 36, 146; on women's emancipation, 30, 187n20
WORKS: "A Conversation in the Kremlin" ("Razgovor v Kremle"), 37, 38–39, 192n87, 193n95; "The Crone" ("Starukha"), 22; *A Double Life* (*Dvoinaia zhizn'*), 24, 35; "Lanterna magica," 124; "Three Souls" ("Tri dushi"), 185n2 (chap. 1); "To Countess R" ("Grafine R"), 18, 23–26; "We are contemporaries, Countess" ("My sovremennitsy, Grafinia"), 5, 18, 25–27, 30–31, 34–35, 64; "We came together strangely" ("My stranno soshlis'"), 36; "You, who have survived in my destitute heart" ("Ty, utselevshii v serdtse nishchem"), 124
Pedrotti, Louis, 34, 190n59
Pisemsky, Alexei, 29
Pletnev, Petr Aleksandrovich, 43, 50, 55, 63, 196n22
poetic tradition. *See* women's poetic tradition of Russia